The Student Teacher's Handbook
Fourth Edition

The Student Teacher's Handbook
Fourth Edition

Sara L. Schwebel
Harvard University

David C. Schwebel
University of Alabama at Birmingham

Bernice L. Schwebel
Douglass College of Rutgers University, Retired

Carol R. Schwebel
Columbus, Ohio, Public School System, Retired

LEA

LAWRENCE ERLBAUM ASSOCIATES, PUBLISHERS

2002   Mahwah, New Jersey   London

Sponsoring Editor:	Lori Hawver
Textbook Marketing Manager:	Marisol Kozlovski
Cover Design:	Kathryn Houghtaling Lacey
Textbook Production Manager:	Paul Smolenski
Full-Service & Composition:	Pre-Press Company, Inc.
Text and Cover Printer:	Hamilton Printing Company

Lawrence Erlbaum Associates, Inc., Publishers
10 Industrial Avenue
Mahwah, New Jersey 07430

Library of Congress Cataloging-in-Publication Data

The student teacher's handbook/Sara L. Schwebel ... [et al.].—4th ed.
   p. cm.
   Prev. ed. Andrew Schwebel listed first.
   Includes bibliographic references and index.
   ISBN 0-8058-3928-3 (cloth, alk. paper)—ISBN 0-8058-3929-1 (pbk.: alk. paper)
   1. Student teaching—Handbooks, manuals, etc. I. Schwebel, Sara L.

LB2157.A3 S9 2001
370'.71—dc21

2001033001

Dedication

We lovingly dedicate this book to the memory of Andy and in honor of Milt: scholars, activists, and fathers who have touched so many students' lives, including our own.

CONTENTS

Part III: What and How We Teach

Preface

We wrote this fourth edition at the dawn of a new century. It is a time when the population of American youth is growing steadily, and is projected to continue to grow throughout the coming decades. It is a time when television sets, video games, popular music, and the Internet are transmitting violence into children's homes. It is a time, like many in the past, when K–12 test scores have raised alarms across the country, emboldening calls for higher academic standards and an end to social promotion. It is a time when teachers—not just good teachers, but exceptional teachers—are desperately needed. It is a time when you can make a tremendous difference.

This edition of *The Student Teacher's Handbook,* like earlier ones, was written expressly for student teachers. It is designed to be practical and useful, especially during the weeks of the student-teaching assignment, but also throughout the early years of teaching. In the pages that follow we hope to encourage, instruct, guide, and cheer you as you begin the journey of becoming the kind of exceptional teacher who makes a real difference in students' lives.

We are aware that there is no substitute for the instruction, advice, and counsel that student teachers obtain from their cooperating teacher and, in particular, from their college/university supervisor. The personal and professional relationships with those individuals cannot be duplicated or replaced by a book. The book can only supplement, and perhaps maximize, the potential of those relationships.

Over the years, student teachers have told us what the student-teaching assignment meant to them: excitement and challenge, concern, and anxiety. They shared that information with us in personal conversations, in their written journals, and during discussions in student-teaching seminars. What they shared forms the heart of the book. In essence, they reported to us that they were experiencing the normal and typical human reactions to a brand new undertaking.

This book is about those reactions and how best to cope with them. It is about turning concerns and anxieties into opportunities for personal and professional growth. This book is also about the challenges facing educators in the 21st century: classroom management and discipline, special-needs students and inclusion, multicultural education, gender equity, technology integration, standardized test scores, legal issues in the classroom, partnership building with parents, and more.

The book is divided into four distinct parts. Part I, *Beginnings,* focuses on the preparations you make as you move from student to student teacher. Part II, *Relationships,* examines your developing professional identity as you build relationships with your cooperating teacher, college/university supervisor, students, principal, parents, and others. Part III, *What and How We Teach,* centers around your multifaceted work in the classroom. Finally, Part IV, *Today and Tomorrow,* focuses on the preparations you make as you begin to move from student teacher to teacher.

We strove to make this book as user-friendly as possible. Major topics are highlighted at the beginning of each chapter and indexed at the back of the book. An expanded Critical Issues section raises important points in the form of questions at each chapter's close.

We wrote this book as experienced professionals sharing ideas with those entering our profession. We visualized the very real challenges student teachers face and the down-to-earth solutions they need. When possible, we were simple and direct in our analyses and recommendations, but sometimes the problems in our schools are complicated and without easy solutions. We recognize that reality; in fact, we believe that is what makes teaching continually challenging and gratifying.

ACKNOWLEDGMENTS

As we write this fourth edition of the *Student Teacher's Handbook,* we first express our deep and loving gratitude to Drs. Andrew I. and Milton Schwebel, who co-authored the first three editions of the book. They are central not only to this book and the ideas in it, but to all aspects of our lives.

As in previous editions, this book was a cooperative venture in more than just its multiple authorship. We could not have undertaken it without the benefit of what we have learned from our many students over the years. Of special importance are the journals that our student teachers so generously shared with us. We are deeply indebted to them.

We wish to thank Linda Kozusko of the English Department at Rutgers University for her perceptive observations and graphic descriptions of teachers at work, which we incorporated in the book.

We are also indebted to the many educators who generously shared their thoughts with us and, especially, the following three whose constructive advice enabled us to enrich the content of this book immeasurably: Dr. Frances Cagnassola, a teacher in the Newark, New Jersey, school system; Professor James Raths, University of Delaware; and Professor Richard Wisniewski, former Dean of the College of Education, University of Tennessee.

We thank Sherley Keith, a middle school teacher at St. Stephen's & St. Agnes School in Alexandria, Virginia; Claudia Mason, of the University of Washington and Children's Hospital in Seattle; and three anonymous reviewers for the useful perspectives they provided for the fourth edition. We also thank Karen Schwebel for preparing the book's index.

We have profited enormously from the support of our publisher, Lawrence Erlbaum, his senior associate Joe Petrowski, and on a day-to-day basis from Lori A. Hawver, Sponsoring Editor, and Naomi Silverman, Senior Editor.

Finally, our thanks go to family members: Ruth Lubinsky for freeing the authors to complete the first edition by lovingly tending two young children; and Robert Schwebel and Yikun Schwebel, also educators, for raising challenging questions and providing thoughts and comments to help keep us close to the grindstone of reality.

Sara L. Schwebel
David C. Schwebel
Bernice L. Schwebel
Carol R. Schwebel

PART I

Beginnings

1

Introduction:
On Being a Student Teacher

TOPICS

- Some Keys to Success
- The Student Teacher as Apprentice
- Concentrating on *Your* Needs
    Concerns
    Optimism
- How This Book Can Help You
- Journals: Student Teachers Share Their Experiences
- The Contents of This Book

Our aim in this book is to help you make the student-teaching experience a rich and successful one. When deciding what to include from the vast literature on education, teaching, and learning, we examined studies in which student teachers reported their concerns. We also reviewed journal entries of our own student teachers. And we drew on our own experiences as student teachers, teachers, cooperating teachers, and university supervisors.

SOME KEYS TO SUCCESS

Student teachers say they know they are taking on a responsible job. They feel the pressure of having to teach 20 to 30 students in elementary school or 100 or more students in middle and high school, to do it well, and especially to do it in the presence of the cooperating teacher and the college/university supervisor. They have to contend with the pressure.

Our experience suggests that the student teacher's comfort on the job is a central key to success. By *comfort,* we mean that the individual is able to manage the inevitable worries and stresses and enjoy the challenges of preparing for and teaching his or her classes. We devote much attention to those worries and stresses not only to help you manage them, but also to help you gain maximum learning and fulfillment from your experience.

Other keys to success include planning, preparation, and problem solving, as well as understanding and accommodating the diverse students in your classes. In the pages that follow, we pay much attention to these important topics.

Another topic of vital importance to the student teacher is relationships. If student teaching had to be characterized by one word, *relationships* could well be it. As a student teacher, you will be developing relationships with a supervisor, a cooperating teacher, students, and, to a lesser degree, administrators, other teachers, parents, office workers, and custodians. Your success will depend on the quality of relationships you build, especially with your supervisor, cooperating teacher, and students.

THE STUDENT TEACHER AS APPRENTICE

In the field of education, the experience of student teaching is unique. That uniqueness is due in particular to the relationship you form with the cooperating teacher, truly an apprenticeship one. It is the only time in a teaching career that one is an apprentice under the close guidance of an experienced mentor.

For many centuries, beginning at least during medieval times, young people were trained for work through practical experience. For skilled or professional occupations, learning took place through the relationship between masters and apprentices. The masters were experts in one of the arts, crafts, or trades of their time (a barrister or cobbler, a miller or stone mason), and the apprentices served as assistants for various lengths of time. Apprentices learned by observing the master; by engaging in the activities of the calling, first in small, then in larger ways; and finally, under the close scrutiny of the masters, by completing an entire product on their own.

In the process of learning to use the tools and materials of the occupation, the apprentices also acquired the special language of the field, adopted the habits and specialized garments, and absorbed the general mode of thought of fellow artisans. The apprentices became trained (acquired the knowledge and skills) and socialized (acquired the language and habits) in preparation for a lifetime's work in the occupation. They also learned to do more than imitate their master: They were free to be creative within their specialty.

Your student-teaching experience will have almost exact counterparts to the medieval apprenticeship system. One of its purposes is to help you become socialized into the teaching profession: Through student teaching, you go beyond your textbooks. You observe and physically experience how real-life teachers behave in classrooms, in schools, and in their relationships with students, other teachers, administrators, and parents.

Also, as the apprentice, you will be working with an experienced teacher. Under his or her scrutiny, you will use the tools and materials of your trade. Guided by the cooperating teacher, you will move toward ever more challenging teaching experiences. When this time comes, you will probably find that although the courses and fieldwork that preceded student teaching helped prepare you for it, the teaching experience itself caps and gives fullest meaning to all your previous education.

CONCENTRATING ON *YOUR* NEEDS

The weeks of student teaching offer unusual learning opportunities, and you will want to gain the best possible results from your apprenticeship period. For this reason, you should devote extra attention to your needs during the weeks of student teaching. Specifically, focus your energy on developing a large variety of skills (e.g., communication, relationships, assessment) and on gaining confidence in leading a class of students. Because this process of professional growth can be physically and emotionally draining, it may be helpful to remind yourself of your reasons for choosing the teaching profession in the first place. Were you attracted by the way of life, by the opportunity to work with children or adolescents, by the time given to reading and study, by the doors it opens to serve other people, or by the work schedule? Recalling your goals will give you a clearer perspective on your priorities, enabling you to make decisions that best serve your interests.

The long hours involved in your commitment during student teaching may interfere somewhat with your personal life. If so, remind yourself of the limited time frame and the satisfaction you will have when the training is over. If you have a spouse or partner who expresses concern about your restricted time schedule, explain that the student-teaching assignment is short in duration but great in its long-term career significance.

Concerns

It is perfectly understandable that you should have some concerns. The student teacher's position is a demanding one: A novice, still a student, enters a new setting to use newly acquired skills, under the watchful eye of experienced professionals. This is not easy. Yet, most students meet the challenge successfully.

Furthermore, teaching is a high-pressure occupation. At the elementary level, teachers share 6 hours a day, 5 days a week, 40 weeks a year with 20 to 30 children. At the middle school or junior high school level, teachers contend with more students and the students are facing major transitions: rapidly maturing minds and bodies, greater social assertiveness (they speak up more), and the rainbow of emotions expressed by individuals in the throes of peer pressure. At the high school level, teachers experience continual turnover of students during the course of the day. That means getting acquainted with 100 or more adolescents, all of whom are going through the personal and social changes of preadulthood. It also means managing a sizable number of classes of young people who are at their peak of activity and energy. Some of them will be intellectually curious and excited by what teachers offer. Others may be unwilling students, simply waiting for the chance to legally end their formal schooling. Some, although interested in class material, may be continually distracted by thoughts of after-school activities such as athletic contests, band rehearsals, or social gatherings. Still others, although willing students, are drained by parental demands for help in household duties, by the pressure of holding after-school jobs (sometimes to help their families financially and sometimes to earn personal money to purchase cars, clothes, and entertainment), or even by the demands of their own children.

As if all of that were not enough to make teaching a high-pressured career, during a typical school year, teachers can be confronted with problems that ordinarily are in the province of psychologists, psychiatrists, social workers, speech and language specialists, occupational and physical therapists, and the juvenile justice department of the police or legal systems.

Many student teachers wonder whether they will be prepared to deal with all the issues and questions they will encounter in their subject fields (What if students ask about my political views during a discussion of presidential elections? What if a child of Haitian parents repeatedly questions my pronunciation and knowledge of French idioms?). They also ask these questions: Will I be able to manage the class? Will I be able to plan and conduct high-quality lessons? As you prepare for and begin student teaching, you may have occasional frightening thoughts about the class getting completely out of hand. You may worry that you will become preoccupied with special problem cases, including the obviously disturbed child. Having these questions and concerns is perfectly normal. You are moving forward into what, for you, is uncharted territory.

Then there are the worries related to the unique role of the apprentice: You work in the proverbial goldfish bowl, under the observant eyes of the cooperating teacher and college supervisor. You know you will learn much from their observations, but will you ever get used to their presence?

Optimism

Hopefully, your answer to all these questions is a resounding "yes." Hopefully, you have an optimistic outlook on life, and you expect that, come what may in the form of problems, you will confront them as best you can. If you cannot resolve them at first, you will not blame yourself, lose self-esteem, or become depressed.

In his influential book *Learned Optimism*, Seligman (1991) wrote that optimists are not fazed by problems or setbacks. Unlike pessimists, who think their misfortune will last a long time and is their own fault, optimists perceive setbacks as temporary and as challenges to try harder and succeed. The difference between the two habits of thought has substantial effects: Many studies show that optimists perform better in school and college, on the job, and at play. In fact, they tend to surpass predictions based on aptitude tests. Even their physical health is better. Being optimistic in outlook, or acquiring that outlook through methods spelled out by Seligman, can be advantageous for student teaching and, in fact, for the rest of your life. As an optimist, you will probably regard the diversity of knowledge and skills required in teaching as a great attraction. You will also find that the daily challenges and bits of the unpredictable that arise from time to time add spice to your working life.

HOW THIS BOOK CAN HELP YOU

We could go on telling you about the enjoyment and growth you will experience in your profession. Instead, we have highlighted the demands and pressures of the job because those are most likely foremost in your mind. We believe that right now you want help in solving problems you are likely to face and in acquiring skills you do not yet possess. We have written this book with that in mind.

The problems student teachers encounter have myriad causes. Some student teachers create dilemmas for themselves, unintentionally of course. These may be the result of inexperience-driven misjudgments or anxiety-driven misstatements. Some are the problems inherent in the day-to-day life of teaching. Others are peculiar to the special circumstances of being a student teacher, such as feeling inadequate as a result of comparing one's own work to that of the experienced cooperating teacher.

In this book we confront each of these problems in turn. We show how they relate to the life of the student teacher and we provide you with the tools, the knowledge, and the problem-solving strategies we think will help you contend with difficulties.

In writing this book we had one primary objective: to present material that will help you make your student-teaching experience optimally rewarding. In doing this, we have been guided by an orientation of realism. As you complete your student teaching, your thoughts will be on effectively meeting the day-to-day demands of your job and also on securing a teaching position for next year. We concentrate on those concerns. In doing so, we are straightforward about what you can do to prevent problems and how you can deal with those that cannot be circumvented. To accomplish this, we draw on theory and research and our very practical experience as teachers and supervisors.

As you use this book we encourage you to consider the ways each idea or thought presented bears on your life in the classroom at the present time. Although we expect that what we have written will be useful to you next year and perhaps beyond, our aim is to help you make your life as a student teacher easier and more successful today and tomorrow.

A final point: One of the most important objectives of education—yours and each of your student's—is to reach the point of being an independent thinker. Those free to think about and solve problems for themselves have enormous control over their own destiny. You can make much progress toward such independence during your apprenticeship. We believe this book can help you do that.

JOURNALS: STUDENT TEACHERS SHARE THEIR EXPERIENCES

To help you more fully understand and learn to cope with the real problems of student teaching, we have incorporated excerpts of many student teachers' journal entries. Some were written in the white heat of emotion, perhaps at the beginning of the student teachers' assignments when they were feeling frustrated, inept, or powerless. Other entries were written while student teachers were burning with anger over a sense of having been treated unfairly or close to panic about their difficulties in controlling the class. Still other entries were authored at moments of warm satisfaction about seeing progress in their students' work and in their own skill to effectively teach and manage a class.

The journal entries were written by student teachers to serve as aids to themselves. Although most of the entries were shared with supervisors, they were not graded. Instead, the supervisors wanted the journals to provide their students with the opportunity to:

1. Recall, review and reflect on the day's events.
2. Experience release from the emotions of the day.
3. Work at solving problems that they face.
4. Cope with relationship issues, with students or others.
5. Share thoughts and feelings with their supervisor.
6. Recognize and record their growth as professionals.
7. Look to their future as fully accredited teachers.

Many dozens of journals were collected during several different academic years. Seven states in the Eastern and Midwestern parts of the United States are represented. The journals were written by men and women of diverse racial and ethnic groups who came from families of upper middle, middle- and working-class backgrounds. Although the journal authors ranged in age from 20 to 35, most were in their early 20s. Their assignments were at the preschool, elementary, junior (middle school), and senior high school levels and their schools were located in urban (including inner city), suburban, and rural settings. They student taught at both public and private schools.

The instructions given to students writing the journals quoted in this book were essentially those proposed for your use in chapter 2. They were asked to reflect on their classroom experiences each day and to write about them freely. They were to review events that went well and those that did not and to try to explain why the events turned out as they did. They were encouraged to express their feelings about the day and the people involved. They did, sometimes tearfully, sometimes joyfully, and sometimes with passionate anger. Their openness has made their documents valuable to themselves and to others.

The anonymity of the authors of the journals has been carefully safeguarded. Names of student teachers, cooperating teachers, college supervisors, and students are pseudonyms. The school names have also been changed, and no localities are identified.

Besides the journals, we have drawn material from personal interviews with student teachers in several regions of the country. As with the journals, pseudonyms are used and the interview excerpts are marked by a date.

THE CONTENTS OF THIS BOOK

Part I of this book is devoted to *beginnings*, by which we mean the beginnings of your student-teaching experience. We place great stress on this early stage (and even the weeks before it) to help you prepare for early successes.

Two themes that are repeated often are developed at great length in chapter 2: (a) The most effective way to deal with anxieties about new experiences is by preparing for them, and (b) the best way to avoid teaching problems is by thoughtful preparation for the work to be performed. One of the features of chapter 2 is the elaboration of a problem-solving method you will find useful in your student-teaching period, and later as a fully accredited teacher.

Part II is devoted to the *crucial relationships* of the student teacher. Your success depends on quality relationships with your students, cooperating teacher, and college supervisor. In chapters 3, 4, and 5, we indicate how to go about building constructive relationships with each and how to cope with the kinds of problems that inevitably arise. Chapter 6 is about building relationships with parents, the school principal, and others important to school life.

Part III focuses on *diversity and expectations, curriculum, and classroom management*. Linkage of these topics is deliberate; the content and presentation of lessons plays a central role in shaping students' classroom behavior. In other words, what and how you teach can foster student involvement and discourage disruptive behavior just as easily as it can fail to hold learners' attention and, in this and other ways, lead to classroom disruption. The problems of classroom management and control are discussed in great detail because from countless conversations with student teachers, we expect these issues loom large in your mind.

Part IV addresses some of the *student teacher's special concerns.* These include concerns of "today," by which we mean those prevalent during student-teaching days, and those of "tomorrow," the stress associated with ending your college career and beginning your teaching one.

CRITICAL ISSUES

- What rewards am I expecting from student teaching?
- How do I feel about being an apprentice?
- What personal resources can I tap to make my student-teaching experience a rich and rewarding one?
- How do I feel about the difficulties student teachers are likely to confront? What can I do to remain optimistic?

2

Preparing for Student Teaching

TOPICS

- Recognizing Your Expectations
    Self-Expectations
- Preparing for Your Assignment
    Exploration and Investigation of a Community
- Becoming Part of the School Community
- Acknowledging Your Concerns
- Mastering a Problem-Solving Method
    Assumptions
- Using COURAGE
    C: Collect a Bank of Information
    O: Organize Thoughts About the Problem
    U: Understand the Problem by Taking Others' Perspectives
    R: Reflect on Possible Solutions to the Problem
    A: Act on a Solution
    G: Gather New Information
    E: Evaluate Effectiveness
- Four Stages to Student Teaching Success
    Stage 1: The Early Days
    Stage 2: Becoming a Member of the Teaching Team
    Stage 3: Soloing as a Teacher
    Stage 4: Feeling like a Teacher

"When I think about teaching my own classes, I'm excited, anxious, and a little scared. Especially I wonder if I can be a real teacher to them, someone they will accept as the equal of their own teacher. I also wonder if the teachers at the school will respect me." Those were James's feelings a few days before beginning his student teaching.

His feelings were normal. Certainly, you will feel excited as you embark on the first phase of your teaching career. However, it is also normal to feel some anxiety in anticipation of a new experience, especially one in which you will be observed and evaluated. Do you remember other first experiences—your first date, the first time you drove a car, or, earlier yet, the first time you gave an oral report in class? Chances are you showed the normal human reaction of anxiety of one kind or another: "butterflies" in the stomach, a bit of sleeplessness, a lowered appetite, overeating and some digestive problems, or some combination of these symptoms. Chances are, moments after the new experience got underway, your anxiety level dropped considerably.

That is what you might expect about the impending "firsts": when you first report as a student teacher, when you first lunch in the teachers' room, when you first take over the class for a lesson, when you first teach a whole day.

Anticipating a new experience is usually worse than the reality. Worry about failing can grow out of proportion, especially considering that most cooperating teachers will go to great lengths to help you develop as an independent teacher ready to take over the class on your own. The same is true for the college supervisor, who wants to see you through a successful teaching assignment. The school principal wants that too, if for no other reason than the fact that your success means a smoother running school.

The students? They are children or adolescents, with all the feelings and problems and stresses that go with their stage in life. They expect and want you to behave like the adult you are. They do not want you to be one of them: friendly, yes, but not their friend; understanding, yes, but not with the intimacy of a parent or peer. In other words, they want you to be the teacher, the adult who sees to it that they and their peers keep to the limits of behavior expected of them. They are not your opponents; on the contrary, most will be friendly to and supportive of the student teacher.

RECOGNIZING YOUR EXPECTATIONS

"I'm happy when I think about taking over the class. But I guess I'm also apprehensive because I don't know what to expect. It's like the unknown," a student teacher shared with her seminar group.

"What are you apprehensive about?" she was asked.

"That's just the point," she replied. "I know that my fears are groundless. My cooperating teacher is friendly and decent, and she likes being helpful. But sometimes the kind of help she wants to give is not what I want. But that doesn't take away from her wish to be helpful! I don't know. I just don't know what I'm worried about."

When a stressful future experience has a lot of unknowns connected with it, we tend to fill in those unknowns with uncomfortable scenarios that, frequently and thankfully, are far from what actually develops. Here are examples taken from the journals of student teachers:

> I expected the school to be modern, the climate to be cold and impersonal, and the staff to be distant. How different it all turned out! There is a very warm, close atmosphere among the teachers. They made me feel very comfortable. As to my cooperating teacher, she is warm, helpful, cooperative and very understanding. I really enjoy working with her.

This student teacher, a bright young adult, had a bleak outlook about the important experience ahead of her. Fortunately, circumstances corrected her false expectations. Here is another student teacher:

> I thought most of the children would be from middle-class families and that the teacher would be an older woman and probably very set in her ways. As it turned out the children are great; each is so special. Many of them stay full days because their mothers work. They are all friendly and most are not the prima donnas I expected. There are 23 children in the class, all from very different backgrounds. The teacher turned out to be young, innovative, sensitive, very open to new ideas and she's going to be fantastic to work with and learn from.

Not everyone is as pleased with the cooperating teacher and children as these student teachers were, but hardly any of the worst expectations ever materialize.

The inaccurate expectations of the student teachers just quoted were corrected only after their student teaching got underway. One said, "I sure wasted a lot of energy and time with my worries. And I lost some sleep—not to mention peace of mind—needlessly. Oh well, now it's just water over the dam."

Of course, it does not have to be this way. A student teacher can test out some fantasies and fears. It is reassuring to visit the school to which you are assigned in advance of your starting date. It is better yet to see the classroom, and best of all to meet your cooperating teacher and the students. "I visited my school back in October," wrote one student teacher whose assignment started in February, "so I knew more or less what I could expect. The school I found was lovely and the room itself appeared to provide warmth and color and is conducive to learning. That's the way I found it when I started here a few weeks ago."

Often, an early visit serves as fine medicine to reduce anxiety, especially when the picture you get is both positive and inviting. It is true, of course, that early visits do not always reveal the kind of school or conditions one would prefer. The school might turn out to be old and forbidding in appearance. Worse yet, the teacher might appear to be remote. Worst of all, the students might seem to be so different from you that you become concerned about your capacity to understand and cope with them.

Your early observations may be disappointing. Still, it is better to know the characteristics of your teaching assignment than to live with untested fears. All one can do with the unknown is toss and turn in bed over it. You can deal with the "known." You can prepare for it. Here is one account of a student teacher's expectations and the real life of the classroom that unfolded:

> 1/15: I expected the school to be an old one in a poor neighborhood, and so it was. I had been told it would be like that, so I expected everything that I thought goes with that: poor equipment and very little at that. I also thought it would be poorly organized and hence that minimal amounts of teaching would occur. Then I expected the children would be wild whether in the classroom or on the playground. They would display minimal self-control, that is, a lot of battling, hitting, and teasing. The teacher, I figured, would always be screaming at the top of her lungs and reprimanding the children. You can imagine that I wasn't very happy about that and it surely didn't add to my confidence.
>
> As it turned out, this old building in a depressed area was very well organized and had many advantages (e.g., a breakfast and hot lunch program, a reading program, a library, and a good gymnasium). The children displayed a lot more self-control than I had expected. They are very verbal and use minimal physical aggression in the classroom. They are also learning self-discipline about finishing their work. The teacher is very firm and consistent with the children. She fosters independence in the children. Nonetheless, teaching here will be a difficult task, as the class is large and there are a lot of cultural gaps as well.

Your foundation courses probably stressed the need to understand the diversity among the students in a school. Chances are you learned the value of demographic information in aiding that understanding. Now is the time to use that knowledge—to find out in advance the composition of your class(es) and to be familiar with the community surrounding the school.

Let us sum up: Anxiety in anticipation of a new experience is normal. Some of it is even desirable, to give you a bit of an "edge." More than a little of it, however, is a burden, and you should work to reduce it so that it does not interfere with your sleep, appetite, or personal life. Reality testing, by getting useful information about your school and cooperating teacher, is the best antidote to worry about the unknown student-teaching experience.

Self-Expectations

Have you ever asked yourself what you expect to gain from your student-teaching assignment? What you expect depends partly on the standards you set for yourself and the confidence you have in your abilities. Both will help shape the outcome of your student-teaching experience. However, other factors, many beyond your control, will also play a role in determining what you gain from the apprenticeship period. Three factors, discussed here, are particularly important: (a) the degree of similarity in philosophy of teaching held by you and your cooperating teacher; (b) the atmosphere in the school, especially in the classroom; and (c) the class composition.

Let us first look at teaching approach. Suppose your personal style and experience in school have given you a preference for a highly structured mode of teaching. Now you are assigned a cooperating teacher who is generally permissive and loosely structured in class organization. Under these circumstances, you have a right to expect more stress than you would if your approaches were similar.

You may have difficulty adapting to the unaccustomed behavior; yet the experience could turn out to be an enriching one. You may find that incorporating some permissiveness makes your teaching more effective. The same expectation is appropriate in the opposite situation; that is, if you are permissive and the cooperating teacher is highly structured.

The second of the three factors, school and class atmosphere, cannot be ignored when you set your expectations. If there is tension in the school, a sense of distrust and perhaps quiet hostility among teachers or between teachers and administrators, the students will be affected. If tension is clearly present in the classroom, it will affect the behavior of the students. They will still learn, but probably at a diminished level. Under those circumstances, you must adjust and do your best.

The last of the three factors that should have a bearing on the expectations you set is the composition of your class or classes. It is unrealistic to expect all classes to perform in the same way. If you are assigned to a large class in an urban school and the students are behind grade level, you may be facing extraordinary challenges. In today's test-oriented environment, level of achievement, like it or not, is an important reality. With a class starting out considerably behind state and national norms, you should generally set your expectations in terms of progress made and not solely in terms of level of performance achieved.

You should, of course, set high standards in all professional work, but you should not expect the impossible. In several months as a student teacher one cannot expect to remedy years of poor school performance and lack of readiness for the grade or subject you are teaching. Moreover, it is not the student teacher's job to do so.

PREPARING FOR YOUR ASSIGNMENT

We said earlier that visiting your assigned school and its surrounding area would probably reduce some of your concerns. Another reason for such a visit is that teachers are at an advantage when they know the context in which they work and in which the children and their families live, work, and play. To obtain such information, you should investigate the neighborhoods from which your students come as systematically as possible before beginning your assignment. Learn what you can about cultural, economic, and political issues in the area. Remember that in schools where a significant number of students are bussed, you may need to investigate more than one part of the city. Your college supervisor can give you a start in obtaining useful information, and your cooperating teacher can help fill in the gaps.

One of us had the good fortune of taking a course in which a useful plan for studying the community was used. (This sociology of education course was taught by Patrick J. Kelley, then at New York University.) The following modified outline indicates the kinds of useful information you can obtain to assist you in understanding your school's neighborhood and its people.

Exploration and Investigation of a Community

Get a map covering a radius of 10 blocks around the school in which you will be doing your student teaching, and obtain a neighborhood or local newspaper, if available.

Using the map and newspaper, plan a visit to the school's neighborhood. If you are assigned to a school in a high-crime area, inquire whether it is safe for you alone, or you and a classmate or a friend, to walk about unescorted. If it is not safe to walk, try to arrange a visit by car. In either case, your aim is to make careful observations. If possible, speak to storekeepers, police officers, community leaders (official or unofficial), nurses in public health clinics, staff members in neighborhood agencies, and citizens in restaurants, laundromats, and other public places.

Become acquainted with curriculum resources, such as factories and commercial enterprises; transportation facilities; museums and parks; libraries and historic sites; and churches, synagogues, mosques, and other houses of worship.

Note the characteristics of the neighborhood, including evidence of problems (e.g., many vacant storefronts) and strengths (e.g., friendly interactions among people on the streets).

Determine the representation of ethnic and socioeconomic groups in the neighborhood based on available statistics (e.g., from agencies or the census) and on personal observation of street signs, restaurants, and means of communication. The information gathered will help you understand the environment in which your students live, and thus make you a more effective teacher.

It is essential to know that the very meaning of education differs from social class to social class and ethnic group to ethnic group. In many instances, a college education, which was obviously important to you, may not mean the same to your students and their parents. It could have less value because in the past, it was generally unrealizable or because a child from a family dependent on welfare support for three generations has had no opportunity to know its meaning.

To use another example, children of upper middle-class professionals may feel relentless parental pressure to succeed in school. Their parents, recognizing the increased competitiveness for admission to top colleges and universities, place an extremely high value on achievement, both in and out of school. Their lifestyle demands fast-paced, high-paying jobs, and they expect their children to gain the skills necessary for this kind of employment. A poor grade that keeps their child off the honors list can be devastating to such parents. They may be willing to do everything from hiring private tutors to "helping" with a research paper to achieve the desired result.

No one socioeconomic or ethnic group is better than another, but members of each group may experience school and even the lessons and homework you assign differently.

BECOMING PART OF THE SCHOOL COMMUNITY

Over the decades, the teaching profession has undergone considerable change in the direction of freedom to live one's private life as one prefers. When your grandparents or great-grandparents were children, the practices were quite different. In most school systems, if a woman married, she lost her job. But that was not all: Teachers seen serving beer in their homes on a Saturday night found their contracts not renewed.

Those days are past. However, that does not mean that all of the public's social restrictions on teachers have been lifted. The proprieties in a school regarding such practices as speech or mode of dress are more conservative than they are on most college campuses. Schoolteachers are expected to impart students with not only knowledge of math or science, but also with certain values such as the importance of sharing, the unacceptability of physical aggression, the necessity of treating authority figures with respect, and so on. In the face of school violence tragedies, public outcry about the need to incorporate character education as a part of public school education has heightened.

Although there has been much change in teachers' attire since the 1960s when slacks were taboo for women in most districts, many styles of dress are still considered inappropriate in a school building. We would like to be helpful to you by being able to spell out what the "well-dressed" student teacher wears today, but that is not possible. Practices differ greatly among geographic regions, school districts, and types of schools (neighborhood public, magnet, parochial, independent). Our recommendation is to carefully note the dress of the faculty in the school to which you are assigned and dress slightly more formally than the average faculty member does. If teaching in the upper grade levels (7–12), it is important to ensure that your attire differs from that of your students. Students this age will recognize your youth, and it is vital that you look the part of teacher, not peer.

ACKNOWLEDGING YOUR CONCERNS

One of the best prescriptions for mental health is to remind yourself that you are not alone in your worries. For that reason we dwell here on common concerns reported by student teachers.

Over a period of several years, candidates for student teaching in one department at the University of Georgia were surveyed about their concerns about student teaching (Murwin & Matt, 1990). At the beginning of their course in methods and curriculum and one quarter before their student teaching, they were asked to identify their 10 major concerns about student teaching (Matt, personal communication, February 21, 1991). The responses of 36 students showed that some or all of the following were very much on their minds:

- Discipline: Uncertain about what to expect . . . and how to handle it . . . and whether their ways of handling problems would meet with approval.
- Student Relations: Anxious that they might not get along with their students . . . might not be liked and respected . . . and that this outcome would develop for reasons over which they themselves might not have any control.
- Faculty Relations: Apprehensive about relationships with teachers and winning their respect . . . troubled about what their relationship with the cooperating teacher would be like.
- Lesson Plans: Insecure about preparing adequate and acceptable lesson plans . . . not confident their plans would be found to be satisfactory.
- Methods and Motivation: Troubled about their ability to motivate and hold their students' interest.
- Self-Image: Unsure about their ability to match the expectations of the people who would make judgments about them.
- Materials and Supplies: Teachers in fields like technology, art, and music wondered if the necessary materials and supplies would be available and adequate in quantity and quality.

The students in this study seemed to be saying, "I don't know what to expect and how I'll handle it. Also, I'm not sure whether students and teachers will like what I do, and will like me. I hope I can live up to expectations." A study 20 years earlier (Cohen, Mirels, & Schwebel, 1972) took a different tack but showed some similar findings.

The 139 participating student teachers were given a 122-item questionnaire built to assess the common concerns of student teachers during their school assignment. The items covered the broadest possible range—from concerns about getting cooperation from the school's custodian to those about getting too personally involved with the students' problems. The student teacher participants were asked to rate each item indicating whether it caused: (a) no concern, (b) slight concern, (c) moderate concern, (d) great concern, or (e) such very great concern that it has led me to consider leaving the teaching profession.

It is comforting to know that only 3 of the 122 items on the common concerns list aroused great concern or very great concern in 50% or more of the student teachers:

• Obtaining a good job placement after graduation (81%).
• Working with students who don't seem to care if they learn or not (52%).
• Finding enough time to give adequate attention to each student (50%).

Not surprisingly, the first of the three was about securing a satisfactory job after graduation. Student teachers know that their performance and the ratings they receive from the cooperating teacher and college supervisor will have considerable bearing on their success in obtaining a job. Next came concern about the "unmotivated" students. Implicit in this concern is fear about controlling a class if the unmotivated become disruptive. The third greatest concern was worry about the time available in today's classrooms. The student teachers wondered, given the press of time, if they would be able to provide attention to individuals, which they were taught was the mark of the good teacher.

It is fortunate in one sense that studies show that not all of student teachers' concerns develop and must be faced at once. Koeppen (1998) described the experience of a high school social studies student teacher, Jared, who initially struggled with nervousness in front of the class. At the beginning of his student-teaching experience, Jared focused his energies on reducing the anxiety caused by standing in front of the class. As he became less nervous at the front of the room, he developed other concerns: defining himself in the role of teacher, feeling he had mastery of the content he was teaching, managing the pace of instruction, and later, feeling socialized with his cooperating and other teachers.

It is not surprising that Koeppen's (1998) prototypical student teacher first struggled to feel comfortable and secure himself and then mobilized energy to focus his attention on problems relating to the children, and later, to fellow teachers. The same pattern emerges in nursing students during their clinical assignments (Packard, Schwebel, & Ganey, 1979). Specifically, they are first concerned about themselves and whether they are performing up to their supervisor's expectations. Then, recognizing this, they feel badly that they are worrying about themselves rather than their patients.

Given the results of these studies, remember when you are feeling overwhelmed early in your teaching that there is a tendency to blame yourself and also to assume that somebody else would be working wonders. Self-criticism is useful because it can help you do better, but self-condemnation is crippling. It drains your confidence while offering you nothing positive. When you are knee deep in concern, remember that everybody faces challenges of one kind or another during student teaching; most problems are remediable and conditions tend to improve over time.

Knowing that you are not the only student teacher with worries can be reassuring. Helen put it this way in her journal:

3/5: My lesson on plants was timed perfectly today. But I'm still having problems getting the children to listen or respond to me. The student-teaching seminar helped me here. It's comforting to know the rest of my classmates are having similar experiences and problems.

For generations, concerns like Helen's and others discussed here have troubled student teachers. Most student teachers successfully manage or conquer their fears, cope with their stress, and go on to become effective educators.

MASTERING A PROBLEM-SOLVING METHOD

In embarking on new ventures like student teaching, individuals who feel confident are at a great advantage. The belief that they will manage to cope successfully with whatever comes their way helps them effectively deal with both the realities of their apprenticeship and the concerns already discussed. As we said in chapter 1, student teachers who train themselves to think optimistically will not blame themselves for setbacks. They will not retreat into helplessness and depression. Instead, they will be challenged to find ways to confront problems more successfully (Seligman, 1991).

One way to reinforce your optimism is by having the wherewithal to deal with problems. You don't have to be a superhero to do that, you just have to develop your skills as a problem solver. We have outlined a strategy, called COURAGE, to aid you in this process. With COURAGE firmly planted in your mind, you will come to believe that you can successfully manage any classroom situation.

A seven-step process, COURAGE outlines a logical way of coping with the problems that every teacher encounters.

Assumptions

In utilizing COURAGE, it is important to understand its three underlying assumptions:

1. There are usually a variety of ways to cope with a problem in teaching.
2. To cope effectively with a problem, you must appreciate the perspective of everybody involved.
3. Not every problem a student teacher faces is solvable.

After these assumptions are discussed, the COURAGE method is presented.

Assumption 1: There Are Usually a Variety of Ways to Cope With a Problem in Teaching.   Because we live in a scientific age, we have come to believe in the invincibility of research and scientific discovery. When we have a problem, we go to the expert and expect him or her to solve it. We have become accustomed to thinking that there is a right answer to everything. However, such simplicity rarely exists in schools.

Usually there are many reasonable approaches to problems, with no one way seeming obviously more right than another. Each possible approach has its own likelihood of success, its own payoffs, and its own costs. COURAGE was designed to help you select your best alternative for a given problem, keeping in mind that the best solution for you may not necessarily be the best solution for someone else.

Consider John, for example. A bright youngster, he finishes homework quickly, then converses with his slower paced peers, interrupting their studies. There are many ways to deal with him. You could move his seat, assign him additional work, scold him when he engages others in conversation, use him as a messenger, develop his talent as a peer tutor, or challenge him with an independent study project. None of these options is obviously correct, however.

Student teachers must select their approach after considering several factors, including their values as educators, their understanding of the child's and class's needs and interests, and their assessment of the relative merits of each choice. If one plan fails, student teachers should choose another.

Assumption 2: To Cope Effectively With a Problem, You Must Appreciate the Perspective of Everybody Involved. For example, finding an effective solution to John's disruptiveness could involve a number of people, including John, his parents, the student teacher, the cooperating teacher, the principal, the school counselor, and the student teacher's college/university supervisor.

Each party has his or her own needs, goals, personality, and so forth, and these affect how each sees the situation and what each wants to do about it. Some of their needs may not be immediately obvious, but the student teacher (or teacher) who hypothesizes that they are there and then investigates their presence will be much more effective in problem solving.

Everybody wants John to be a productive learner and less disruptive to the class, yet everybody is also influenced by covert (i.e., not immediately obvious) needs and goals. The following list shows what some people's needs might be in John's case. Psychologists sometimes call these covert needs hidden agendas. All people have them in situations that relate to their work and personal lives, which means they exist in virtually all relationships. There is nothing wrong with hidden agendas. Having them does not mean these people do not want to help John. Quite the contrary; they all want to help him function better in school. However, if each person were aware of the hidden agendas of the others, the group might be better able to do what they all want—to help John.

The possible covert goals of each person involved with John's problem include:

1. John: To get attention from his classmates and teacher.
2. John's mother: To be judged by the school as a concerned and good mother.

3. John's father: To be judged by the school as a concerned and good father.
4. The student teacher: To appear patient and competent when dealing with John in front of the cooperating teacher and college/university supervisor.
5. The cooperating teacher: To appear to the principal as a skilled teacher who is having difficulty because of John's personality (and not because of his or her handling of John).
6. The principal: To portray himself or herself as a concerned administrator who cares about each student.
7. The school counselor: To show progress in diagnosing and helping John.
8. The college/university supervisor: To demonstrate the usefulness of academic knowledge in problem-solving issues such as John's disruptive behavior.

Identification and recognition of such hidden agendas may help you not only find a solution to the problem at hand, but also make each person feel good about the result.

Assumption 3: Not Every Problem a Student Teacher Faces Is Solvable.   Regrettably, there is not a happy Hollywood ending to every classroom problem. However, most situations can be improved to the point where those involved are comfortable. For instance, John may never be your most obedient pupil, but if he and the class are handled effectively, his behavior can be modified so that he is much less disruptive.

An example of an unsolvable problem may be the actions of a disruptive, undisciplined child whose hyperactivity was brought on by the mother's use of crack cocaine while pregnant. It may be too much to hope that you will end the child's disruptions, but through consistent standards and discipline, you can establish a situation that is tolerable, if not desirable.

USING COURAGE

Your mind is the most important tool you have at your disposal as a problem-solving student teacher. When you inevitably face a problem, apply COURAGE. The raw material for COURAGE is the information you create, collect, and record. You process this information in steps that allow you to gain a deeper understanding of the problem and then solve it in a thoughtful way.

COURAGE includes seven steps:

C   Collect a bank of information.
O   Organize thoughts about the problem and patterns associated with it.
U   Understand the problem by taking others' perspectives.
R   Reflect on possible solutions to the problem.

A   Act on a solution.
G   Gather new information.
E   Evaluate effectiveness.

Next, we explain each step.

C: Collect a Bank of Information

We suggest you collect a bank of information about your life in the classroom by keeping a daily journal of your student-teaching experiences. Problems in the classroom, like problems in everyday life, often build over time. If not addressed, minor annoyances and frustrations can eventually reach a boiling point. When—in the heat of the moment—you explode or panic, it is often not because of a particular incident but because of a pattern established days, weeks, or even months before. Journal entries help in several ways. Most crucially, expressing your thoughts in writing forces you to reflect on the events that have transpired during the course of the day. As a result, journal entries both help you deal with issues as they arise, before they become major problems, and help you reflect objectively on those issues that do build up over time, despite your best efforts. In addition, later steps of COURAGE depend on having a bank of information collected from journal entries or similar recordings.

In your student-teaching journal, enter the key events of your school day and your thoughts, feelings, and reactions to them. Record what you consider positive and negative. Identify those high points where everything clicked. Describe those moments of frustration when nothing seemed to go right. Write out what you might have done differently to make things better and what you could do to avoid problems in the future. Also enter important events in your student-teaching seminar and your reactions to them. Effective journal keeping involves both a logical thinking process and a free-flowing stream of consciousness on the range of emotions emanating from your classroom experiences.

We know that you are likely groaning at the thought of having one more daily task—writing notes after a full day of student teaching—and we can sympathize with such a reaction. Ultimately, the decision to keep a journal (or not) is yours. We can only emphasize the advantages. In addition to serving as a problem preventer, journals (a) help make COURAGE work more effectively, (b) encourage you to regularly devote a few moments to think through and reflect on the events of the school day, (c) provide you with a regular opportunity to relieve stress by venting your feelings, and (d) develop a document that reveals your growth as a teacher.

Carmen provides a strong argument for keeping journals in the document she was required to keep during her student teaching:

I just reread some of my earlier thoughts from the beginning of the month. Sometimes it's easier for me to explore things on paper. When I look back on my thoughts after a time interval, I see that not all of my ideas are logical. That makes this sort of thing valuable to me. I've been doing this journal-type thing since spring quarter. I wish I had kept a journal of my thought-notes during my three weeks in the classroom winter quarter. It would be interesting to see my changes on paper. Easier, too. I've gone through a lot of changes since then. I'll bet this is much more interesting to me than to you [her college/university supervisor].

Example of C. Your journal serves as your collection of an information bank. Examples of journal excerpts are presented throughout this book.

O: Organize Thoughts About the Problem

When a problem develops during your student-teaching assignment, as problems inevitably do, use your journal to make an accurate statement of your concern. Describe the specific difficulty succinctly, preferably in a sentence or two. Initially, focus only on describing the problem rather than presenting a presumed cause or a proposed solution.

Once you have clearly phrased the problem, use the bank of information stored in your journal to organize your thoughts about it. Note patterns. Do particular behaviors by you or others (e.g., your cooperating teacher, students, etc.) lead to particular desirable or undesirable results? Begin to explore causes by listing factors that might be playing a role in the undesirable situation. Be sure to put all possibilities on paper so you can review and reflect on them, now and in the future.

Example of O. Clearly stated problem: My cooperating teacher will not let me teach enough to satisfy me. (Not: My cooperating teacher doesn't think I'm competent and that's why I'm not teaching enough to satisfy me.)

Bank of information:

#1 I didn't control the kids today during my first lesson. We had a long class discussion today, got off into six different directions and covered only half of what we were scheduled to do. Mrs. P. didn't want to go to lunch with me today. I don't think she likes me. She complained about the student teachers she gets from State University, that they're never prepared.

#2 The first class I taught didn't go as well as I'd hoped. I think I'm getting sidetracked by students' questions. Because we spent so much time discussing the lab's setup, the kids didn't get through the experiment. Mrs. P. seemed really frustrated when I dismissed the class before all the equipment was put away. It's so hard to win! I know she values business-like efficiency, letting kids out the minute the bell rings. So how am I suppose to know if that or her rule about putting everything away takes precedence?

#3 Mrs. P. told me she would teach all of the lessons tomorrow. She asked me to assist the 1st and 3rd lab group in 2nd period, the 4th lab group in 3rd period, and the 2nd and 5th lab group in 6th period. My groups have fallen behind. I'm feeling very frustrated—I know I didn't do very well explaining the lab last week, but how can I improve without practice?

Exploration of causes:

—The class sometimes gets out of control when I teach, perhaps because I focus on individual students' concerns. When I'm looking at one corner of the room, the rest feel they can get away with things.

—I seem to get caught up in answering questions and we get off track.

—Sometimes I do not follow class procedures as closely as Mrs. P. wishes.

—Mrs. P. has clearly had bad experiences with student teachers from State University in the past, and I'm just one of the pack.

U: Understand the Problem by Taking Others' Perspectives

Once you have brainstormed possible factors that contribute to the problem, you should consider how other people might perceive the same situation differently. For example, if you are feeling frustrated and cheated out of learning time, then what is your cooperating teacher feeling? How does he or she see the issue?

Remember the hidden agendas we discussed earlier? One of the most difficult challenges of student teaching is working to reach beyond your own impressions and feelings and step into the shoes of the many other people involved with the issue. Work to understand and appreciate their perspectives. Using whatever information you can, including your exploration of the causes of the problem and old and new journal entries, hypothesize what their thoughts might be.

Example of U.   Hypotheses about what the perspective of Mrs. P. might be: Mrs. P. is responsible for the safety of the students. She has to run a tight ship to make sure there aren't any accidents in the lab—she could get into big trouble if one of the kids got cut by a broken test tube or managed to catch their sleeve on fire by leaning over a Bunsen burner.

Mrs. P. might be worried about the state science test the kids have to take in May. She has the reputation of being an excellent teacher and obviously wants to maintain that. She could be worried she won't get through all the material covered on the test.

Maybe Mrs. P. is accustomed to mediocre student teachers coming out of State U., but I got all As and Bs in my education courses. Problem is, she probably doesn't know that. I have to overcome some mistrust I had no part in creating. She might assume I'm like student teachers she's had in the past, even though I'm not.

Hypotheses about what the perspective of the students might be:

The students might think that since I try to answer their questions in a lot of detail, and Mrs. P. doesn't, they should take advantage of the time I teach to ask all their questions. If they try to ask her questions, she might blow them off. So, they ask me questions and we fall behind.

The students might get bored during Mrs. P.'s lectures, but they are excited by my approach and they listen and since they're listening, they ask a lot of questions, but that slows us down and I don't cover nearly as much.

I suppose the students might see me as inexperienced, and try to take advantage of that. They might purposely ask a lot of questions so we don't get through as much material, meaning they can't be tested on it.

R: Reflect on Possible Solutions to the Problem

After clearly defining the problem and working to understand how each person involved may see the issue, you are ready to brainstorm solutions. Use the following steps.

1. Reviewing knowledge about patterns gleaned from current and past journal entries (Step C), and the work you completed in Steps O and U, generate a list of strategies for dealing with the difficulty. Reflect on the advantages and disadvantages of each approach and consider the likelihood that it will improve the situation. Write these down in a chart, as shown in Table 2.1.
2. Consider all the people involved in the situation and the effect each approach would have on them and on you. Add these to your chart.
3. Share the problem and possible coping strategies with people who can help you: your college/university supervisor, cooperating teacher (if the problem is not directly related to him or her), fellow student teachers, or friends. Have these people help you review both your thoughts about the problem and possible coping strategies. Once they have the relevant information, they may be able to provide a fresh view.

Example of R.

1. I could talk to Mrs. P. about my early performances, and how that affected her thinking about my abilities. I could explain that I think I need to practice techniques to improve my skills.
2. I could ask Mrs. P. why she hasn't let me teach much.
3. I could just be really direct and ask Mrs. P. to let me teach more often and see how she responds.
4. She does let me teach occasionally. After I teach the next lesson, I could ask her directly for criticism and go from there.

TABLE 2.1

Problem Analysis Chart

Alternatives	Likelihood of Improving situation	Advantages	Disadvantages	Effect On			
				Me	Mrs. P.	The Students	My Supervisor
1. Talk to Mrs. P. about my early performance							
2. Ask Mrs. P. to let me teach							
3. Ask Mrs. P. why she hasn't let me teach							
4. After next lesson ask directly for feedback							
5. Ask my supervisor to talk to Mrs. P.							

5. I could ask my supervisor to talk to Mrs. P. and explain that it's okay if I take over all the lessons earlier than the last 4 weeks of the term even though that's all State U. requires of me.

A: Act on a Solution

Based on your chart and the information and thoughts you have collected during the previous steps, choose an approach. Plan its implementation and consider how you can evaluate the success of the approach selected. Record this in your journal.

Example of A. Choice of approach: I will ask Mrs. P. directly why she hasn't allowed me to teach more frequently. This direct approach may solve my problem, and I think it will boost my self-confidence. Because I will deal with the issue myself, I think I will have a better chance of earning Mrs. P.'s respect (and it won't hurt the relationship with my supervisor either!)

Plan for implementation: I will ask Mrs. P. first thing in the morning—before the 8 a.m. bell—if we can chat briefly after school.

Plan for evaluation: Tomorrow is Friday. I will compare the number of lessons I teach next week (after the discussion) with the number of lessons I taught this week.

G: Gather New Information

After you have acted on your solution, record the results in your journal. Remember that often the interests and opinions of many people are involved, and things might not always work out cleanly. Change may not occur or, more likely, it will occur gradually. Continue to use your journal to record and reflect on the problem. Repeat many of the steps of COURAGE—organize your thoughts, understand by taking others' perspectives, and reflect on solutions. Remember to look for (and celebrate) even subtle or incremental improvement.

Example of G. Journal entry: I taught only one full class period today, but it went pretty well. Mrs. P. liked my creation of 3-D molecular models. I still had some difficulty handling the questions, but most of the kids were engaged for the majority of the class period, and Mrs. P. seemed more pleased than she has been in the past, which I guess is saying something. During lunch she asked me what I knew about 3-D computer modeling of molecules. She suggested that we might plan a new unit around that. I sense that the "we" really meant "you," and that this might be a chance for me to get more teaching time on a trial basis. We'll see how it plays out. I'll stop at the computer center on the way back to campus and see what I can learn about the software program.

E: Evaluate Effectiveness

The last step of COURAGE is to evaluate whether your plan has worked. This step often takes time, and occurs over the course of a few weeks. If little improvement occurred, consider whether you should continue with this coping strategy or try another. Refer back to your chart from Step R and reconsider the options if necessary. Remember the old adage, "If at first you don't succeed then try, try again."

Example of E.   Journal entry: I taught five more class periods this week than I did last, and I have had several conversations with Mrs. P. about the 3-D molecule project on the computer. I have half the molecules unit planned already. Basically Mrs. P. and I discuss the lesson together, then I go home and write it. She's going to have me do just about all the teaching for the duration of the unit, so I'm satisfied. I've also begun thinking about how in my own class next year I can integrate technology throughout the curriculum, something we spent time discussing in class last semester.

This problem was solved successfully, as many of your own problems will be, when COURAGE is applied. Others problems, however, will end with only moderate success. However, by using sound problem-solving techniques, you can make even a difficult situation instructive.

We give COURAGE prominence here because we know you will inevitably encounter many challenges and problems in student teaching. We also know that you will benefit by having such a problem-solving procedure at your disposal. Once you try using COURAGE, you will find it is not much more difficult to use than the sound reasoning you apply in other areas of your life.

FOUR STAGES TO STUDENT TEACHING SUCCESS

We conclude this chapter with a description of four stages of development typical in the life of the student teacher and the kinds of concerns, issues, and problems you are likely to encounter at each. This is not to say that your experience will follow each stage exactly, or that each will be equally prominent, but you can expect to find at least elements of each stage—perhaps more of some than others—during your teaching assignment. In each stage you will find that COURAGE helps you deal with the inevitable problems.

Stage 1: The Early Days

The first days are no honeymoon. They can be overwhelming, especially because student teachers try to absorb so much information so quickly. They drive themselves: I've got to learn the schedule, I've got to learn my way around the building, I've got to learn each student's name. I've got to learn the school rules and policies, the class routine and procedures, the materials the teacher uses, and the teacher's techniques. Besides trying to master all that, they want to please the cooperating teacher. Feeling overwhelmed and seeing the cooperating teacher handling everything in stride, they feel awed: "Can I possibly do it?" they ask themselves.

Stage 2: Becoming a Member of the Teaching Team

Through observation and immersion in class activities, student teachers begin to get a more accurate picture of their class(es) and its teacher. They begin to see the students as individuals and, at the same time, to gain a sense of the wholeness of the class, a group that operates as a unit. The cooperating teacher is not a name on an assignment sheet anymore, but rather a real live person. Effective as he or she may be as a teacher, he or she is not imbued with superhuman powers, but is simply an able person who, being human and working with humans, has to cope with problems. Student teachers may start to generate ideas about what they would do differently if this were their class. They begin to feel part of the class. The class recognizes them as members of the teaching team. Student teachers, perceiving their cooperating teacher as a person, have feelings that stem from their interaction, including feelings of warmth, respect, and anger.

Stage 3: Soloing as a Teacher

The preliminary period is over and student teachers try their wings: They solo! All of the topics and problems discussed so often in college classes, fantasized, and dreamed about (including an occasional nightmare) are now real life, here and now, today. Preparation, presentation, timing, movement of students from one activity to another, assisting one group while monitoring the class, discipline, and discipline again—all these facets confront student teachers simultaneously.

By Stage 2, student teachers' morale has risen rapidly. In Stage 3, unless they are careful, their morale can nose-dive. If student teachers want to feel bad about something, there is always something to feel bad about. For instance, if they compare their performance with their cooperating teachers', they will surely find themselves inferior—and yet they may fail to attribute this inferiority to the differences in their experience. However, they need not make this comparison. They can instead find positive things to take note of, such as the progress they have made and their success each day in coping with something they were unable to cope with before.

There are no yardsticks for student teachers at this point, only feedback from the college/university supervisor, cooperating teacher, and students. However, they can reflect on and learn much from this feedback. There are three patterns of response to choose from in this stage: Some feel defeated by the situation, label themselves failures, and give up. Others feel defeated, but place the blame elsewhere—usually on the cooperating teacher and sometimes on the college for having prepared them poorly—and give up on the assignment, if not on teaching. Finally, most student teachers feel okay about Stage 3, viewing it as a passing phase, difficult indeed, but one that they will successfully weather and grow from, in part by using a problem-solving system like COURAGE and continually sharing experiences with other student teachers.

Stage 4: Feeling Like a Teacher

After passing through the storms of Stage 3, student teachers settle down to the job of working with their students and in the process, transform themselves into teachers. Their time with the cooperating teacher will be drawing to an end. From here on, whole days are theirs to plan and execute.

From the weeks of classroom experience they have begun to develop their own style, and further, they have come to feel at home in front of the class. They know there is much more to learn, but they accept the reality that one does not become a master teacher in 10 weeks or even 10 months; it takes years. Above all, Stage 4 student teachers have much more confidence: When the new school year rolls around and they take over their own classes as full-time teachers, they know they will be able to handle the job.

CRITICAL ISSUES

- What am I expecting of myself as a student teacher?
- What do I know about the community of my assigned school and the students who attend it? What can I learn?
- What can I do to become part of the school community?
- What are my chief concerns about student teaching? What can I do to face those concerns?
- How can I benefit from the use of a systematized problem-solving strategy like COURAGE?

PART II

Relationships

3

Building a Good Relationship
With Your Cooperating Teacher

Success in student teaching begins with a good relationship with your cooperating teacher. A productive relationship places you in a strong position to learn and become an effective teacher. It also lays the groundwork for a supportive letter of reference that will aid you in securing your first position.

We start with a step-by-step discussion on building an effective bond. This is followed by an explanation of how to avoid potential relationship problems and how to deal with those that do arise. The last section of this chapter deals briefly with substitute teachers, whom you may encounter during your student-teaching assignment.

THE FIRST MEETING

That first meeting with your cooperating teacher is important. You can do much in advance to make it a successful one. Here are some suggestions:

Prejudgments

Before and after student-teaching assignments are announced, you may hear your classmates voice very subjective evaluations of different cooperating teachers: "Hartman is good, but Hellman is a loser." "I hope I don't get stuck with O'Shea down at Lincoln School," somebody might say.

If you hear your prospective cooperating teacher so evaluated, we advise you to ignore the comment. Without prejudgments, you will be better positioned to enter your first meeting with an open mind and with the expectation that in due time, you will make your own judgments and develop an effective teaching team.

Psychological Readiness

The situation is ideal if you come with confidence in yourself and your ability to succeed. If you cannot muster that degree of confidence now, you can work to prepare yourself psychologically and, as a result, present yourself as willing and able to assume classroom responsibilities.

One aspect of readying oneself psychologically is coping with anxiety. Nervousness is a natural human defense to anxiety-provoking situations, and to a degree is sometimes helpful—anxiety raises our heartbeat and gears us for unexpected or difficult situations. Excessive anxiety reduces mental acuity, however, and coping with it is an invaluable skill. Deep breathing, muscle relaxation, and distraction techniques are all useful stress-reduction tools you might explore through self-help books in your local library or bookstore.

In readying yourself psychologically you will want to set aside time to think about what you want to learn. Jot down specific skills you hope to develop, content areas in which you want to prepare units, discipline techniques you would like to use, and so forth. Next, think about the first meeting with your cooperating teacher. What do you want to know from him or her? Are there specific issues about the students or classroom that are worrisome? What information can the cooperating teacher give you to allay these fears? You should also think of what information you want to provide your cooperating teacher about yourself, your training, and your goals. Before your first meeting, rehearse your part of the conversation. Finally, practice the stress-reduction techniques you have learned and use them as needed during the meeting.

The Cooperating Teacher's Perspective

Because you will probably know little about your cooperating teacher, it will be difficult to anticipate the dialogue with him or her. One way you can deal with this ambiguity is by imagining somebody who is both your boss and your instructor. Those are the cooperating teacher's roles. Now, imagine that you were in that position. What characteristics would you want in your student teacher? Would you be pleased to have a student teacher who conveys excitement and enthusiasm about teaching?

While you are imagining yourself in the cooperating teacher role, consider what else you would hope for. The instructor part of you would probably prefer a person who exhibits an appetite for learning as well as an eagerness to use you as a resource person. The boss part of you likely desires a person who is competent, reliable, trustworthy, and hard working. He or she wants a student teacher who generates new ideas, but also understands and follows established procedures.

Scheduling the First Meeting

Although there is much you can infer about your cooperating teacher, you will not begin to get the information necessary to substitute facts for assumptions until you meet. When you are given your cooperating teacher's name, it is wise to telephone (or e-mail) and request an opportunity to meet as early as possible.

The ideal first meeting would be a leisurely one, held before or after school at a time and place convenient to you both. Such circumstances allow you to initiate a pattern of useful communication and thoughtful sharing. You might discuss the topics your class will be exploring when you begin, your role in the classroom over the course of the student-teaching period, and the dates and times you are expected to be at work. If you have allowed ample time, you could also exchange ideas about educational theories.

Unfortunately, the ideal is frequently not possible. Some student teachers will not know details about their assignment until the day before they are to begin. Others will have sufficient notice but a cooperating teacher who prefers not to meet until the term commences. If the cooperating teacher seems to be putting off a meeting, remember it may not be for the reasons you assume. Whenever the meeting takes place, make sure it is the first step in building a solid relationship.

At the meeting you will form your first impressions of your cooperating teacher. You will see whether the teacher is open and comfortable or restrained in interacting with you. You will probably learn something about the teacher's orientation toward education and style of running the class: for example, highly structured, following a well-defined schedule, or loosely structured and flexible.

Before and after meeting your cooperating teacher, remind yourself that a single conference gives only a first impression. If the meeting went well, you may feel fortunate in being assigned an effective and personable teacher. If you thought the meeting was only mediocre, remind yourself that even if your assessments were accurate, feelings often change as student and cooperating teachers get to know each other over time.

THE FIRST DAY

Although you will likely be too busy to realize it, your first day as a student teacher is a milestone in your life and transition point in your professional career. It deserves special attention. Whether things go well or you end up needing two aspirin before noon, take a moment to celebrate the occasion.

Alice, who was not able to meet her cooperating teacher prior to her first day, described her initial impressions in her journal. Note that she made observations that she expected would be useful when she began teaching:

> 1/6: It was a pleasant day. I met Mrs. L., my cooperating teacher, who appeared to be friendly and highly concerned with her pre-kindergartners. I was also introduced to the children, who seemed to be happy and for the most part, eager to learn.

> I observed all day long and noticed how some of the children had very short attention spans. That should be useful to me when I begin teaching lessons. Since I was observing, I didn't have much interaction with the children. They tended to be a little shy with me yet.

> Overall, I think I'm going to enjoy student teaching at Glen Avenue School.

Alice was obviously pleased. Some student teachers leave school after the first day in a state of ecstasy, whereas others are disappointed because the school, the cooperating teacher, or the children were not what they had anticipated. To some extent, Joyce felt this way, but she had hopes, too:

> 1/6: This wasn't what I expected at all! I guess I'm really disappointed with the situation I think I'll be in at this school. Well, it's only for 10 weeks. With a big mental psyche maybe I'll make it. I like the other student teachers. And, if I'm not crazy, I feel an air of disappointment from them too. The staff seems friendly towards us all, but I receive negative vibrations towards me as a Black.

> The class and I will get along fine. The school day in this classroom is so regimented! That's one thing I'd like to change. The kids are always in their seats. The fact that I'm Black may not upset them much, since I'll be the teacher. But, with the staff—things might be different. It's going to be hard working with Mr. P. . . . He's so set in his ways and he seems to be against change. Hope I'm wrong!

To state the obvious, first impressions are not necessarily accurate, and it is a mistake—a very serious one, in fact—to set your expectations on the basis of your initial experience. Why? Expectations prepare us to act as if the expected events were inevitably going to occur. Then, without our necessarily being aware of it, we may help make them occur through our actions.

For example, if, on the basis of very limited experience, you expect your cooperating teacher to discourage you from voicing your views by putting you down every time you utter a word, you will end up censoring yourself and speaking only when necessary. Put another way, you will make your expectation come true and, at the same time, limit your chances to learn from your student-teaching experience. Instead of making premature judgments, you should go into the situation with a positive outlook.

STAGES IN YOUR RELATIONSHIP WITH YOUR COOPERATING TEACHER

Your relationship with your cooperating teacher will most likely pass through many stages of development. At each stage you will face certain challenges and benefit from unique learning opportunities. To prepare you to best take advantage of those opportunities, we trace the development of the cooperating teacher relationship, using the stages outlined in chapter 2.

Stage 1: The Early Days

In getting started, much time is spent absorbing a great deal of information as quickly as possible. You channel energy into (a) becoming familiar with the cooperating teacher's teaching style, (b) becoming acquainted with the students and learning their names, and (c) adapting to the pace and atmosphere in the school and in the classroom. The feeling of being overwhelmed will likely develop; expect to feel drained by day's end.

You also will want to invest energy into building the student teacher–cooperating teacher relationship. As the journals we collected suggest, this relationship does not develop automatically. Although some cooperating teachers take the initiative, others do not. In such cases, it is in the student teacher's best interest to do so.

As days go by during the classroom observation period and you feel more comfortable with both your class(es) and teacher, you will want to assume more responsibility. By then, your cooperating teacher will know you better and may be ready to have you teach. When you reach this point, a student–cooperating teacher planning and goal-setting meeting is useful. At such a meeting, you can review your classroom involvement to date and identify areas in which you would like to work. Perhaps through give-and-take discussion, the two of you can develop your learning goals.

Sandra asked Darla, her cooperating teacher, if she would be interested in having a planning and goal-setting meeting. Darla thought it was a great idea, and it was she who suggested a lunch meeting. Much was accomplished, as Sandra described in her journal:

1/26: Darla and I went to lunch. The first part of the meeting turned out to be more of a social situation than anything else. Later, we did discuss my position in the class and Darla was concerned how I was or wasn't enjoying the observation days. She informed me I could begin teaching lessons on Monday and we planned the procedure for the day. We also set up a series of long-range goals. These were for me to:

a: rearrange the reading corner and that side of the classroom

b: plan a measuring unit

c: fully acquaint myself with all materials in the room

d: design a unit on transportation

e: review the science manual and classroom laboratory kit and start science with the kids

f: individualize with Stephen and Kevin

g: work on being a creative teacher

h: create a backlog of 5-, 10-, and 15-minute classroom activities

i: by the middle of March, see how much of the above has been accomplished

For Sandra, building an effective working relationship with her cooperating teacher, Darla, was easy. Most student teachers who call on their social skills and the knowledge acquired in their courses will also find this task easy. In fact, they will find it much like forming a friendship with a willing person who shares common interests.

Not every student teacher will be this fortunate, however. If you have difficulty building an effective working relationship, reassure yourself that others have been in a similar position and have succeeded in bringing about change. Try using COURAGE to think about the problem systematically. In analyzing the situation, consider a range of potential causes, including those that involve your cooperating teacher's style and behavior as well as your own. For instance, ask:

1. Is your cooperating teacher by nature the type of person who takes time to warm up to people?
2. Is your cooperating teacher an unwilling participant in the student teacher program?
3. Are you your cooperating teacher's first student teacher and, if so, is he or she learning how to make the cooperative effort work?
4. Did you do or say anything your cooperating teacher might have thought out of place? If so, could that account for the difficulty you are experiencing?
5. Do you represent a threat to your cooperating teacher because of your personality, appearance, or some other trait or quality?

COURAGE may lead you to discuss the problem with a friend, fellow student teacher, or your college/university supervisor. They might be able to suggest alternative coping methods or, if necessary, your supervisor may intervene on your behalf. As you know, the supervisor's job is to help you as well as evaluate you. Supervisors know that a poor relationship with a cooperating teacher deprives you of an optimal learning experience.

Stage 2: Becoming a Member of the Teaching Team

As the first days pass, student teachers recognize the cooperating teacher's substantial professional ability, while also discovering that the halo of perfection has disappeared. Cooperating teachers are not perfect. They make mistakes and do some things differently from the way the student teacher was taught. For example, they do not handle June's disruptive behavior head-on and they seem to ignore Harry who, with all his potential, will soon turn 16 and drop out unless somebody persuades him to complete high school.

A frequently voiced concern during this stage relates to the cooperating teacher's classroom style and philosophy of education. For example, Patrick wrote in his journal, "The teacher is so traditional. . . . She shouts at the kids all day. . . . Even an adult couldn't sit still for as long as those kids have to."

Student teachers airing such criticisms note the differences between their philosophy of education and teaching style and those of their cooperating teacher and often hasten to add comments like, "I'm never going to teach my class that way." However, making such observations and declaring that one is going to teach in a different way does not eliminate the worry. These student teachers doubt whether they can learn from a mentor whose approach seems so different.

Fortunately, student teachers do benefit from an experience with a teacher whose approach is very different from their own. Richard and Beth are good examples. Although they first feared they would be unable to tolerate a semester-long relationship with their cooperating teachers, they ultimately found that their classroom experiences helped them crystallize their own thoughts about teaching and learning. As Richard wrote:

> 2/5: School went well today. I have vowed to myself I will not teach in the same manner employed by Allyson. . . . My obedience to this vow remains to be seen. Also the question comes to mind, how will I teach?

> . . . How? I am really not sure, but I will try to avoid shouting . . . and asking them silly or irrelevant questions when they act up.

> I will try to let them look at more books, have their work areas less cluttered, and come up with more imaginative ways of introducing a lesson's learning objective.

Beth's philosophy of teaching also differed from her cooperating teacher's. As she wrote:

> 3/15: I finished grading the test on *A Tale of Two Cities* tonight. What a chore! I still think it's a ridiculous test, but I've learned there is little I can do about that— Mr. O.'s been throwing students multiple choice questions like these for years. I do know, however, that I will never ask such obscure, minute nonsense when I write my own exams. They do little more than tell you that the kid memorized overly detailed notes put on class handouts (or that he made a lucky guess!). My assessments will test for understanding and comprehension, not memorization. And they will let kids WRITE. They are in English class, after all.

The reason we confidently state that you can learn in any cooperating classroom is that you are the key ingredient in what is learned. Regardless of your assignment, you can derive great benefits from your interactions with your students. It is true that with certain assignments you will have more extensive experience and more opportunity to experiment, but wherever you are, if you commit yourself, you can develop professionally.

At some point during Stage 2 you will probably compare yourself with your cooperating teacher. This may occur when you are reflecting at your desk or watching your cooperating teacher call on a student you might not have selected to answer a question posed to the group. When you do compare yourself with your cooperating teacher, you will invariably find differences, some of the most obvious of which are discussed here.

First, you obviously differ in years of experience and perhaps in the kind of training you received. You have come on the scene with fresh ideas from your college or university that may contradict the ideas and practices that your cooperating teacher has developed through the "school of hard knocks."

Second, you have different roles and responsibilities in the classroom. Your main job is to learn. In contrast, although the cooperating teacher has some responsibility for instructing you, his or her first responsibility is to the class; that is, to see that certain instructional goals are achieved.

Third, the two of you may have different personalities, work styles, and so forth. You may be energetic and bubbly, whereas your cooperating teacher may be quieter and steadier, or vice versa.

These differences, and others, may create divergences in the ways you approach students and in the preferences you have on how lessons should be taught, class order maintained, and student work evaluated. As a person without the yearlong responsibility of maintaining discipline, you may be critical of aspects of your cooperating teacher's approach. For example, you might think he or she shouts too much, is too tied to routines, and is oriented to the middle-of-the-road students, ignoring high achievers and those with learning deficiencies. After you have drawn these mental conclusions, you may well be tempted to suggest changes to your cooperating teacher or to indicate how you would handle things differently. Should you? Resist that temptation and instead:

1. Avoid being judgmental or assuming the cooperating teacher's way is wrong and yours is right. Consider the advantages and disadvantages of both approaches. When he or she handles a situation or teaches a lesson in ways different from how you would have, enter that in your journal and list the pluses and minuses of both approaches.
2. With an open mind, approach your cooperating teacher to discuss his or her approach. Ask "why?" questions and share your perspective. You may find that your cooperating teacher is insightful and has carefully considered reasons for selecting the approaches used.
3. Follow your cooperating teacher's way, unless you have permission to experiment. Do so for several reasons, including the fact that you are a guest in the classroom. If you give the cooperating teacher's approach an all-out effort, you can see how it works for you. With that experience, the two of you can assess whether that approach works for you or whether another approach would be worth trying. For example, one of the authors was assigned a male cooperating teacher in an urban school. The rough, tough, masculine approach to disciplining students did not work well for her. As a result of several discussions, the two of them worked out a plan she could use for disciplining that was comfortable for her but also consistent with his approach.

The journal entries that follow show that differences in teaching approaches, which seem terribly important in the early days and weeks, generally get resolved satisfactorily as time passes. Discussions of methods, assessment, discipline techniques, and differences in style become more fruitful and comfortable as the student and cooperating teacher get to know each other as people. Moreover, many student teachers find that after they win the confidence of their cooperating teacher, they are allowed to experiment. Marsha reported this:

2/19: When I first observed Mrs. H.'s split first and second grade class, I saw she was much more strict and traditional than I wanted to be. Her room was very orderly. She asked the children to raise their hands before they talk and tried to stress manners. I don't object to an orderly class, but it seemed to me that the children were too regimented. They all sat in their seats and were not allowed any paper or objects in their hands.

I think that they need quite a bit of direction to begin with. Also, they do need help in working quietly. But then gradually, they could work in groups, and be given a little more "room." Those are thoughts which occurred to me at the start. . . . Within a month Mrs. H. and I had a good relationship. She let me open things up more and try some of my ideas. She was surprised at how well they worked, even though I let the children go some.

When you get permission to try things your way, the results are not always satisfactory to you or your cooperating teacher. For example, Phyllis tried to give the students more freedom and, when she did, she was pleased with the results. However, her cooperating teacher was not at all happy about what developed. The two of them spoke about their different views on classroom atmosphere and about what was tolerable in terms of control. Phyllis hoped they could define a middle ground between them, but they were not able to. Wisely, Phyllis accepted the fact that she had to run a "tight ship" for the rest of the term.

Although many students are fortunate because they are assigned to cooperating teachers who give them opportunities to experiment, not everybody will find this. If you are not permitted to try your way of teaching, bear in mind that the cooperating teacher is the boss. The relationship is not an equal one; the cooperating teacher has the authority and you have only that which is delegated to you when you teach a lesson and grade the related student work. In any situation when somebody must yield and the cooperating teacher is not willing to do so, you must.

In summary, if you are convinced that you are not getting the chance to use your abilities effectively, try COURAGE and talk with your cooperating teacher, supervisor, or both. Then, if it becomes clear that there is no way of obtaining the teaching opportunities you want, think about next year when you will have your own classroom.

Stage 3: Soloing as a Teacher

This is it! Although student teachers learn much by immersing themselves in the life of the classroom and observing the process of teaching and learning, the heart of student teaching is in teaching itself. You will learn most when your teaching is accompanied by constructive criticism. Student teacher–cooperating teacher relationships often get rocky around the time that criticism is given and received. Sensitivity and fortitude, respectively, are essential to giving and receiving criticism. If you feel resistance within you when your cooperating teacher begins to offer criticism, tell yourself, "Here's an opportunity for me to learn how to be a better teacher. He or she is not evaluating my worth as a human being but rather how I might be more effective in a realm of functioning that is important to me." With practice, the process of receiving criticism in a healthy way will become second nature.

Few of us get a great deal of experience in giving and receiving criticism in a professional setting. This lack of experience can cause problems that manifest themselves when cooperating teachers prepare and provide feedback to their student teachers. The kinds of problems that may emerge include these:

1. Receiving no feedback from your cooperating teacher.
2. Getting only negative feedback.
3. Getting only positive feedback.
4. Being criticized while you are teaching.
5. Having criticism of you publicized.
6. Getting angry at the cooperating teacher.
7. Finding yourself in a difficult relationship with your cooperating teacher.

Each of these is discussed in turn with an eye to helping you overcome such a problem should you encounter it in your relationship.

Receiving no Feedback. Perhaps the most frustrating problem is not receiving verbal feedback. Without it, you do not know how your cooperating teacher feels you are doing, leaving a gap you must fill by wondering and guessing. This hampers your learning, often forcing you to search for signs of approval instead of concentrating on your students.

Joyce had problems getting feedback and commented in her journal on how that made her feel:

4/8: Today, I was supposed to take the class over for the entire day. The only thing I wasn't supposed to teach was history . . . (after lunch). And that is how it went. The day went along great. Everyone got along and I feel my lessons were successful. The children really got involved with the math lesson. My first one! Boy, I was glad. Sometimes I wonder what Mr. P.'s bag is. He glares at me with approval (I think) but he'll never say anything. But then the glare could be envy or dislike. I wish he'd say something because as it is now, I don't feel at ease with him watching me. I just don't know what he's thinking.

What can you do in a situation like Joyce's? Here are general suggestions that may help:

• When you have a good opportunity to talk, meaning that students are not present and your cooperating teacher is not busy, ask specific questions about your work, various class procedures, the functioning of individual youngsters, and so on. Remember to phrase your questions so they do not sound critical or threatening. Stress instead your interest in learning the art of teaching.
• Ask about the possibility of establishing a regularly scheduled time to discuss your progress as a student teacher.
• Receive any criticism you get graciously. If you appear intimidated, angry, argumentative, or annoyed by feedback, you will likely make it more difficult for your cooperating teacher to criticize you and, in fact, may discourage future sharing.

The basic idea here is that you need to take the initiative. We recognize that asking for criticism is often anxiety provoking, even in cases where the student teacher and cooperating teacher have a fine relationship. Ed's journal entry illustrates his concern about receiving specific feedback from his cooperating teacher:

> 4/4: Mrs. R. is fantastic. She spends so much time talking with me, suggesting, and giving me books to read. I also feel comfortable with her because I feel that we have ideas and beliefs that "mesh" and work together well, with the main objective being the benefit of the kids.
>
> I still wonder if I am doing enough. . . . Does Mrs. R. expect me to do more? Does she think I'm lazy or afraid to take on more? I feel as if I am not asserting myself enough with her, that I should ask her more. I guess I am a bit afraid to suggest taking over more . . . than I do, and I can see that I am slowly doing more and gradually taking my place. . . .

Ed needed evaluative information from Mrs. R. but was afraid to ask for it. As a result, he had needless worry and spent time feeling he was not meeting her expectations. When he finally asked, he felt reassured because Mrs. R. was very pleased with his work.

There are at least three widely used but ineffective ways to get feedback on what you want to know. We do not recommend them. The first is dropping hints. You know how that operates. In a matter-of-fact way, you say, "Something just came to mind." Then you mention it and hope the cooperating teacher will catch on and tell you what you want to know. Sometimes this strategy succeeds, but you cannot depend on it.

The second method is to start a conversation and hope. This involves talking first about an issue related to what you want to know and hoping the teacher will catch on and move to your topic. This is not a reliable approach, as an entry from Vicky's journal shows:

> 3/8: I made plans for today and informed Mrs. B. of them. But things didn't turn out as planned. I was very upset at one point when I told the children to go to their small groups and Mrs. B. decided they should have some exercise. Since I had already told some children (Group I) to get their books, there was a lot of confusion. ("Are we supposed to get our books now or get in a circle?" etc.) Besides the fact that she interrupted my plans and completely undermined my authority in the classroom, she chose to play an exercise song that half the children refused to participate in because the other half of the children get so rowdy. . . .
>
> Later, when I asked her if she had any comments about what I had done today (I was hoping she would bring up this part of the day so we could discuss my intentions), she only said she liked what I had presented, especially the Bear Hunt.

Vicky started a conversation and hoped, but the conversation did not turn to what she wanted to discuss. As a result, the air was not cleared and she went home frustrated. Whatever caused Mrs. B. to interrupt Vicky's plans was left unclarified, so a repeat of the incident at a later date was possible.

A third ineffective method is mind reading. Mind reading is not a prerequisite for being a cooperating teacher! This method is unreliable because it assumes the cooperating teacher knows what you want feedback about—or that you want feedback at all.

Getting Only Negative Feedback.   A hazard of student teaching is encountering a cooperating teacher who gives you only negative feedback. What problems can this cause? First, people want to hear the good news about what was right as well as the bad news about what was wrong. When you hear one without the other, your opportunity for learning is accordingly reduced. Second, hearing only negative criticism can erode your confidence, even if you have the strongest of egos.

If you find yourself receiving only negative feedback—and becoming angry or frustrated about that—take action. Use COURAGE to think about the situation systematically. Ask whether you need the teacher's positive words to learn better, build confidence, or boost your ego. The answer will help you plan a course of action.

In one journal entry, Leslie reported that she was facing nothing but negative criticism. After analyzing the situation, she concluded that she needed positive feedback to improve her teaching. She said to Mrs. R., "I need to know what I'm doing right so I know what not to change." Mrs. R. smiled and replied, "You are doing everything fine," but that was all the positive feedback Leslie got that week or the next.

More thought about the situation led Leslie to decide that Mrs. R. was not the "positive feedback type," and that she would have to learn without hearing from her the positives that she craved. Because Leslie's need for "positives" stemmed from a desire to improve her teaching through feedback, Leslie decided she could obtain it another way, by watching her students and providing positive feedback to herself through the "reading" of their faces and actions.

After each lesson she presented, Leslie asked herself, "What did I do well? Did they learn what I intended to teach? Did they seem challenged and effectively stimulated by the material?" She also looked at their papers to document the reliability of her observations. Did the students master the material taught as evidenced by their homework, quiz responses, and test answers?

Leslie also used conversations with her supervisor and informal talks with her friends as a way to gauge whether or not her progress in student teaching was on track. Although Leslie did not change Mrs. R.'s behavior, she did develop a plan that made life tolerable. Of course, she wondered why Mrs. R. would not give her positive feedback. She thought that Mrs. R. might have been taught to avoid complimentary comments, or, perhaps, that Mrs. R. was experiencing her as a threat because of her high energy level. Leslie also considered the possibility that Mrs. R. might be going through difficult times in her personal life. Without further speculation, however, Leslie made peace with the situation. She accepted Mrs. R. for what she was, took advantage of the negative feedback she provided, and learned to use her students as an indirect source of the positive aspects of her work.

Like Leslie, Lorraine was concerned with the negative feedback she was receiving and the effect it was having on her feelings of competency. Lorraine's journal entry shows how she worked at understanding possible hidden agendas in her cooperating teacher's negative feedback. Note how liberating it was for Lorraine when she sensed that it was a personal quality in Mrs. C. rather than one in herself that had resulted in the flow of negatives.

> 3/4: Today went all right, and for the most part I taught for the entire [day]. . . . I really like when Mrs. C. gives me corrective criticism or suggestions, but sometimes I feel as though she is stressing or pointing up to me that she has had much more experience. In a subtle way, at times she makes me feel inferior or not as intelligent, and I'm beginning to realize that this is just her personality.

As you might expect, when Lorraine came to this realization, she was much better able to profit from Mrs. C.'s expertise and criticisms. Lorraine managed to deal with the negative feedback situation without asking for help from her supervisor; this is not always the case. For example, there are times when the amount and intensity of negative feedback from the cooperating teacher is such that it is defeating to the student teacher. Kate's journal entries, written over a period of a few days, describe what it is like in such an extreme case:

> 2/25: As I was leaving today, Mrs. N. said, "I can see by your face that you're not happy about today." I said, "I don't like the way things went." She answered, "Neither did I." I was glad she had answered me honestly. But at the same time, I think I was hoping more for reassurance.

> Essentially my dissatisfaction came from the fact that whenever I tried to do something with the class today I never seemed to have their full attention—they wouldn't listen to me when I asked them to be quiet, etc. Mrs. N. said that I lacked control. (I don't know if I would choose that word. To me it connotes a dictator.)

> On the way home I began developing a "fear of failure" feeling and I started dreading tomorrow morning. But after I sorted out my thoughts I realized my teaching strategy was not totally at fault.

> 2/27: As I walked out of the building today, the tears started pouring down my cheeks. I had held it all in for almost 3 hours, enduring the worst day of my life, and I was now ready for a good cry. When I got home I was crying so hard I couldn't even explain what had happened.

> It took me all afternoon to sort out what had occurred, and I'm not sure now what brought about my noontime discussion with Mrs. N. She told me (the obvious) that I am responsible for the children or I will be when I take over full time.

> [Mrs. N's criticisms included:] . . . I tend to get engrossed in one activity and have trouble keeping track of everything else that is going on in the room (a character

flaw, perhaps?). I am not disciplining the children. And she went on and on, the criticisms pouring out all over me. I tried to explain that I need time to get everything coordinated and that by the time I took over I was sure things would have improved.

I also tried to point out that because she always overpowered me I did not jump right into discipline situations. I would be standing there trying to talk with a child who had done something. Seeing it, she would be right behind me, with a "Stop it now!" directed at the child. Yes, the kid would stop, my discussion was over or I felt I might as well not bother. Anyway, our talk ended with her telling me that she didn't think I would make it and my numbly saying, "Don't worry."

I was so upset when the children walked in for afternoon classes. I don't remember how I taught my lessons. How could she do that to me? Hours later I'm still upset. I'm hoping that by morning Mrs. N. will be calmed down, the whole thing will be forgotten. Maybe she was having a bad day, because I think many of her comments did not take into account the fact that I am still learning and need time to absorb everything.

For the next days, Kate went through a great deal of suffering with Mrs. N. During this difficult period, she sought and received support from her supervisor, who eventually spoke to her cooperating teacher. Kate's persistence and the aid of Kate's supervisor paid off, as the following entry shows. Note that it concludes with thanks to her supervisor:

3/2: No more tears. Today was so much better. Mrs. N. liked my plans a lot. She was pleased with the way the day went and I was pleased too. The encouragement she gave me built up my confidence and I could teach again.

She told me that she could have cheered me up . . . but that then I wouldn't have done the soul searching I needed to do. Strange reasoning, in my opinion. There must be an easier way than coming close to a nervous breakdown.

Now I realize that perhaps we just weren't communicating, and I really didn't understand what she expected of me. I just hope there isn't a repeat. Although I would know what to expect, I don't think I could go through it another time. Thanks for the hours you spent.

Getting Only Positive Feedback.   At first glance, you might think this problem is nonsensical. How could it possibly be problematic if one receives only positive feedback? However, a crucial part of student teaching is learning, and it is difficult to learn without sensing what you could do better along with what you are doing well. Receiving negative feedback on aspects of your work you might improve—and everyone, even master teachers, has aspects of work that need improvement—will only help you as you begin your professional career.

Our advice for fixing this problem is very similar to the recommendations for overcoming reception of only negative feedback. Use COURAGE. Consider how the lack of negative feedback is affecting your development as a professional and how you can resolve that problem. Consider reasons for the situation: Perhaps your cooperating teacher is a novice at working with student teachers, is having personal problems at home, or is concerned about how you might react to negative criticism. If necessary, turn to your college/university supervisor for support.

Being Criticized While You Are Teaching.   Two things we know for sure are: (a) you want criticism of your work but not while you are teaching, and (b) you want assistance in learning to control the class but not in the form of having the cooperating teacher step in during your lesson. Nobody benefits from being contradicted in front of others. When this does happen, not only do you feel put down and worry that your authority has been undermined, but you also have to rebound from those feelings quickly so that you can overcome the interruption and maintain the flow of the lesson.

To some extent, you can take steps in advance to try to prevent your cooperating teacher from stepping in while you are teaching or handling discipline problems. The most important preventative measure is forming a healthy relationship with your cooperating teacher. If you accomplish this, chances are good he or she will feel better about electing to withhold criticism until the two of you can have a private discussion. Realistically, however, even when a solid rapport exists there are times when the cooperating teacher may unknowingly countermand your directions.

Let us first look at an instance in which the cooperating teacher, perhaps unknowingly, gives a set of directions that contradicts the ones issued by the student teacher only moments before. Sheryl's diary entry describes an incident during her fourth day of student teaching:

> 1/8: The day didn't start out well. We were going to the museum and the bus was due at 9:00. I told the class to keep their coats on—why have them in and out of the coat room? Mrs. R. came and screamed, "What's going on? Take your coats off and hang them up now." She really laid it on and made me feel stupid and sorry for the kids.

The incident struck Sheryl hard because it seemed at the moment to halt the progress she was making toward achieving something important to her: establishing her authority and winning respect from the class. The episode resulted from lack of communication. Sheryl had not had a chance to tell Mrs. R. that she had told the children to keep their coats on. Of course, Mrs. R. could have assumed that or even inquired of Sheryl, but she did not. Fortunately, the events of the next few days proved Sheryl wrong in thinking she had lost face with the children.

At the time of an incident like Sheryl's, it is natural to feel that single episodes like this one are very important. Generally, they are not. However, when episodes of this kind recur, there is reason for concern. Here are specific steps you can take to help prevent being repeatedly interrupted, contradicted, or countermanded.

1. Learn class and school rules.
2. From the beginning, try to establish a before-the-school-day-begins routine of speaking to your cooperating teacher about the day's plans. Besides what has already been scheduled for you to do that day, find out if there are any other specific tasks your cooperating teacher might want you to handle and the thoughts he or she has about these.
3. When you are observing, attempt to train yourself to know at what point your cooperating teacher reacts to events. For example, note at what point he or she speaks to a student who has been restless or disturbing, and how long after a group of youngsters becomes noisy does he or she put a stop to it.

Rose, who had been having trouble with in-class criticisms, reported how, by learning and applying class rules, she saved the children from criticism and herself from embarrassment.

3/3: Spring may be here at last. We went outside today for the first time. I really had the urge to slide down the sliding board with the kids, but I had the feeling Mr. N. would not approve. So I stood around with the other teachers on the playground and occupied my time by observing the large-muscle coordination of the children. I saw a lot more about their physical coordination out there where they were free to run around than I could ever have observed within the confines of the classroom. I also tried to absorb all their playground rules. Mr. N. has a lot of rules that I am unaware of until I let one of the children break a rule and he hurries over to correct the situation. (I, of course, always feel like a jerk.) So before we went out today I decided to learn as many as possible, so that I wouldn't end up embarrassed and the children wouldn't be needlessly confused. Mr. N. seemed pleased to list them for me.

Student teachers differ in what their predominant emotional reaction is when they feel their cooperating teacher repeatedly and inappropriately interferes with their lessons. Although some will be embarrassed or hurt, others will be angry or even infuriated. The least effective reaction is to slough it off with an "I don't care, it doesn't bother me" attitude.

Regardless of student teachers' emotional reaction to the interference, they must let the cooperating teacher know that interrupting their lessons frustrates their efforts to learn classroom management. Student teachers should use COURAGE to think through the issue systematically, then broach the subject with their cooperating teacher.

In the next example, we focus on a situation where the student teacher was repeatedly criticized in front of the children. Although this example merits attention in its own right, here it illustrates how a student teacher can use feelings to motivate a search for solutions. Note how Alice handled her problem over a 2-week period.

2/10: As I walked out of the doors of Glen Ave. this afternoon, I felt as if I had been a complete failure. Though I spoke with Mrs. L. about the day and accepted my criticisms well, I still felt something was missing.

Because I was 10 minutes late, I was scolded by Mrs. L. for being irresponsible as an adult. The children were restless throughout the entire day. I got very upset because Mrs. L. got angry because the day did not go smoothly—she criticized me in front of the children and before I had done my Valentine story. I told her that I would appreciate criticism after school. She said, "No, I'm going to tell you what you do wrong whenever I see you doing something wrong." I further explained that I could not function to the best of my ability if she did not save her criticism for later. "Well, that's the way I am," she said, "and besides, if I said something to you after school, I would just blow up."

I told Mrs. L. that I am student teaching for the purpose of learning, and it seemed as if she wasn't allowing room for any mistakes. She neither agreed nor disagreed but continued to talk about how I had done this wrong and that wrong.

This was a start for Alice and Mrs. L. Two weeks later they made further progress.

2/24: Each morning Mrs. L. writes assignments on the board. Today she put my lessons at the end, because yesterday I lost control of the group and she couldn't do anything with the children and had to punish them because of me. I asked her if she felt this was fair. "No," she said. When I asked why she punished them then, she said: "Because they must learn and learn to listen." I explained my feeling about having my lessons put at the end. I felt as if I was being punished for making a mistake. I asked her how I was going to develop control if she didn't give me a chance. Agree? She agreed. Then she put my lesson back on the board at the top, but she warned me, "The children must learn, and if you can't keep control, I'll have to take them."

Mrs. L. did not interrupt during the lesson, perhaps because Alice had handled the situation so well. Alice's success illustrates that forcefully but diplomatically stating your side of things can be effective.

Having Criticism of You Publicized. Any real professional understands that criticism should be private, shared only with the student and college supervisor. Yet that is not always what happens. Remember the game called "Telephone"? The way you play is that the first person in a line whispers a secret to the second, who in turn passes it on to the next, and so on. By the time the story gets to the last person, who announces the message as he or she heard it, it is typically vastly different from the original.

Dorothy faced a situation in which she was not getting constructive feedback from her cooperating teacher. Instead, as with the telephone game, the cooperating teacher was telling another teacher, who was in turn passing the information on to her student teacher. This student teacher was a friend of Dorothy's and kept Dorothy posted on how Dorothy's cooperating teacher was feeling.

Dorothy was never sure how accurate the information she heard was and, moreover, she wanted direct feedback. Dorothy's supervisor intervened, asking the cooperating teacher if she would give Dorothy more direct feedback and refrain from unnecessarily sharing feedback with other teachers.

Getting Angry at the Cooperating Teacher. The student teacher's partnership with the cooperating teacher has the potential for being quite intense. You will know soon enough whether the mix of your personalities might at times lead you to uncontrollable anger. Because favorable outcomes rarely follow outbursts, plan a method of keeping your temper in check if you spot such potential.

The following strategies may be useful in preventing a volatile situation:

- If at all possible, wait at least 1 day before you react to an upsetting situation.
- Ventilate your feelings daily in your journal and then, using COURAGE, develop suitable means of handling them after you have calmed down.
- Talk the situation over with your supervisor and with friends and get their reactions to your proposed ways of handling it.
- Remind yourself that next year the class(es) you teach will be your own.

Becky was ready to explode with anger at her cooperating teacher, but instead kept her temper. Following several of the steps just suggested, she handled the situation smoothly:

3/9: Class-wise today was OK, but I had some problems with my cooperating teacher. She voiced her opinions on what I planned to teach when I take over the class. She told me exactly what materials I should use, rather than let me use my own plans, and exactly how I should go about it. I became annoyed, frustrated, aggravated, and just plain angry. But I kept my temper and said nothing and went along with what she said. I will be planning activities for all reading groups, as well as teaching them (these activities) to the individual groups.

After my first week, she informed me, the aide will no longer help me. I will be completely on my own. I understood her logic of wanting me to have experience teaching without an aide, because, true, I might not have one. But for three weeks? I think that's a little ridiculous. I have to work my butt off while they are lollygagging in the teachers' room. Blah! I have decided I will try it for one week or 1 1/2 weeks, but no more. After that, if the aide doesn't help I'm going to Mr. Y. and tell him he is paying his teacher and aide to gossip in the teachers' room. I know I will cause "fireworks," but tough stuff. I have my limit too! Today was a terrible day. I was MAD!

Becky did not vent her anger on her cooperating teacher, which was fortunate because, as two of Becky's later journal entries show, her initial concerns and fears did not materialize:

3/10: Today was all right. My teacher came out of her witch act today. She was nice. She even offered to help me with my lesson plans for next week. And she gave me my very own plan book. Hurray! I'm going to let bygones be bygones because after all I still have to work with her and teach her class. And she has to give me my grade. I explained to her that I will be unable to stay for the afternoon tomorrow, because of a prior commitment. She understood. So I hope we are on the road to a better relationship.

3/14: Today was the first day I took over the class completely. My lesson plans are now done for a full week and my cooperating teacher is pleased. The day went pretty well. I came in extra-early to be organized, and it helped a lot. I planned the activities for reading groups, but we continued to teach as is. I taught my group, Mrs. C. taught hers, and Mrs. A. taught hers. . . . I was pleased. I left tired! But pleased.

Finding Yourself in a Difficult Relationship With Your Cooperating Teacher.   Ann was successful in building a relationship with her cooperating teacher despite an unhappy beginning. Ann considered herself a low-key person and presented herself that way in class. Unfortunately, at least as she perceived it, she was placed with Mrs. K., a vivacious "snappy" teacher, who wanted Ann to be a carbon copy of herself, even though she declared that every teacher should develop his or her own style.

Ann's success did not come easily. She worked very hard to attain the good relationship she wanted, and she spent many long hours discussing her situation with her supervisor.

She found herself uncomfortable with Mrs. K. and unable, she thought, to talk with her. To complicate things further, Mrs. K. had already established a close relationship with the classroom teacher's aide. This left Ann feeling like an outsider. The first time she was able to get the teacher's ear at all was the day the aide was absent. Ann took advantage of this situation, for she felt she had to grab at every straw.

The first day Ann asked for feedback on her science lesson the cooperating teacher responded with, "How do you feel about it? How would you mark yourself?" Ann's silent reaction to those questions was that she wanted Mrs. K.'s opinion, not questions. At this point Ann was not ready to evaluate her own lessons.

Ann and her college supervisor discussed the initiative she could take to improve communication. First and foremost, they decided, she had to be open and honest if she expected to establish a good relationship. She had to communicate her needs to Mrs. K. one way or another.

Ann knew that she would have to ask her cooperating teacher for time to discuss her feelings, time to discuss future lessons, time for feedback, and suggestions for improvement. To get this she had to be flexible and willing to come in early or stay late. The situation, she came to realize in discussion with her college supervisor, was unlike social ones she was accustomed to, and she had to make a distinction between her personal and professional life.

When Ann's cooperating teacher turned down a request for a meeting, Ann had to ask again, although in her social life she would not have done so unless the rejection had been accompanied by an explanation and a request for a postponement. Instead, Ann persisted. She ended up treating Mrs. K. to lunch.

With support from her supervisor, Ann continued to arrange meetings and make progress with Mrs. K. About a month into her assignment, she made this comment in her journal: "I am starting to build up a very nice rapport."

Ann learned that she had to compromise on certain things while she was in Mrs. K.'s classroom; this included working with students in a style acceptable to Mrs. K. She came to realize that sometimes you do things because your cooperating teacher expects it, but that you do not have to incorporate these things in your mode of teaching in the future. In fact she wrote, "One good thing I'm learning is exactly what I don't want to do as a teacher!"

The process was turbulent for Ann. At times her spirits were so low that she doubted whether she would ever succeed as a teacher—or even if she still wanted to be one. But she pressed on, saying, "I don't want to adopt her style. It isn't me. I'm not the snappy type; however, I probably do need to improve my voice inflection and I am going to work on it." And so, out of persistence and effort, Ann built her relationship, won her cooperating teacher's respect, and received a top grade.

After Ann's last day at school, Mrs. K. asked to see the university supervisor. The supervisor thought that Mrs. K. was coming to discuss Ann's grade, but instead, Mrs. K. opened a floodgate of feelings. Mrs. K. began apologetically, explaining that this was the first time she had a student teacher. During the early days she found it hard to relinquish her class to someone else—even the student teacher she had requested. "I was very unsure of myself from the start," she explained.

When Ann tried her first lesson, Mrs. K. was shocked at her quiet but diligent style. "But she is so different from me," Mrs. K. thought. That observation led her to remember what had been said by the supervisors at the introductory tea: Each teacher has to be himself or herself. So for the next few days, Mrs. K. tried not to impose herself as a model. Instead she tried to allow, indeed to encourage, Ann to do things her own way. However, that did not work. Mrs. K. saw the children changing under Ann's leadership. Discipline was loosening and the class was falling apart. She saw all her months of efforts "going down the drain." Eventually, Mrs. K. reached her limit and found it hard to refrain from imposing her standards on Ann and directly on the class.

Ann responded to Mrs. K.'s silent (and not so silent) impositions as harsh criticism of her teaching ability. It was then with the help of her supervisor that she undertook her campaign to improve communication and persisted until she set up the luncheon appointment. At that time, however, Mrs. K. explained during the conference:

> I hadn't realized Ann thought I thought she couldn't teach. . . . I tried to interfere as
> little as possible. It was difficult to hold myself back. I thought my class, my chil-

dren, were at stake, but I did hold myself back and much to my surprise it was not as disastrous as I had anticipated. Then when the end of the term came, and Ann began tapering off in her teaching and I began getting back into the act, I had another surprise. I didn't find teaching or disciplining to be a problem. . . . The children were exposed to both styles of teaching, and I think they grew and developed as a result.

In reflecting on the term that had just ended, Mrs. K. also mentioned with satisfaction that although Ann's style was different from hers, Ann had nonetheless acquired some of her ways. Mrs. K. mentioned that even the children noticed this, and had said to Ann, "That's the way Mrs. K. would do it."

The conversation ended with Mrs. K. and the supervisor agreeing about how important it is for the student and cooperating teacher to establish rapport. Mrs. K. said that unfortunately she and Ann did not have instant success, but at least they made it. Smiling, the supervisor said that in some cases it never happens.

We have seen both perspectives in the two-sided experience of forming the student teacher–cooperating teacher relationship. Basically, the essence of Ann's and Mrs. K.'s problem is a universal one, and it reduces itself to this: Student teachers must function in established classes and under the direction of others who, over the years, have developed their own way of teaching. On the other hand, cooperating teachers must share their classes with someone new, someone different, probably younger and more idealistic, and surely less experienced— characteristics that are likely to lead students and cooperating teachers to have different perspectives.

Stage 4: Feeling Like a Teacher

By this point, the major problems you will face during student teaching are probably behind you. With the end in sight, the negative part of your experience will seem more tolerable and under control; concomitantly, the full meaning of the positive part of your student teaching will come into view. Gerald describes what he experienced:

> 5/17: Just a couple of weeks left. So much stuff to do and learn. Oh, well, there is always next year in my own class. My own class. I have to write that to believe it will happen.
>
> This is my second week of planning and doing the whole day. Before I couldn't imagine how I could [manage] the whole day. Now it seems so natural. Mrs. R. was gone part of the afternoon, and I felt like it was next year. I've learned so much from her—even the hassles we had now seem unimportant to me. I'll miss her, but I feel I'll be ready to do it on my own next September.

Some "Feeling Bads."   As the term progresses and you take over more teaching duties, many thoughts will come to mind, including some that you may find surprising. We review a variety of these here, primarily so that you will know that they are normal and typical.

1. Feeling bad because you want the cooperating teacher to leave you alone in the room. This feeling is particularly annoying if you have had a good relationship because, in this case, you may feel guilty wishing him or her away. Vicky made the following entry in her journal: "I can't believe it. Even after 3 months she (the cooperating teacher) still never leaves the room, and I wish she would every once in a while."

2. Feeling bad about having to teach a lesson you think lacks excitement or having to teach a concept using an approach you believe is ineffective. Laura provided an illustration: "The day basically went well. The one activity that I was requested to do was pretty bad. It was a video on maps and globes. The kids were bored with it and so was I, but I had to do it. There are a lot more interesting ways to present maps and globes."

3. Feeling bad because you see time being used ineffectively. Ted bemoaned what he considered excessive use of new technologies:

> I'm getting frustrated with the seemingly endless practice of getting on the Internet or popping in a CD-ROM. It's great to have access to these tools and to expose kids to them, but there's something to be said for plain old human creativity in teaching. I think at times Ms. H. uses the computer just because it's there. And all that time we have the kids spend online could be used to hold the discussions and class debates we always seem to run out of time for!

4. Feeling bad about being successful and worrying about whether your cooperating teacher will resent your success—and your time with the kids. Brenda shared:

> I am beginning to feel more confident and I love the children. I really hope that Mrs. C. does not resent or mind my taking over sometimes, because I don't want to offend her. I decided that I wanted this to be a good learning experience, and I hope we can really make it one."

These feelings hardly deserve to be called problems. They sometimes develop during student teaching, and will not be problems if you reflect on them and put them in perspective.

HOW YOU AND YOUR COOPERATING TEACHER MAY DIFFER IN ASSESSING YOUR PERFORMANCE

Rarely do any two people agree 100% on assessments, especially if one is the novice performer and the other the expert mentor and evaluator. Williams

(1995) designed a study to test this issue in regard to student teaching. Williams's results may help you better understand the difference in opinion between you and your cooperating teacher. Using an instrument containing 54 specific items to measure student teacher performance, Williams administered her survey twice to 200 Tennessee State University student teachers and their 200 cooperating teachers. She found statistically significant differences on 23 items. In most of those differences the cooperating teachers gave more favorable ratings to the student teachers than the student teachers gave to themselves. Specifically, during the ninth week of student teaching, the cooperating teachers gave more favorable ratings than the student teachers on the following items:

- The student teachers' lessons were not boring.
- The student teachers got the students actively involved.
- The student teachers seemed to have had time to plan adequately.
- The student teachers managed all the paperwork.

Thus, although student teachers in their ninth week of internship might feel inadequately prepared, overwhelmed by paperwork, and unable to hold students' attention, they often do not appear to be.

Williams's (1995) study also pointed to areas where student teachers were perceived by cooperating teachers to be less adept during the ninth week of their internship. Namely, cooperating teachers saw their student teachers as having trouble:

- Managing small groups.
- Revising lessons while teaching if lessons were not going well.

As Williams pointed out, these are instructional skills that are acquired with experience. They are not likely to be in the repertoire of beginners.

Two points should be emphasized: First, cooperating teachers in this study generally saw the work of the student teachers in a more positive light than the student teachers themselves; second, cooperating teachers need to be reminded of something that most of them probably know: Some essential skills can only be acquired through experience over time. Remind yourself of these two findings during your student-teaching assignment to help keep your morale high and self-assessment on target.

RELATING TO SUBSTITUTE TEACHERS

The chances are good that your cooperating teacher will miss at least a few days of school during the course of your internship. On these occasions, you will most likely team with a substitute teacher.

A day or two with a substitute provides a good learning experience for the simple reason that a new set of circumstances is introduced. Treat the cooperating teacher's absence as a quasi-experiment. The substitute is the one variable that has been changed while everything else has been held constant: the students, the physical setting, your presence, and so on.

Of course, the substitute's personality and skills as a teacher partly determine the kind of opportunities you will have, as do several other factors, including whether the absence occurs early or late in your experience and whether you have lessons prepared for the day your cooperating teacher is out. Regardless of the circumstances, treat the substitute's presence as a learning opportunity. Whether you end up teaching (with a substitute observing) or watching a substitute teach is not as important to your learning as it may seem at the moment. If the substitute teaches, observe closely. Be attentive to how the substitute introduces himself or herself. What first impression is made? Watch the methods he or she employs. Assess the substitute's approach and note whether it is one you would be comfortable using. By observing, you can often gain insights otherwise unavailable in your student-teaching classroom. Laura reported:

> 3/19: The substitute today was fantastic. She was so bright and cheerful. The minute she walked into the room, you knew things were going to be good.

> In fact, Mrs. J. was one of the most enthusiastic teachers I have ever seen. After seeing how effective she was, I wanted to work on my own enthusiasm even more.

Laura saw a style she wanted to try to emulate, and she was exposed to certain techniques that she might not have otherwise seen. By contrast, Stan had a useful day because he saw what he did not want to be as a teacher and what effect cynicism can have on a professional's performance. He entered the following in his journal:

> 1/4: I worked with a substitute teacher who informed me that teaching was boring. It was evident he was not at ease or content, for his introduction of concepts was hastily completed, which led to impatience when Anne and Blanche and several others . . . asked several questions. He failed to follow the lesson plans Mrs. H. had left for him. I can imagine how much damage a permanent teacher could do to a class if she or he didn't want to be there.

If you are scheduled to teach lessons on the day a substitute covers, be ready to utilize the substitute's expertise. You could find yourself with an opportunity for constructive criticism from yet another professional. If your initial contact suggests that the substitute is willing to observe, explain how eager you are for feedback and how valued his or her opinion would be. You may also get a chance to teach for an entire day, with the substitute acting as a backup on an "as-needed" basis. Such an outcome can be exhilarating, as Irene reported:

> 2/26: Today was absolutely fantastic! Mrs. L. was out sick today and I felt I was the teacher and not just an assistant. She called me last night and told me about the things she had planned. She said that it was completely up to me whether I wanted to do them or give it to the substitute. I decided that I wanted to try to handle the entire . . . [day] and fit her plans into the ones that I had. The day went very well. The substitute was there but always in the background. I accomplished everything that I wanted to and . . . the day was over before I knew it. The more time that I spend in the classroom the more I dream about having a job in September doing what I want to do.

Of course, problems can also arise between substitutes and student teachers. Sometimes the situation is such that you choose to overlook them; other times you may decide to take action. An example of each is provided in the journals of Carl and then Dorothy. Carl wrote:

> 2/19: Today we had a substitute. Was today ever horrendous! I had to raise my voice more today than I've had to in the past four weeks. It seemed as though their "routine" was broken by Mrs. B.'s absence. They behaved in ways they never had (i.e., acted dumb to the previously established rules and routines).
>
> The substitute was a sweet person, but she constantly interrupted me and challenged my authority on several occasions. I only hope it really is for one day. I got the impression she wasn't working with me but against me at some points. An example of this feeling of opposition . . . [was] her reinforcing behavior that was contrary to the established rules in the class, like talking, etc. . . . I'm really thankful it's only temporary.

Carl wrote off the experience, knowing his cooperating teacher was returning in the next day or two. He could have been more assertive, but at the time felt it was not worth the risk of causing friction. A few days later in a seminar, however, he reported that if it were to happen again, he would have privately approached the substitute during lunch and said, "You know, while I was setting up the first lesson you interrupted me to discipline Brad. I felt the kids saw that as your challenging my authority. What do you think?"

Dorothy did take action, as she reported in this journal entry.

> 2/8: Miss K. is gone for the entire week due to some illness. The substitute is an elderly lady. She is very sweet, but as she said, "The children are too much for me to control." The main problem was that she continuously sent students to the principal's office. This is not appreciated by Mr. R. (which I will hear about when Miss K. returns), and I don't think it helps the class. Therefore, I discussed the problem

with the substitute. She said this was the last means of control and that she felt it necessary. After we talked, though, no more children were sent.

Dorothy took action in the interest of the class and also of herself and Miss K., because of the principal's anticipated reaction. The substitute did not welcome Dorothy's comments but seemed to respect her for speaking her opinion. Most important, Dorothy's comments changed the substitute's behavior.

Occasionally student teachers find themselves spending several days with one or a series of substitutes. If that happens, the important concept to keep in mind is that these days represent a significant proportion of those you will have as a student teacher. Use them as best you can for your own learning. Elaine, who experienced a lengthy absence of her cooperating teacher, did just that:

5/16: Mrs. R. told me today she has to go to the hospital. I know I can handle the [full] responsibility . . . because I did it the week she was out and part of last week. But I feel bad—I learn a little more every day from her and feel I'll be missing out. Besides, I'll miss her—I've gotten close to her. Well, the substitute they will be getting in her place will have much to offer on things too.

The presence of student teachers, especially after they are familiar with the students (and vice versa), is reassuring to cooperating teachers who face a prolonged absence. Often, knowledge that the student teacher will be there to provide continuity is enough to sway conscientious but ill teachers who might have otherwise come to school against their best interest. That they have that much faith in you will make you feel good.

YOUR STUDENT-TEACHING ASSIGNMENT
AND THE REALITIES OF SCHOOL LIFE

By their very title, cooperating teachers are those professionals who cooperate with your college or university and with you for the purpose of providing you with real-life experience in an apprentice–master teacher relationship. Cooperating teachers are selected for the role because they are considered skilled.

Although cooperating teachers want you to have a rich experience, they are subject to the policies of the school and under the direction of the principal. They are obligated to meet state standards, which places enormous pressure on teachers to shape lesson plans with standards—and test scores—in mind.

After finding that state standards were simply a reality she, like her cooperating teacher, must face, Brooke set about looking for the positives. As she wrote:

9/12: During the first few days of school I have been introduced to the state standards and the necessity to teach and guide lessons around the standards. After thoroughly reading through the standards I am slowly coming to better understand their purpose and direction. I think they can be extremely effective in ensuring that all students learn essential skills and theories. The textbook for the seventh and eighth grade curriculum is extremely good and presents a well rounded historical approach to American history and geography, but it still seems difficult at times to ensure that all activities are geared toward meeting certain standards.

As Brooke found, a school that values teachers who strictly adhere to state standards will produce cooperating teachers who may be resistant to devoting long periods of time to topics that, although of interest and value, are not included in state goals. Similarly, a school that values teachers who maintain quiet, order, and a highly structured teaching environment will produce cooperating teachers who are unlikely to encourage you to use a teaching approach that carries the risk of disorder. That does not mean that most cooperating teachers object to innovative class material or less structured teaching approaches on professional grounds. It does not necessarily mean that they would prevent you from trying them under other circumstances. It only means that in many cases, they accept (even if begrudgingly) the realities of professional life in their schools.

Realities like that will be very much part of your life, both as a student teacher now and as a teacher with your own class in the future. Perhaps the most helpful advice we can offer is that you make peace with the real limits you face in today's schools. Give yourself permission to function at your best within the boundaries available to you. Whatever limits are imposed on you by your cooperating teacher, your supervisor, your cooperating school, or your state department of education, remind yourself that there is still much you can learn and much you can teach.

Delight in the fact that you are a student teacher teaching in a real community and a real school. That community and school may have social, moral, and educational values similar to or different from yours. Your cooperating teacher may have an instructional orientation similar to or different from yours. Whatever the case, accept it and tell yourself, "This is my one and only student teaching experience—and I'm going to make the most of it."

Be good to yourself. Gain confidence in teaching in the ways that circumstances permit. Except for those your cooperating teacher allows you to try, save innovative ideas for your own future classes. Be sure to record them so you have them available when you might be able to use them in the years ahead.

In summary, recognize your cooperating teacher as a helpful person and work to build a strong relationship. Understand that your cooperating teacher will be affected by your response to him or her. If you show that you are eager to benefit from advice, you are more likely to have good rapport. If you appear annoyed when criticisms are given, you will make life difficult for both your cooperating teacher and yourself, and you will probably discourage your cooperating teacher from offering helpful suggestions again.

Even with the best of intentions and greatest efforts in relationship building, however, problems will arise. When you encounter them, remember that your supervisor and COURAGE are invaluable resources.

It seems appropriate to conclude our discussion of student teacher–cooperating teacher relationships with a brief summary of how researchers have studied the issue. Research over the past several decades suggests that a student teacher's orientation toward educational practice typically evolves during the student teacher experience. Most frequently, this evolution is from a more liberal, progressive, or emergent approach to education toward a more conservative, traditional approach favored by cooperating teachers (Harty & Mahan, 1977; Hoy & Woolfolk, 1990; Jones & Vesilind, 1995). As an example, Harty and Mahan (1977) asked 159 student teachers to complete the Educational Preference Scale before and after their 16-week student-teaching experience. The scale was also given to their cooperating teachers halfway through the 16-week internship. The Educational Preference Scale measures the teacher's orientation toward education on a number of different domains, yielding a general sense of how progressive or conventional the teacher is.

The results from Harty and Mahan's (1977) study were clear-cut. The student teachers were more liberal (progressive or emergent) than their cooperating teachers before they began their classroom assignment. By the end of the teaching, their orientation had shifted in the direction of their cooperating teacher and was more conservative or conventional. In fact, a substantial number of student teachers ended up with more conservative scores than their cooperating teachers. The investigators concluded: "Student teachers tend to become more like their cooperating teachers with respect to their expressed orientations toward education as a result of a 16-week student teaching experience" (p. 40).

This change occurs, we believe, not because cooperating teachers force it on student teachers. Rather, it occurs because of a bias toward conventional, custodial forms of schooling in our communities and in our society at large (Sarason, 1982). Student teachers discover this during their apprenticeship.

However, the question remains, should student teachers' orientations change from the relatively more progressive and emergent to conservative? Recently, some colleges and universities have begun experimenting with alternative models of student teacher training that may alter the results described in Harty and Mahan's (1977) study. For example, the teaching internship program at the University of California at San Diego lasts 2 years and allows the student teacher (called an intern) to work in several different classrooms under several different master teachers to varying degrees of intensity (Smith & Souviney, 1997). One goal is to avoid the situation common in traditional student-teaching programs where the preservice teacher enters a cooperative classroom with an established routine and, because of this, feels tentative about trying out his or her own ideas for fear of failure.

The Professional Development Schools (PDS) model also has gained national prominence. In this model, collaborative supervision is emphasized and interns are encouraged to explore their own approaches to educational theory, minimizing the evolution toward the cooperating teacher's approach. In fact, in many PDS schools, not only the student interns are enrolled in the university, but the cooperating teachers (many of whom are pursuing master's degrees) are as well. Classroom instruction often becomes a cooperative effort involving university professors, classroom teachers, and student interns.

CRITICAL ISSUES

- How can I ensure a successful beginning to my relationship with my cooperating teacher?
- How do I feel about working under the watchful eye of another person?
- What can I do to make the most of my student teacher–cooperating teacher relationship?
- How can I cope with problems in the relationship with my cooperating teacher?
- What can I do to get the most benefit from criticism provided?
- If I believe I am being unfairly assessed, how can I cope with that constructively?
- How can I make the best use of my contact with substitute teachers?
- How do I feel about the realities of teaching in today's schools?

4

Building a Good Relationship With Your College/University Supervisor

TOPICS

- How Your Supervisor Can Help You
  - As a Classroom Observer and Constructive Critic
  - As a Problem-Solving Resource
  - As a Source of Emergency Help
  - As a Seminar Leader
  - As a Support Figure
- What Supervisors Look For
- Classroom Conditions That Set Limits
- How You Will Be Evaluated

College supervisors are a special group of people. Typically, they are knowledgeable about the schools in the community where you will teach and are familiar with the problems of daily classroom life. They have a good working relationship with principals and teachers, which is helpful not only during your student teaching, but also in your job hunt. Because of their practical knowledge of teaching, they are a rich resource for the student teacher.

Who are the people who serve as supervisors? Some universities employ education graduate students, teachers who have returned to the university to further their own education by pursuing an advanced degree. Other institutions employ recently retired teachers as supervisors. All universities, however, select supervisors who have had experience as teachers, some for many years. Having themselves been student teachers, they understand what it is like to be in that position.

Supervisors differ in experience, personality, educational background, and approachability. Regardless of the mix of those qualities, your supervisor will be interested in your professional development. You will want to develop a trusting professional relationship with that person, whoever he or she is.

HOW YOUR SUPERVISOR CAN HELP YOU

College supervisors have a broad set of responsibilities and often carry a heavy load. Their tasks may include:

- Scheduling and holding observation sessions for each student teacher, including meetings with cooperating teachers and principals involved.
- Writing reports on the observations they make.
- Conducting a seminar for student teachers.
- Planning and hosting professional social activities for student and cooperating teachers.
- Maintaining cordial relationships with principals, department heads, and other school personnel (this for its own purposes, but also as the college's "ambassador").
- Serving as a confidante, problem-solving aide, resource person, and supporter to student teachers.
- Keeping records, including supplying information to the registrar for official school documents.
- Keeping informed of position openings for teachers.
- Evaluating student teachers and providing official letter grades, often in conjunction with the cooperating teacher.
- Composing letters of reference for student teachers.

The supervisor is very much a middle person, an agent of the college working to satisfy the needs of many people. In the following pages we review some student-teaching issues that arise as supervisors perform their duties.

As a Classroom Observer and Constructive Critic

Your college supervisor will likely observe your teaching several times. It is only natural to want to teach your best on those days. Because of that, student teachers often make the mistake of trying something innovative and new on the days of their observations. This is an unfortunate choice for two reasons. First, most supervisors want to observe you and your students under typical conditions in the natural setting of the classroom. Second, and most important for student teachers, differing greatly from the normal routine adds new dynamics that may lead you and your students to feel uncomfortable. This, in turn, may invite the unpredictable to emerge. The accustomed routine puts both you and your students at ease, increasing the likelihood that you will teach at the same level as on other days.

Although an observation day should be treated like others, the days preceding it should be treated differently. Your supervisor's several visits allow you to demonstrate the diversity of your skills, so you will want to think carefully about which particular approaches or techniques you will highlight in the upcoming observation. As at other times, prepare your lesson plans and materials thoroughly and well in advance. You may want to discuss them with your cooperating teacher and peers. This will help you gain confidence in your choices.

Prepare yourself psychologically for the observation by mentally envisioning the day unfolding. Imagine yourself entering the room in the morning with carefully planned lessons well suited to your abilities and the students' needs. When your supervisor arrives, picture yourself handing him or her a copy of your lesson plan for the day, including your aims and behavioral objectives for each lesson. Picture yourself handing him or her a copy of the student textbook and other materials assigned for homework. Then, because your classroom has an accepted procedure for introducing classroom guests, picture making the introduction. Your cooperating teacher smiles, and so does your supervisor.

If at any point a negative thought comes to mind, banish it. For instance, if you start thinking that you have chosen the wrong lessons, reassure yourself immediately. Remind yourself that the class has previously responded well to lessons like the ones planned. If you start worrying about a student asking a question for which you do not know the answer, remind yourself that it is fine to respond with, "That is an excellent question, and unfortunately I do not know the answer. I will do some research and let you know tomorrow." Remind yourself that you are well prepared to lead the class.

Picture yourself remaining effective throughout the observation period. Imagine the supervisor asking, "Do you have time for critical feedback now?" The words *critical feedback* ring in your ears: You remind yourself that this is the evaluation your supervisor promised to give you after the observation. You are alarmed again, but only momentarily. Remember that your supervisor has your development as a teacher at heart, and wants to help you become the best teacher you can possibly be.

Playing out the imagined scenario of a forthcoming observation is an effective preparatory mechanism. It helps you deal with the worry and stress evoked by your thoughts about the supervisor's scheduled observation. Some uneasiness is natural under the circumstances. Your supervisor is there to evaluate you: You alone are in the spotlight, and you want to excel. Thus, despite careful preparation and the attempt to keep the observation day as normal as possible, some nervousness will most likely remain. As Phyllis wrote:

3/8: I was tense about the observation at the beginning . . . in the back of my mind I was hoping that the children would be easily managed and my lesson would go all right. As it turned out, an early part of my lesson failed but everything else seemed to go well. Afterwards my supervisor gave me some good advice I have really thought about, and now even the failures of the day seem unimportant.

Because Phyllis prepared extensively, much of her nervousness passed once she began her lesson. Further, she was well enough in control of herself so that she was not devastated when—early in the period—her lessons did not go as planned. Under the pressure of being observed, that minor misfortune might have upset some student teachers. However, Phyllis had prepared for contingencies and thus was able to handle the situation.

Phyllis's nervousness was short-lived. Stephanie was never able to free herself of anxiety, even though her supervisor had worked especially hard to make her feel comfortable while being observed. Stephanie wrote to her supervisor in her journal after two successive observations:

2/25: Today I must admit, I was a little edgy and nervous. It's funny, but I feel very comfortable and relaxed speaking with all of you in college, but I felt nervous just knowing that I was being observed by you, Mrs. S. Also, the lesson I had planned did not go according to my plan, though it went pretty well. . . . I was very glad that you spoke with me immediately afterward and gave me many interesting suggestions.

The next month, she still experienced substantial anxiety about being observed, although she was becoming a more confident and able teacher.

3/30: Today I must admit again I was a little nervous. As I explained to you, Mrs. S., you're one of the nicest people I have ever known and I feel very comfortable talking outside the classroom, but I guess that just knowing I am being observed can throw me a little. Well, anyhow, my day was planned and everything went pretty smoothly. Afterward, I felt very comfortable speaking with you, because I felt by criticizing and making creative statements about how I could improve certain things you were helping me. One other thing that I felt very pleased about was when you told me that you thought I had good control and was doing a good job teaching. As you once said in a seminar—a little praise never hurts anyone!

Although intelligent and insightful, Stephanie could not manage to free herself of anxiety about being observed. That was not disabling, however, because she managed to keep it at levels that did not materially affect the quality of her work. Although Bev taught in a situation similar to Stephanie's and Phyllis's, because her level of anxiety was higher and she was unable to control it, her student-teaching experience was less satisfactory. Bev wrote:

6/2: . . . I'm a high strung person . . . the presence of my supervisor and at times my cooperating teacher made me uneasy, and unsure of myself. I had the most faith in myself when no one was there, and I feel that's when I did my best work.

Bev assumed that because she was a high-strung person, the presence of adults observing her in the classroom would inevitably affect the quality of her teaching. Once Bev accepted this assumption as fact, she handcuffed herself. Instead, she should have used COURAGE or another logical problem-solving procedure to tackle her anxiety. If you find your stress level uncomfortably high during an observation, especially if it continues after your first one, take action.

Identify factors related to your anxiety and talk with a friend or, better yet, your supervisor about ways to reduce or modify them.

Remember that observations are not unique to student teaching. Teachers' classrooms, in sharp contrast to the offices of fellow professionals such as lawyers, computer programmers, and physicians, are always open to the scrutiny of others. Effective teachers need to be comfortable teaching in the presence of their principal, students' parents, and outside guests. It is best to work on developing the confidence to do this while student teaching. If you find the process difficult, seek help. Nancy, who struggled with self-confidence during observations, initiated contact with her supervisor through the following journal entry:

> 1/20: I feel very loving and warm today. I like myself. I was thinking about our talk last week: You must think I'm immature. It's really weird that I can't talk with you. I'm usually pretty open. I guess I'm intimidated by roles. Nope, that's not it, because I basically feel that you deserve no more human respect than anyone else. I respect the fact that you have gone to school a lot longer than I and are valuable and helpful as a resource person. But I'm not in awe of professors. I wonder why I am uncomfortable, uptight with you. I'm sorry.

When Nancy discovered that she had considerable difficulty in dealing with the student teacher–supervisor relationship, she treated her problem in an effective way. Although some might have been tempted to delay taking action, Nancy immediately raised it with her supervisor and the two of them together were able to help her resolve this difficulty successfully. As a result, Nancy was able to capitalize on the guidance and insights of her supervisor during her student-teaching assignment.

Carole, in contrast, never gave her supervisor a chance to be of any help. The problem arose early in the term when Carole had a direct conflict with her supervisor. Unlike Nancy, Carole did not foresee the value of tapping her supervisor's resources and took no steps to resolve their differences. Instead, she simply let things drift, trying—without enthusiasm—to please her supervisor by her behavior in class.

Let us follow events that took place in Carole's relationship with her supervisor, starting with comments in her journal about their first meeting:

> 2/8: Wednesday was the first session with my supervisor. . . . I brought up the question of the role of the student teacher in the classroom, giving my opinion that it is a dual role: (1) the cooperating teacher aided the student teacher by contributing to his development and guiding him, and (2) the student teacher contributed to the cooperating teacher by bringing new approaches and developments that were being introduced in university classes. My supervisor stated, "But most teachers and principals would not agree with you." I answered, "But ideally this is what we want." Her response was, "But ideals don't exist in city public schools."

This is a 7-credit course and I have already antagonized the supervisor. That's all I need today!

One month into the term, Carole had already been having a difficult time with her class. Frustrated by classroom conditions she had no power to change, Carole seemed to release her frustrations in her first session with her supervisor by defining the student teacher-cooperating teacher relationship in a "radical" way. She did this without forethought about how her comments might be perceived by her supervisor, a person charged with the responsibility of maintaining good relationships with the cooperating teacher and school.

Carole would have been better off if she had recognized what was really going on inside of her. She was frustrated by her mixed success in the classroom and could have benefited greatly had she asked her supervisor to observe and discuss with her how best to approach the situation. Fortunately, Carole's supervisor returned to her school the next week. This time Carole handled the situation differently.

2/17: Mrs. W. stopped in briefly for a conference with the other three student teachers and me. We had an interesting conversation. She'll never really see things my way, but at least I used my head more today in the discussion. That helped us to be more open with each other.

The relationship between Carole and her supervisor had taken a step forward. She knew that her supervisor would be making four visits to her classroom and that her grade for student teaching would be based on the outcome of these. Carole wrote about the next visit:

2/29: My opinions about my supervisor have changed somewhat. At least I must admit she's a well-meaning person. I also must realize that she had a rather strange first encounter with me. The things I was saying weren't things one would normally say to a supervisor just like that. . . . As far as Mrs. W.'s actual observation went today, there is nothing particularly exciting to say. My lesson went well. . . . I spoke to her briefly right after the lesson. She commented that I should be more dramatic. Things should be gre-e-ee-at and w-o-o-onderful when kids get them right. Mrs. W. was surprised (and she said so) at how well things seemed to be going in the class. She mentioned that after our first talk she was a little disturbed and had prepared herself for the worst.

Carole's classroom assignment was not an easy one. Her cooperating teacher, although considerate, was not fully committed. She was holding a second job, going to graduate school, and raising a child in addition to teaching and serving as a cooperating teacher. Carole's frustration with the situation led her to make a "radical" observation to her supervisor about a student teacher's role. It also prevented her from more fully tapping what her cooperating teacher did have to offer, and thus strengthening her teaching skills.

Carole's second observation went poorly. Her supervisor arrived early, the class had been having a bad day, and in teaching her lesson, nothing seemed to go right. Although the third observation was better, the final one, she felt, was a great success:

> 5/9: Today was my last observation. I must admit that it was a relief to have it over with. I learned my lesson well. I put on a show for her, and she obviously liked it. The kids really enjoyed the African folk dancing lesson. You can tell. It just shines all over their faces.

Each time Carole had been observed she went through severe anxiety and tension, made worse, most likely, by her doubts about her relationship with Mrs. W. Had she employed COURAGE at the outset, she would have spared herself unnecessary pain and gained more from her student-teaching assignment.

Carole's experiences offer many lessons. The first is this: The student-teaching experience is brief (although at times it may feel endless). When you identify a problem in your relationship with your supervisor, try to correct it immediately. Carole knew a problem was brewing after the first meeting, and she expressed her concerns in her journal. If at that point she had obtained information about the purposes of student teaching, she would have learned that they did not include providing continuing professional education to the cooperating teacher, even if that sometimes is a by-product.

If Carole had used COURAGE and sought this information, she would have confronted questions such as the following (all related to her February 8 journal): Where did I acquire the concept of the dual role? What did I mean when I responded to the supervisor, "This is what we want?" Whom did I mean by "we"? What motives were involved in confronting her? Why do I think I antagonized her? What will I do now? Presumably, faced with those questions, Carole would have evaluated her motive in challenging her supervisor and would have acted to correct any damage done. Why did Carole allow herself to remain alienated from a professional whose help and support could have been greater than it was—which was considerable under the circumstances? Think about that question. By supplying your own reason you can alert yourself to motives that might hamper you in making full use of your supervisor.

Three further points are worth noting. First, Carole had moderate success in overcoming the initially poor relationship. Although this improvement was partly due to her supervisor's professional behavior, Carole's efforts were also helpful, even if they were primarily driven by concern about her course grade and not the desire to make the most of this unique experience.

Second, an important aspect of professional development is strengthening one's skills of communication with peers and supervisors. During a successful experience, the student teacher learns from interactions with the supervisor and cooperating teacher as well as with students. Because the student-teaching assignment is of such short duration, you would be wise to immediately set to work in making the best of it, even if you are not happy with your supervisor or have a difference of opinion about educational issues. An important principle in working with others is to recognize and utilize their strengths and learn from their weaknesses.

Third, Carole's supervisor, like yours, wanted her student teachers to be successful and have the kind of experience that would help them become effective teachers. Besides caring about students, supervisors take pride in the quality of their own work and are concerned about their professional reputation, both of which depend partly on the success of their student teachers.

As a Problem-Solving Resource

The journals we collected contain hundreds of examples of supervisors making suggestions that aided student teachers in solving a variety of problems, such as developing materials, teaching lessons, and coping with challenging students. Although the assistance they provided was similar to that offered by the cooperating teachers, supervisors had the advantage of different perspectives. First, they are able to see many teachers at work in many different schools and school systems. Second, they are able to view situations as an outsider, someone not mired in the day-to-day concerns of a particular class and group of students. Third, they have knowledge of the most current and advanced outlooks on teaching.

An important area of supervisors' specialty is helping student teachers deal with difficulties in their relationships with cooperating teachers. Here we explore three examples that illustrate this supervisory role.

Brent, whose student-teaching experience seemed to be going well, came to see his supervisor because he was unhappy about the grade his cooperating teacher had given him. He thought that he had established good rapport in the classroom and that his work had been well received by both the class and the teacher. True, he might have been a little weak in disciplining, but Mr. H. had never expressed any dissatisfaction; in fact, he had praised Brent often. "So why the mediocre grade?" he asked himself.

The supervisor supported Brent's questioning of the situation. After some discussion it was agreed that the supervisor would take the initiative and set up an appointment with the cooperating teacher. This was done and, after the usual niceties and a general discussion of Brent's classroom work, they turned to the subject of Brent's grade.

It turned out that this was Mr. H.'s first experience as a cooperating teacher and he had decided it would be wise to mark Brent low on the first grading period and then on each successive marking period to grade him progressively higher. Mr. H. felt this would be advantageous because it would show Brent's growth during his student-teaching experience. After a constructive discussion during which the supervisor explained to Mr. H. the consequences of his well-intended actions, he decided to change Brent's grade to one that reflected his actual performance.

The supervisor intervened directly in Brent's case, solving the problem for him. More commonly, supervisors help you address problems by sharing their ideas or perspectives. Ann's cooperating teacher wanted her to work with the whole class, but Ann felt she was ready to work only with groups. The supervisor could see that Ann's protests and worries were not consistent with observable fact—fact even Ann herself acknowledged. Ann wrote:

> 3/10: I also had quite an experience reading a story to about one hundred children while they waited for the film to be ready. I'm not sure how I did. They were all quiet, so I guess I must have been doing something right.

Ann's cooperating teacher kept urging her to "feel self-assured." Ann insisted that this feeling would come to her only with time. The supervisor scheduled a series of appointments to discuss with Ann just what was involved in being self-assured.

The supervisor argued against the position that you were either self-assured or not. She noted that Ann was hardly devoid of self-assurance, reminding her of the previous journal entry, although it was written as if Ann were reluctant to admit her assurance. The supervisor explained that teaching the whole class would bring Ann success that, in turn, would yield greater self-assurance.

A supervisor can also help you better understand some unexpected reactions on the part of experienced teachers. The example we use is a poignant one, illustrating the harsh fact that it is not only students who are victims of stress when the college supervisor comes to observe. Unfortunately, some cooperating teachers feel that they themselves are being observed and assessed.

The following are reports written by Leslie about two of her observations and her cooperating teacher's reaction to them. We have also included in brackets the comments the supervisor wrote in Leslie's journal.

> 3/9: I was quite anxious to see how Mrs. J. was going to react with my supervisor in the room. After the assembly program, the kids were very excited. Mrs. J. was getting nervous because they weren't being quiet. She kept giving me these frantic looks. I don't know what she wanted me to do, because I certainly didn't expect them to sit like angels after having attended such an exciting program. [Supervisor: I thought the kids were great.]

> 3/31: Mrs. J. was so hyper when I reminded her my supervisor was coming tomorrow. It really bothered me. She told me to make sure I had control. I don't know whether she expected them to sit around like silent bodies or what, but I didn't like the idea that she wanted them to be little angels just because there was going to be a visitor in the room. At lunch Mrs. J. suggested I tell the children to be extra quiet to help me out during my observation. I told her I didn't want to do that and she assured me that she used to do it and it worked out well.

> [Supervisor: Her reaction—it is a pity, but I see it time and again, though usually not carried to this degree. I think it's basically a lack of security, which I can

understand in a student teacher, but not in an experienced one. You handled the situation well. I hope you will not allow these experiences to interfere with your learning from her. She does have much to offer.]

Only pressure of great intensity would lead professionals to be so concerned that instead of being a source of strength and security, they add to the student teacher's anxiety. Because some cooperating teachers see the success of their student teacher as a reflection of their own ability, they unknowingly create unrealistic expectations about what their student teachers should achieve.

Part of the process of student teaching involves working with adults as professionals. As you begin to assume and function within the professional role, you will see that everyone, even "masters of the trade," has his or her faults. Although some cooperating teachers may have their own problems to contend with, we urge you to concentrate instead on the strengths of those assigned to help you, even as you recognize their frailties. Leslie had been incensed by her cooperating teacher's suggestion that she ask the children to be "extra quiet," and she made an appointment with her supervisor to discuss her annoyance. When they met, the negatives poured out. As Leslie came to understand her own attitudes, through talk and her supervisor's input, she became less self-righteous and more understanding of Mrs. J. Then, she was able to recall the various ways Mrs. J. had been helpful and could appreciate her despite the inappropriate advice in this instance.

As a Source of Emergency Help

"May I phone you at home?" supervisors are often asked by their student teachers. If your supervisor makes no mention of that possibility early in the term, ask about it, and if the supervisor approves, obtain the home number and preferred calling hours. If a telephone number is given, unless you are explicitly instructed otherwise, use it only for genuine emergencies, by which we mean that you are very troubled and cannot resolve a dilemma or reach a decision necessary for the next day. You might also ask your supervisor if he or she regularly checks e-mail in the evenings; if so, an electronic message can be an equally quick and somewhat less intrusive way to seek advice.

In the journal entry that follows, Kathleen shared her reflection on an emergency discussed in seminar class.

4/17: In seminar today we discussed how supervisors can help if an emergency should arise during your internship. Mrs. L. told us about the experience of one of her colleagues, who received a late night phone call from a student teacher about this time last year. Mrs. L. stressed—and this was reassuring—that if we face a problem that keeps us tossing and turning, she would rather know sooner than later, but we should call regardless of the hour. I just hope I never need to! Basically, this is what happened: The student teacher's internship was in a large, urban city school. The fourth graders she taught were behind grade level, but she and her cooperating teacher worked well together and the experience had been a good one. On a Tuesday in early April, the student teacher left school early in order to attend a special lecture at the university. While she hadn't planned on returning to school, she ended up coming back around 3:30 because she had forgotten some papers she wanted to grade for the following day. When she walked into the classroom, she came upon her cooperating teacher taking notes from what appeared to be the fourth grade state proficiency tests—they had been delivered to the classroom in sealed boxes early that morning. When she entered the room, the papers were quickly put away and the cooperating teacher began chatting with her. The next day, the cooperating teacher's math lesson included warnings that the students "better pay attention" because this material was "important stuff." The math section of the state exam was to be administered the following morning. What should she do, the student teacher asked her supervisor.

When Mrs. L. finished, we all looked for her answer, but she threw the question back at us, and we discussed it for the rest of the seminar.

As a Seminar Leader

In many universities, the supervisors conduct a seminar for student teachers. This seminar, designed to supplement the internship, differs from other college-level classes in several important ways. First, there are typically no exams and sometimes no letter grades. Second, all the students are having the same kind of preprofessional experience (student teaching), and that preprofessional experience is the major focus of the class. Third, the primary objective of the seminar is to give the support—professional, academic, and psychological—that will help student teachers be most effective and profit from their experiences.

How can you best use this resource? First, use it as an incentive to organize the thoughts and feelings you have about your classroom. Your journal can be an invaluable resource in this process. Prepare for seminar by reviewing the classroom events of the previous days. This will help you gain fresh insight into what you have been experiencing and may also ready you to participate more actively in discussion. With the help of the seminar group, you will be able to see that the barrage of stimuli you experience in class with your students is not just a mass of unrelated events. They fit together and relate to theories you have studied.

Second, use the seminar to discuss problems you are confronting. Be open with your thoughts and feelings. Some student teachers are hesitant to be frank, feeling that such disclosure will reflect badly on them. However, if one person is experiencing a particular difficulty, there is a high probability other student teachers are, too. Your fellow seminar participants will be pleased and perhaps relieved that you mention it, as will the seminar leader, who knows that active participation by the group makes for useful meetings.

Third, the seminar provides an ideal forum for exchange. Participants derive benefits useful not only for the present, but also for the school years ahead. You can trade ideas, lessons, methods and materials, and teaching strategies. During the course of seminar meetings you will find that you can learn a great deal from your peers who, like you, have been rapidly acquiring skills in the classroom.

Mark spoke of the benefits of sharing in his seminar:

> The second period English class is awful. Four senior girls sit in the back corner and giggle. I know one or two of them have a crush on me. I brought the matter up during seminar and found that several other students, both male and female, faced the same difficulty. Together we figured out several ways to tackle the problem.

As a Support Figure

The college supervisor also functions as a support figure, sometimes by being a good and sympathetic listener. Student teachers may need such support. They have been working toward this gateway to teaching for years and may have exaggerated notions of what they can accomplish. Anthony, for example, first had hopes of changing his cooperating teacher's class in ways he felt were pedagogically superior. He commented:

> 3/3: I have become aware of something—that is, that any changes that are going to be made in the class are only going to be incremental.

Anthony expected Ms. V. to change in his direction, and he expected to be able to teach exclusively in his own way, not Ms. V.'s. As his next comment suggests, he felt there was something inherently wrong or undesirable about trying out the cooperating teacher's "routine":

> 3/10: I'm a little worried. I seem to be getting the idea that I will be following Ms. V.'s routine when I finally take over. I realize the children need some type of a steady schedule, but frankly there are times when I'm bored with her routine.

With help from his supervisor, Anthony came to understand the following:

- The class routines had been established before he arrived.
- Ms. V. and the class would have to work together after Anthony finished student teaching.
- He should try to accommodate himself to fit her teaching style.

With support from his supervisor, Anthony had an "a-ha" insight. His supervisor could understand some of his frustration and disappointment, but also made it clear that to be an effective teacher, he had to develop skills in recognizing and taking others' perspectives. His supervisor explained that from Ms. V.'s perspective, he was a guest. From the perspective of the students, the issue was not whether their new teacher (Anthony) was bored by Ms. V.'s lesson, but whether they were learning and at ease.

WHAT SUPERVISORS LOOK FOR

Your supervisor probably will inform you of his or her expectations at the outset of your experience as a student teacher. If he or she does not, it would be appropriate for you to ask.

Even without asking, however, you can be sure that certain dimensions will be factored into your supervisor's evaluation of your work. Your college/ university supervisor will want to see you develop the basic qualities of the professional—qualities that all educators value. Promptness, for example, is essential. Reliability and fairness are also of vital importance.

If you are ill and cannot work or if your car breaks down and detains you, phone the office to inform the principal and your cooperating teacher at the earliest possible moment. If you are scheduled to prepare some material for school or to give a report at the college student-teaching seminar, have it ready by the due date. If you are annoyed with your cooperating teacher, your supervisor, or both, do not allow your anger to build silently or explode in an angry outburst. Bring the matter up directly and professionally.

Absences should be reduced to essentials. A person who phones in ill repeatedly is not one who is going to be recommended for a position. A person who tends to schedule medical and business appointments during school hours is going to leave an indelible impression on the supervisor and cooperating teacher, and not the kind that leads to good ratings when grades are due or reference letters are written.

Natural and normal appreciation of what others do for you should be expressed. Supervisors, being human, get satisfaction from knowing that advice they gave you about making a difficult phone call to a parent or about more effectively using a recently launched Web site meant something to you. They also like to be appreciated when they help you understand that your cooperating teacher, although perhaps lacking a diplomat's tact, is nonetheless pointing out a way for you to make better use of the chemistry lab or improve the questions you raise in class. If their interactions with you are not rewarding and their critiques not penetrating, they want to know that, too, and early.

Before turning to the final section of this chapter on evaluation of student teachers, we want to elaborate on some elements of your classroom that are beyond your control. Your supervisor knows that you will be constrained by the existing conditions.

CLASSROOM CONDITIONS THAT SET LIMITS

As we have said before, there is no one right way to teach. Each of us formulates a personal approach. It is based on our beliefs, personality, and personal strengths, as well as our experiences with teachers in schools, colleges, and other areas of life, our interactions with students, and the influence of the school system in which we teach. How we teach may also depend on some factors beyond our control. For example, the physical structure of our classroom, availability of materials, and school rules or state laws may limit us. Further, important limits are imposed by the classroom climate already established by the cooperating teacher and others in the school.

Here we review two studies that speak to limits that exist in cooperating classrooms. These studies, although somewhat dated, are valuable because they point to subtle factors often overlooked by student teachers.

As a rule, student teachers have been exposed to many different kinds of teacher behavior. As elementary and secondary students themselves, they have experienced diversity in instruction, and as college students they have learned about varied instructional techniques. They have a right to wonder, before they begin to take over the class, whether there is some way of knowing if certain kinds of teacher behavior are likely to be more effective than others.

Copeland (1978) studied a significant teacher behavior, probing questioning. The kind of probing teacher questions Copeland examined were those that followed a student's verbal statement and were based on the substance of that statement. Such questions were intended to encourage the student to go further into the thought previously expressed. Copeland wanted to find if there was support for either or both of the following:

1. Cooperating teachers, by asking probing questions, encourage student teachers to use the skill.
2. Cooperating teachers, having accustomed the students to the skill by using it prior to the arrival of student teachers, foster and support the use of that skill by student teachers.

Copeland used 32 student teachers trained to ask probing questions, and 64 experienced teachers (Grades 2–5), 32 of whom were high users of probing questions and 32 of whom were low users. Of the student teachers, 16 were assigned to high users as their cooperating teachers and 16 were assigned to low users. That means that half the student teachers had cooperating teachers who modeled the use of probing questions and half did not.

In the meantime, the other 32 experienced teachers (16 high users of probing questions and 16 low users) were teaching their own classes without having any student teachers. Here is how they entered the study. After 3 weeks, the student teachers were asked to spend 30 minutes each day for a week teaching reading groups in another classroom, classrooms taught by those other 32 teachers. The question was which student teachers would ask probing questions during those 30-minute sessions with the reading groups. Would it be those student teachers whose cooperating teachers had served as probing question-asking models?

The findings were as follows:

1. Student teachers who taught reading groups in classes accustomed to hearing probing questions used them themselves—whether or not the co-operating teachers in their regular student-teaching class used them.
2. Student teachers who taught reading groups unaccustomed to probing questions did not utilize them extensively whether or not their regular co-operating teachers modeled that skill.

The conclusion of the study was that the ecological system in the class (what the students are accustomed to) has a large influence on what skills a student teacher uses. Students become accustomed to behaving in a certain manner in a certain class and are likely to respond to their student teacher much as they do to their teacher, even when their student teacher initially behaves differently.

This important study demonstrates that your ability to experiment in your co-operating class is limited by the style and approach to which the students are accustomed. This finding makes sense at an intuitive level. Keep it in mind early in the term when you are trying to establish yourself. To hold their attention and to maintain the necessary order for learning, find out—and use—the practices to which they are accustomed.

Classroom climate, a subject of much interest to both student teachers and teachers, was studied by Hearne and Moos (1978). The researchers went to 19 high schools (11 general and 8 vocational-technical) to study the relation between subject matter and classroom climate. To do this they gave the 4,000 or so students and their teachers in the 207 participating classes a 90-item questionnaire. This was designed to measure the extent to which the following nine characteristics were present in their classroom:

1. Involvement: Assesses the extent to which students have attentive interest in class activities and participate in discussion.
2. Affiliation: Assesses the level of friendship students feel for each other.
3. Teacher support: Assesses the amount of help, concern, and friendship the teacher directs toward the students.
4. Task orientation: Assesses the extent to which it is important to complete the activities that have been planned.
5. Competition: Assesses the emphasis placed on students competing with each other for grades and recognition.
6. Order and organization: Assesses the emphasis on students behaving in an orderly and polite manner, and on the overall organization of assignments and classroom activities.
7. Rule clarity: Assesses the emphasis on establishing and following a clear set of rules, and on students knowing what the consequences will be if they do not follow them.

8. Teacher control: Assesses how strict the teacher is in enforcing the rules, and the severity of the punishment for rule infractions.
9. Innovation: Assesses how much students contribute to planning classroom activities, and the extent to which the teacher attempts to use new techniques and encourages creative thinking in the students.

As you examine Table 4.1, note that the researchers grouped the participating classrooms listed in column 2 into the categories (based on the nature of the subject matter taught) listed in column 1. The characteristics of the climate they expected to find in each category is listed in column 3 and what the students reported about climate is shown in columns 4 and 5. As you examine the table you will see that in some cases, but not in all, they found the climate as they expected.

These results illustrate several important points:

- Each class has its own climate.
- Students tend to describe it similarly.
- Classes offering the same subject matter tend to have similar classroom climates.
- The class you enter for your student teaching will already have a climate of its own.
- Studying the dimensions of classroom climate described in the table will suggest the kind of climate you might find in your student-teaching class.
- Bearing in mind the results of the previously mentioned Copeland (1978) study, you will undoubtedly work most effectively if you operate within the limits of the classroom climate already established by your cooperating teacher.

HOW YOU WILL BE EVALUATED

Evaluation will be important throughout your professional career. Understandably, at this point in your life you are most interested in the evaluation that will be made of your student teaching. Therefore, our comments about evaluation focus on that. Nevertheless, the general principles of evaluation discussed apply equally to those assessments made by your cooperating teacher, those that will be made by your principal next year, and those you will make of your students' work in classes this year and in years to come.

Evaluation involves the process of making judgments. Your cooperating teacher and college/university supervisor (with different degrees of influence, depending on institutional policy and individual differences) will make judgments about your student teaching.

Those judgments will be of two types. The first, known as *formative*, will be made for the purpose of advising, not grading, you. As a result of their observations,

TABLE 4.1

Classroom Categories and Expected and Observed Characteristics

(1) Classroom Category	(2) Classroom Subjects Assigned to Each Category	(3) Expected Characteristics of Classroom Climate in Each Classroom Category	(4) Characteristics Rated High by Students in Each Classroom Category	(5) Characteristics Rated Low by Students in Each Classroom Category
Realistic	Auto repair, carpentry, electronics, general shop, machine shop, power mechanics	Asocial, conforming, frank, genuine, materialistic, persistent, practical, stable, thrifty, uninsightful	Involvement, affiliation, competition, rule clarity, teacher control, innovation	Task orientation
Investigative	Algebra, biology, chemistry, geometry, mathematics, physics, physical science, science	Analytical, curious, independent, intellectual, introspective, introverted, passive, unassuming, unpopular	Task orientation, teacher control	Involvement, affiliation, innovation
Artistic	Art, band, composition, drama, English, French, German, Italian, literature, music, Spanish, theater	Complicated, disorderly, emotional, imaginative, impractical, impulsive, independent, intuitive, nonconforming, original	Innovation	Competition, rule clarity, teacher control
Social	Civics, economics, government, history, political systems, social studies, sociology	Friendly, helpful, idealistic, insightful, persuasive, responsible, sociable, tactful, understanding	None stood out in the analyses	Task orientation, rule clarity, teacher control, involvement, affiliation
Conventional	Bookkeeping, clerical office practice, retailing, shorthand, stenography, typing	Conforming defensive, efficient, inflexible, inhibited, obedient, orderly, persistent, practical, prudish	Task orientation, competition, rule clarity, involvement, affiliation	Innovation

Note: Portions of this table are from Hearne and Moos (1978, p. 113). Classes offering the same subject matter tend to have similar classroom climate. The class you enter for your student teaching will already have a climate of its own. Studying the dimensions of classroom climate described in the table will suggest the kind of climate you might find in your student-teaching class. Bearing in mind the results of the previously mentioned Copeland (1978) study, you will probably find yourself working most effectively if you operate within the limits of the classroom climate already established by your cooperating teacher.

your mentors will indicate, perhaps through questions or direct comments or a combination of the two, some of the ways in which you could be more effective. They may, for example, suggest how to arouse more student interest in classroom activities, or how to manage the class with fewer discipline problems. Their aim will be to help promote your development as a teacher—or, as we might say, to help you "form" yourself professionally.

The second type, known as *summative* evaluation, will indicate by means of a grade whether or not you have successfully completed student teaching. This will be a judgment of your all-around effectiveness, taking into consideration your strengths and weaknesses. This type of evaluation can be thought of as a form of "summing up" your current level of performance.

One of the greatest gifts you can give yourself is to recognize that the evaluation you get at this time in your career is worth a fortune. Two experts are going to share their time, observations, and advice for "free," something you are unlikely to get to this extent at any other point in your career.

If you find that you want to avoid their observations and hide your usual practices from them as much as possible, think of the following example: A young singing artist, hopeful for a career in opera, goes for a voice lesson with an expert teacher who will listen, advise, and listen again. Can you imagine that young singer thinking "I pay that teacher $100 a lesson, but I want to hide my usual style, and when I get advice I won't take it because I think the instructor is wrong"? Student teachers should not allow themselves to become uptight about being observed and evaluated. They should not allow themselves to be closed-minded about another person's point of view, even if they believe the observer holds a different philosophy of education.

The specific manner in which student teachers' summative evaluations are conducted differs state by state, university by university, and at times even university department by university department (in particular, elementary and secondary school student teacher evaluations sometimes differ even at the same university). However, certain basic criteria are present in nearly all evaluations (Fant, Hill, Lee, & Landes, 1985; Reynolds, 1992; Unrau & McCallum, 1996).

Here, we summarize basic criteria present in two evaluation systems. Note how they overlap in most domains although they use different terminology and descriptors to outline the areas of assessment. Note also that the second system, designed for secondary school (Grades 7–12) student teachers, emphasizes knowledge of course content and pedagogical techniques. We begin with an outline of eight factors of primary concern in student teacher evaluations, as identified in a review by Fant and colleagues (1985):

1. Clarity: Classroom objectives are clear and understandable to students, the content is well organized, important points are stressed, and there are sufficient reviews and summaries of information.

2. On-task behavior of students: Classroom atmosphere includes a high percentage of time when students are involved in learning, in contrast to time spent trying to keep order or discussing unrelated topics. (This is not an argument against discussing the World Series or the circus coming to town, but for managing a high proportion of on-task time.)

3. Use of feedback: Student teacher appropriately, effectively, and frequently provides students high-quality feedback about their work.

4. Task-oriented: The class climate is task-oriented, meant for learning, not entertainment. Learning objectives and tasks are clear, class starts and ends promptly. (A business-like atmosphere does not, however, exclude humor and lightness.)

5. Warm, supportive environment: Student teacher is kindly in relationships with students, showing respect and acceptance of all of them. Students feel that the teacher is available to help them when needed.

6. A flexible, adaptable teacher: Student teacher can change as the situation demands it, and can adapt plans as student responses dictate.

7. An enthusiastic teacher: Student teacher is excited about learning and students know it. (This teacher quality is believed to be important to motivation and students' tendency to concentrate on learning tasks.)

8. High expectations of students: Student teacher has high expectations, which are thought to foster higher student achievement.

Next, we present a summary of the K.A.R.E. (Knowledgeability, Authenticity, Reflectivity, and Engagement) evaluation system developed by Unrau and Mc-Callum (1996) for use with secondary school teachers in California.

1. Knowledgeability, including:
   a. Content area knowledge (e.g., knowledge of the topic being taught, the curriculum being used, and ways to learn more about the topic being taught).
   b. Content knowledge use and access (e.g., ability to use knowledge and ideas, to transfer ideas across domains, and to access resources when needed).
   c. Desire for content knowledge (e.g., interest in learning and understanding more about topics being taught).
   d. Critical attitude toward content knowledge (e.g., desire for truth, flexibility to search for alternative explanations and take a position on debated issues).
   e. Pedagogical knowledge base (e.g., knowledge of strategies to teach and ability to understand differing student learning styles).
   f. Pedagogical knowledge use and access (e.g., ability to use a range of effective teaching strategies, to transfer teaching strategies across domains).

g. Desire for pedagogical knowledge (e.g., desire to learn and understand new strategies to teach).

h. Critical attitude toward pedagogical knowledge (e.g., desire for truth about teaching strategies, flexibility to search for alternative teaching strategies).

2. Authenticity, including:

a. Honesty (e.g., honest and direct in interactions and actions, model of honesty to students).

b. Commitment (e.g., committed to growth of self and others, to teaching, and to the belief that all students can learn).

c. Empathy (e.g., concerned with self-appearance to others, ability to show empathy, understand alternative viewpoints, and relate to students and others professionally).

d. Confidence (e.g., confident to present self as teacher to students and to share thoughts and thinking pattern with students).

e. Openness (e.g., openness to change, to adversity, to diversity, and to personalities different from own).

f. Sincerity (e.g., sincere in desire to solve tasks and make decisions).

g. Interaction (e.g., concerned with interactions with students, parents, staff, and fellow teachers).

3. Reflectivity, including:

a. Self-evaluation, monitoring (e.g., evaluates own strengths, weaknesses, errors, and successes).

b. Initiation of repair, fix-up (e.g., learns from mistakes, responds effectively to coaching).

c. Value/attitude toward reflectivity (recognizes value of self-analysis, uses journal to reflect on and change teaching behavior).

4. Engagement, including:

a. Field-based engagement (engaged in student-teaching assignment, including a willingness to take risks, preparedness for teaching, and concern about quality of teaching).

b. Commitment to problem solution (e.g., willingness to work on problems, to succeed in placement, and ability to fulfill contractual agreements).

Although the two lists clearly differ in some aspects, they overlap in many others. When assigning a grade for your student-teaching assignment, your supervisor will evaluate your performance in relation to university standards that most likely match the preceding assessment lists to a large degree. Your university standards will also be based on the specific education requirements of your state government.

Your supervisor will, of course, consult with your cooperating teacher prior to finalizing a grade. As we noted in chapter 3, Williams's (1995) study showed that on a survey questionnaire of 54 student teacher performance items, the co-operating teacher generally gave higher ratings than the student teachers gave themselves when a difference in ratings was noted, especially at the 3-week mark of student teaching. At the 9-week mark, two unfavorable ratings by co-operating teachers stood out, for handling small groups and being able to revise unsuccessful lessons while teaching. Should your cooperating teacher be un-aware that these more difficult skills of teaching come with experience, your su-pervisor is likely to point that out. In any event, these are skills that you will want to work on, perhaps by seeking the advice of your cooperating teacher and supervisor.

At this point it is useful to examine a study explicitly exploring how student and cooperating teachers view the same salient events during a student-teaching assignment differently (Gonzalez & Carter, 1996). In one example, a student teacher brought the children outside to tend a small vegetable garden the class had planted. Because only a small number of the students could weed and water at one time, the student teacher asked the other children to wait outside the gar-den and watch. As you might expect, the student teacher experienced difficulty with the students assigned to watch, as they soon became unruly.

The student teacher's analysis of the situation was "how different the kids are whenever they are not in their normal surroundings . . . [and therefore] how much harder [it is] having control over [them]" (Gonzalez & Carter, 1996, p. 41). The cooperating teacher saw the situation in a different light, explaining that the student teacher should have considered the details of the activity—the size of the plot and the necessity of engaging all students in the process, for example—ahead of time. This could have prevented the discipline problem in the first place.

Gonzalez and Carter presented several other vignettes paralleling this one and concluded that student teachers and cooperating teachers are likely to remember the same key events during a student teacher's assignment, but will analyze the components of those events differently. They discussed the importance of com-munication between the cooperating and student teachers and, although they ad-mitted experience is necessary for becoming an expert educator, suggested that student teachers work to understand and consider the interpretations of salient events as their cooperating teachers do.

One of the great benefits of student teacher evaluations is the opportunity to learn how to conduct self-evaluations. Come September, you will have to de-pend on yourself for critical feedback, and that is not always easy. As one teacher said in an interview after her first full year of accredited teaching, "I got constant, constant feedback when student teaching. I missed that this year. If a lesson didn't go the way I wanted it to, I didn't have anyone there to tell me why."

You stand to gain enormously from learning how to evaluate yourself in the thorough, systematic way your supervisor and cooperating teacher evaluate you this year. By reflecting on specific questions about your student-teaching experience and discussing them with your supervisor, you will gain invaluable self-confidence, self-knowledge, and problem-solving skills that will serve you well now and in the years to come.

CRITICAL ISSUES

- How do I feel about being observed by someone who will grade me?
- What can I do to manage to "be myself" when I'm being observed?
- How can I best tap the skill and expertise of my supervisor?
- What can I do to get the most benefit from my student-teaching seminar? What benefits can I get—and give—from sharing experiences with other student teachers?
- How will I react to the preestablished limits posed by my cooperating classroom?
- What can I do to improve my skills in self-evaluation?

5

Building a Good Relationship
With Your Students

TOPICS

- Learning About the Students in Your Class
- Recognizing Temperamental and Intellectual Differences in Your Classroom
- Dealing With Troubling and Troubled Students
- Preventing Problems
- Understanding How Students and Student Teachers Feel About Each Other
- Defining a Teacher–Student Relationship: How Friendly Should You Be?
- Analyzing Your Classroom Work

The first day. Ms. V. introduced me to the class. I looked them over . . . like a sea of faces. I smiled and they did too. I just hoped I'd be able to be a good teacher and that I would have some beneficial impact on their lives.

These were the thoughts of one of us during the first day of student teaching. In fact, by the end of the term this student teacher did have "some beneficial impact on their lives." As a student teacher you, too, can have a positive influence on your students and make significant contributions to their development.

Students are the central characters in the classroom. Your objective is to give them the best possible opportunities for learning. As we have said, because you are a guest in your cooperating teacher's classroom, you must work within limits set by him or her. Nevertheless, you are still free to do meaningful things. Most important, you are free to develop a trusting relationship with students. You can do this with classes as a whole by acquiring a reputation for kindness, fairness, and consistency, and with students individually by showing an interest in them as people and by helping them learn.

LEARNING ABOUT THE STUDENTS IN YOUR CLASS

Start looking at individual students from the outset, preferably on your first day at school. Guard against having your attention predominantly focused on the obvious ones, such as the attractive, extremely vocal, or undisciplined. The quiet and restrained students deserve just as much attention. All learners, fast, average, or slow, have something that interests them. It is worth discovering that something, whatever it may be, and making use of it in your teaching.

How well you know students partly determines how much they will achieve in your class. When you know students' current level of academic development, you know what assistance they need to make additional progress. Careful observation of questions, comments, and attitudes in class can help you gain a sense of developmental levels. So, too, can careful examination of student work. During the early days of observation, it may be worthwhile to ask your cooperating teacher for samples of students' papers, tests, or projects. Just as in the work of the physician, diagnosis is needed before you write the prescription (i.e., plan of action) that will enable you to help students take the next steps in their intellectual and social development.

Here, Ruby, in her first week as a student teacher, was working to get to know students so she could more effectively assist them in learning:

1/6: Kids—I'm getting to know them better, to know their names and personalities. A lot of them have problems or unusual home situations that they want to tell you about; questions aren't necessary, they just want to be listened to. Felicia likes to tell about her family, and even though it doesn't seem ideal, she seems happy about it. Stan is supposed to be in a primary special [ed] class, but because there is no room, he is in a regular third-grade class. Mrs. W. says that he cannot do a lot of the work, so a lot of it isn't assigned to him. He seems bored.

My first impression was that Stan needed personal attention. I didn't question the idea that Stan has learning difficulties, but he does a lot of the work that the other children do and with just a few minutes of personal attention he has done work for me that wasn't expected.

Daniel is another child that I am concerned about. Mrs. W. says that he consistently receives F's on his work and has expressed her dislike for him because of his attitude. She says his family is on welfare and his mother is a real "slut." My first impression of Daniel was that he was a nice boy who needed a good one-to-one relationship and a lot of motivation. Today on the multiplication test Daniel missed 8 out of 12. After the test he asked me his score. I showed it to him and he said, "I had both of my fingers crossed hoping I'd get a hundred. I haven't got hardly any hundreds all year."

1/7: Mrs. W. seems concerned about my interest in Stan and Daniel, and I'm afraid she feels that by showing concern for them I'm questioning her success in teaching them. Today in the lounge the principal mentioned a chance at getting help for some of the kids. Mrs. W. told him Daniel had already been tested and still no outside help has been made available to him.

After going back to the classroom Mrs. W. and I talked about Daniel a little more. Mrs. W. explained that there wasn't time for her to give Daniel 15 minutes of personal attention each day. I agree. But Stan and Daniel need that attention and help, and the school system has a responsibility to provide it for them.

Yes, Ruby made the kinds of observations an effective teacher makes, but her attitude may not have been helpful. Sensing that her cooperating teacher felt threatened, she could have made this a more successful learning experience for herself and been more helpful to the children by approaching her cooperating teacher in a sensitive manner. Because it was early in the term she might, for example, have asked Mrs. W. for suggestions on how she could help Daniel and Stan or, alternatively, developed a plan and asked for Mrs. W.'s reaction.

People sometimes get a false sense of self-worth because they recognize something another person missed. They feel superior because of another person's oversights. Ruby should feel good because she got to know her students and learned about their needs, but not because of what may be seen as her cooperating teacher's inadequacies. As all teachers come to learn, when there are 20 to 30 youngsters in a classroom, even the best of us cannot single-handedly attend to everyone in need.

Classrooms are active and busy places. Elementary school students demand constant attention; four children may be calling for you at once. Middle and high school students breeze in and out of your classroom in a mere 40 or 50 minutes. Then they—and you—rush off to another class. Accurately assessing the problems students face is unquestionably a challenge. So much is going on that our mind tries to adapt by unwittingly stereotyping the students and treating them according to certain expectations—one child is conscientious, another lazy, this one quiet, that one the bully, the troublemaker, the dull one, and so on.

Juan's comment addressed this point:

> My day brings me into contact with over 120 different kids in my classes and 1,000 more in and around the building. During my first few days I formed impressions about many of the kids—and the impressions tended to stick. I was really surprised yesterday when Jacki—who I thought was a tough, too-cool lady—came up to me after class and asked for extra help. Was I surprised! I had to revise my thoughts about her and now I'm wondering about all those early impressions.

Let us look at how other student teachers experienced stereotyping and what they did to correct it. Making a last entry in her journal, immediately after her student teaching ended, Patty reflected on her experiences:

> 6/6: In the beginning, I watched the children closely, finding that certain ones appealed to me more than others. I guess this must be quite a natural, automatic feel-

ing, but I knew these feelings shouldn't influence my attempts to reach all the children. To deal with this, I tried to talk more with the children I thought would be harder to handle. I would ask them questions on an interpersonal level, and in handling discipline, I talked to the child individually, hoping to build some rapport. In doing this, I hoped to let each child know that he was equally important to me . . .

I found getting to know the needs of each child to be quite difficult . . . I'm quite sure that sometimes I interpreted, underestimated, or expected too much or too little from some children. I feel that if I would have had more time with them, I would have understood more.

Anyway, I was very conscious of showing the children that I did care for each as a person. In group activities, I tried to build confidence in certain children by allowing them to perform successfully. When I showed them my pleasure, they became pleased with themselves.

Rita recognized that she was apt to attend to certain types of children and neglect others. Her journal entry is unusual in that she found herself paying special note to shy children.

1/28: I have a tendency to attract and pay more attention to the shy and introverted children. . . . Since both of those girls [referred to earlier in her journal] are extremely outgoing, I think I might have been passing over them. I'll have to correct that.

Today seemed destined to "prove" to me the difficulties of finding a balance in your relationships with children in the classroom. How can you accept, without rejecting, those children who want to almost cling to you so that they can learn to be independent and yet also friendly and at ease? How can you relate to the child who seems to be afraid of you, without intruding? Perhaps the answer is just to be friendly and at ease to all and let time and their individual personalities decide the outcome.

It is clear from reading her journal entries that Elaine took the problems she faced in stride. No wonder she did, the way she saw the children as individuals. In reviewing her student-teaching experiences she reported:

5/25: My feelings about my children and my profession are fantastic! Each of my children was beautiful in a unique way. Each was capable of a certain amount, and I made each know that I believed in that capability. I always tried to include all of them, especially those who were less secure about themselves. They all knew that I liked them and I have no doubt that they all liked me. Being with them was a great ego trip.

My greatest faith in myself as a teacher concerns my ability to love and understand each child equally, and deal with them accordingly. I enjoy very much, and am proud of, the profession that I have chosen. There is something very special about working with children.

It is because of all this that I want to teach. I value myself, and what I am doing, and I have faith in my abilities. Student teaching succeeded in backing up my confidence.

You can guard against stereotyping students by being alert to instances when this might occur and actively working to circumvent it. For example, at the end of the first few days of your student-teaching assignment, note which students you observed and the time spent watching each. After a few more days, note whose names you know and whose you do not. Every half-day or class period, single out one student for your attention, go to him or her, say something supportive, have a conversation, or ask a question—even if you have to do so as he or she packs up school books and heads out the door to the next class. You may find that small efforts to encourage or inspire do wonders.

RECOGNIZING TEMPERAMENTAL AND INTELLECTUAL DIFFERENCES IN YOUR CLASSROOM

When you observe a class of students of any age seated at their desks, you find marked individual differences in behavior. Some students sit quietly, others periodically shift position in their seats, and still others seem to be in almost perpetual motion, moving restlessly from one position to another. To a considerable degree you are witnessing evidences of difference in temperament.

Psychiatrists Chess and Thomas (1987), who pioneered work in this field, defined *temperament* as the behavioral style of an individual. It is the style of behavior, not the "why" (what motivates them) or the "what" (the content and abilities that go into behaving). They found that normal children from early infancy differ in nine categories of temperament, five of which are explained here.

Activity level refers to motor functioning. Even from infancy some children tend to be active in their behavior, whereas others show this trait to a low degree. You will see some students wiggle continually as they work, whereas others sit still.

Approach or withdrawal refers to the individual's initial reaction to any new stimulus, be it food, people, places, toys, or procedures. You will see some students stand back, not ready to respond to a new stimulus until they have grown accustomed to it, whereas others go out eagerly to meet a new situation.

Rhythmicity refers to the regularity of an individual's behavior. Some children, from early infancy, eat, sleep, eliminate waste, and socialize almost by the clock, whereas others, the arrhythmics, are at the opposite extreme of normality; they do these and other tasks irregularly. Some students will settle in for the class period but grow restless toward the end of the lesson, showing signs of being influenced by their internal clock, whereas others will behave in a studious fashion, regardless of the schedule or whether lunch is at hand.

Attention span and *persistence* are two other categories of temperament with educational significance. Knowing about some of the ways in which people differ is important. It explains, for example, how perfectly normal children who are arrhythmic but assigned to rhythmic teachers can become behavior problems without anyone's realizing that at the root of the situation is a difference of temperament—probably present from birth. Further, knowing about temperament enables you to recognize that you will have all of these types in the classroom, and you are also one of these types. You will find it useful to be aware that different behavior—very active or very inactive, eager or leery about meeting new experience, very rhythmic or the opposite—is still normal and may be more or less unchangeable in some students, even into adulthood.

As a student teacher, you can work to bridge the temperament gap by thinking about your own temperament, that of your cooperating teacher, and those of your students. Sometimes classroom adjustments need to be made to cope with temperamental extremes. For example, the highly active child will likely need more "breaks" or changes of activity to maintain focus on lessons. The student who becomes anxious when the typical classroom routine is modified may need some extra attention when an unexpected fire alarm rings during his oral presentation or when her highly anticipated field trip to the zoo is postponed due to rain.

Along with temperamental differences, your students will vary in dozens of other domains. One of the domains in which your students will most likely differ is areas of intellectual strength and weakness. Gardner (1983, 1993) proposed a theory of multiple intelligences, arguing that individuals might be more "intelligent" in one domain—whether it be musical, kinesthetic, or logical-mathematical—than in others. Just as recognizing temperamental differences among your students will help you react to those students' needs and desires most effectively, recognizing intellectual differences among your students will help you prepare lesson plans that help those students learn in ways they learn best.

DEALING WITH TROUBLING AND TROUBLED STUDENTS

Although all students need your attention, two groups in particular place special demands on the student teacher. It is helpful for you to know the difference between the two, troubling and troubled students. The *troubling students* are those whose behavior creates difficulty for the class and the teacher; their actions distract or disrupt the ongoing teaching and learning process. *Troubled students* are those who are unhappy with themselves and their lives and who often have great difficulties in interpersonal relations. Of course it is possible for students to be both troubling and troubled.

Troubling students will "identify" themselves to you quickly. Troubled students, however, can go unnoticed for a long time. They tend to struggle with internal problems that are not easily noticed or recognized by outsiders. Carla wrote about an experience 2 months after she started student teaching that made her first realize the nature, and something of the depth, of the problem of one troubled boy, Christopher.

> 3/3: One thing happened today that did upset me. When the kids were lined up waiting for the buses some punching occurred. I asked the children to stop, saying that I thought we were all friends in our class and that I was upset they were doing something that might hurt a classmate. At this point one little boy, Christopher, said that nobody liked him. I said that I didn't know why he said that—that I really liked him (he's really a very sensitive and likeable child). I was hoping that some of the kids would also contradict him, since they could all hear him—but nobody spoke up.
>
> Christopher always sounds as if he has a cold and does not enunciate any sounds well. I feel this is a big factor in his lesser communication with classmates and maybe a reason why he feels "unliked" by his peers. I feel bad for the kid. I really do like him and would like to make him feel more comfortable with his peers. I'm not sure how to go about it, however.

Carla applied her commonsense knowledge of human behavior in dealing with this difficult situation. Although she might not have realized it, she was indeed on the correct road to helping Christopher in the classroom by her interest and sensitive understanding. However, this kind of problem is not quickly remedied. Her supervisor, after rightfully complimenting Carla for her handling of the situation, explained that Christopher did not need pity or sympathy; he needed understanding and the kind of creative teaching that would give him experience with success.

Adolescents are often more reluctant to open up to adults, and those student teaching in a middle school or high school need to be extra observant in noting subtle changes in behavior, dress, and social activities. The young man with the new cell phone, pager, and group of friends may be dealing drugs. The young woman adopting loose clothing might be pregnant. A good student whose work has slipped and whose attitude has soured may be experiencing problems at home—a parent with a new romantic interest or a parent who lost a job. Be mindful that changes in behavior could be a sign of trouble.

Troubling and troubled children and adolescents vary in how troubling or troubled they are. Some discussed here are tame compared with those who express their anger and frustration in overt acts of aggression against classmates and teachers. These "tame" examples are useful, however, because they are much more frequent than the very serious cases. Moreover, their greater simplicity facilitates learning the principles involved in acquiring effective coping techniques.

For example, consider the principles implicit in Mrs. S.'s management of a situation described in Jean's journal:

1/19: Through observing Mrs. S. handle an emotional incident today, I learned how to handle it. The incident consisted of Margaret telling Mrs. S. that another girl had called her a bad name. Mrs. S. asked Lauren, the accused, to apologize to Margaret. Lauren walked over to Margaret but couldn't say that she was sorry; and then Mrs. S. said to her (very effectively), "Lauren, it's so easy to say nasty things, but very hard for us to say we're sorry." I thought that the lesson was well conveyed and made a positive impression on the child. Had the situation been mine to handle, I'm not sure I would have been able to do such a good job. Now, however, I feel that this can be incorporated into my way of thinking.

Before you read further, consider how you would have dealt with the problem. Did you wonder why Mrs. S. did not first ask Lauren if she was guilty as charged? In all probability Mrs. S. saw enough of this student's behavior to assume the report was correct. Furthermore, Lauren did not deny it. Mrs. S. was effective because she was not riled up by the use of a "bad name" and was not vindictive. Being clear-headed, and in command of herself, Mrs. S. was able to express matter-of-factly the kind of human wisdom that hits home, no matter what age group it is applied to.

Besides having the desired immediate impact on the children, Mrs. S.'s behavior, when followed consistently, has long-term consequences. With regard to this episode, Margaret had the satisfaction of knowing that her teacher would protect her against abuse in the classroom. She would not have to accept abuse and internalize it (i.e., "swallow it," which is never good for mental health) or carry on some kind of a fight in the class and suffer negative consequences.

Lauren learned that antisocial behavior was unacceptable and also that her teacher was a human authority figure who did not condemn or humiliate her but could actually understand and reflect her difficulty about apologizing. Also the rest of the students, or those within earshot of the conversation, learned all of these lessons, although at lower levels of intensity than the leading characters.

The troubling student can be the bane of the student teacher's existence. Because your effectiveness in the classroom depends on your success in coping with troubling youngsters, we deal with it further in later chapters.

Whatever the age group or class level, coping with the troubling student poses a challenge. It will take you time to learn which techniques work for which child. For all students, however, coping requires an attitude of respect, understanding, and openness combined with consistency. You may not unlock the secret to success with every troubling child in your short stint as a student teacher. That is why a basic principle of this book is defining success for you, the student teacher, as the fostering of your own development so you can feel and react like the adult authority figure and class leader your students perceive you to be. If you are like most student teachers, it will take you time to make a transition—to move from the relatively passive and subordinate role of student, which you have played for years, to the active and superordinate role of teacher. That change is probably the most crucial professional adjustment you will face during student teaching.

PREVENTING PROBLEMS

We refer again to Jean's journal about Mrs. S.'s handling of the situation involving name-calling. Besides reaffirming her position as a fair, humane, but forceful teacher, Mrs. S. avoided unnecessary confrontation and subsequent damaged relationships and negative attitudes. She did not threaten: "Now, Lauren, either you apologize to Margaret this minute or I'm sending you to the principal." Never—yes, we use the absolute here—compound problems by creating unnecessary confrontations. They do nobody any good.

Student teachers must also guard against whatever vestige remains in them of a childlike grudge (e.g., She did it to me, now I'll get back at her). Once the offending student is disciplined, the episode is terminated, even if the offender shoved you or used an obscene word. For the sake of your professional effectiveness, the experience of such unpleasant interactions should be the occasion to think more about preventing them.

There are many ways to prevent avoidable problems with students, no matter what their age. A few are described here, first by Roger:

5/18: Mrs. M. feels it is more beneficial to reward good behavior than to reprimand bad behavior, and I agree with this. While this is something I try to keep in mind, and remember to do at times, it comes more naturally to me to ask a student to stop an inappropriate behavior than to praise another for an opposite, acceptable behavior. However, I will continue to work on this.

Bored students find ways to stimulate themselves. Sometimes they do it by provoking classroom trouble. Laura found a creative way to deal with one boy's boredom:

2/15: Leonard is extremely bright. For the most part, the group activities are below his level. Today when we were going to have a story I decided to let Leonard read it for the class. He did great. It solved the problem of his being bored, and the kids enjoyed it too.

At the end of her student teaching, in a discussion with her college supervisor, Dorothy said that a most valuable lesson for her was learning to listen to the children. She discovered this principle after the following incident:

3/25: I felt so bad today. Actually I felt like an ogre. Tracy asked me to go to the bathroom twice while she was doing seat work, but she had just gone to get water. I said, "Wait till you finish coloring." Well, a few minutes later she peed in her pants and gave me this look. I told her I was sorry. I just hope Tracy doesn't hold it against me. I took her aside and said that I was really sorry.

Another student teacher reported that she wished she had more closely listened to and trusted her students, who had protested that a unit test on Monday conflicted with their weekend-long championship soccer tournament. The student teacher, who chose not to move the test despite the fact that many of her students had limited weekend study hours, was faced with alarmingly low scores. In a frustrated journal entry, she explained her decision to give a retest the following week.

Another student teacher, Nancy, also learned that by listening to students she could avoid the kinds of problems that develop when a teacher has unrealistic expectations:

2/2: The kids put on their plays for the other ninth-grade English classes today. We explained that these were works-in-progress, not finished productions. The second-period group's play was a fiasco, but fun. They were disappointed and mad at themselves. Definitely a learning experience.

I'm more relaxed and accepting again now that it is over. I think I was taking these plays too seriously and expecting too much. The "mad" notes the kids wrote me, after I asked them to, said I was asking too much, and I think they're right. We went into these plays with the idea of having fun and learning to work together. I got too hung up on technical things. I guess it's been a learning experience for me, too. I hope so.

When deviating from the usual classroom routine, problems can be prevented by anticipating how students will react and be affected. For example, when students board a bus for a school field trip, will some feel left out if no one wants to sit with them? Will chaos ensue as students fill seats in a haphazard manner, leaving you at a loss as to the number of seats remaining open? Will you be able to tell which student is missing if your head count comes out one child short?

Problems can often be prevented if students are informed of rules—and the consequences of failing to follow them—before difficult situations arise. For example, if students know that for safety reasons, baseballs may only be thrown in the far corner of the playground—and that they will lose the privilege of using any sports equipment if regulations are not followed—they are much more likely to play safely.

Rewarding good behavior, listening to students, anticipating youngsters' reactions, outlining rules clearly, and making lessons interesting for every class member are teacher behaviors that both make for good teaching and help to prevent problems. They also contribute to a positive atmosphere and sense of community in the classroom.

UNDERSTANDING HOW STUDENTS AND STUDENT TEACHERS FEEL ABOUT EACH OTHER

Expect certain thoughts about your students to cross your mind. Some of them will be pleasant, such as the interesting and exciting way they responded to a lesson or the funny comment they made during homeroom. Some of them will be disturbing, such as your use of a particularly difficult student as an excuse for a personal failure. In a very human way we may even have fantasies or dreams in which we punish the challenging student severely, or even eliminate him or her entirely. If you tend to be excessively self-critical, you may condemn yourself for this contemplation. If so, remember that such transient thoughts are natural and widely experienced.

The other side of the coin, however, is worrying about how students think and feel about you. A student teacher with an excessive need to be liked by the class is at a great disadvantage. Students cannot be used to satisfy personal needs. Your relationship with them, although at times quite personal, must remain professional. That does not mean, of course, that you should deny yourself the natural pleasure that comes from meaningful relationships. In the first of two journal entries, Stephanie expressed warm feelings about her students.

> 2/17: Today was my first day back in over a week. I really missed the children, and it made me feel good knowing they remembered me. Since I had written out their Valentines before I got sick, I brought them in and the children liked the late surprise. I was sorry that I had to miss their Valentine's Day party, but they told me all about it. I even got some Valentine cards from the children. It was nice.

Almost 2 weeks later, however, Stephanie's journal puts her behavior in a different light. Her report suggests that her need to have the attention and affection of the children was excessive and not constructive.

> 3/9: Yesterday when I met the afternoon class . . . I walked around, spoke with them, and by the middle of the session, a few of them were even fighting with one another to hold my hands.

We all want to be accepted and liked, and if this happens, it makes the student-teaching experience that much more pleasant. The problem here is not Stephanie's gratification over the children's apparent feelings about her, but that she could report with obvious satisfaction that she also liked that they fought over her. This is not a teacher devoted to the needs of the pupils, but rather a teacher inducing the pupils to satisfy her needs. Needs like this that dominate classroom functioning interfere with the kind of clear thinking we, as leaders in the classroom, must engage in if we are to see to it that the students have the necessary opportunities for learning.

That very kind of clear thinking enabled Erin, then about 2 months into her student teaching, to use a child's ordinary drawing as a projective technique. By doing that, and by avoiding self-centered temptation, she gave a child an opportunity for emotional release. She herself was able to gain important insights about the child that would otherwise have been difficult to obtain.

3/19: Today went great. I had the children draw something they like to do and then tell me a story about it. Some of the children were very creative and I gained a lot of insight into how well they express themselves. This one little girl did two pictures, one with me in it and one about home. I wanted to ask about the one with me, but I decided I'd learn more from the other one. Her story about that painting was amazing and I felt it reflected a lot. In it she had different objects and whenever she went to play with one, her mother would yell at her or beat her. It was amazing how well she could tell me a story about this picture, and it probably reflected her home.

Erin's supervisor praised her for creative use of the pictures and for developing hypotheses about the meaning of the girl's statements. However, she urged her to treat it as no more than a hypothesis and to discuss her observations with her cooperating teacher. If the cooperating teacher suspected child abuse, she would be obligated to report this to the appropriate authority. Although specific laws differ, teachers and administrators in all 50 states and the District of Columbia are required to report any reasonable suspicion of child abuse.

DEFINING A TEACHER–STUDENT RELATIONSHIP: HOW FRIENDLY SHOULD YOU BE?

One question repeatedly asked by student teachers is, "How friendly should I be with students?" Our answer: A teacher is not a friend. Teachers and students have different roles in the classroom and different responsibilities: Being a close friend to students conflicts with being a teacher. Contrast friendliness—an attitude of interest in the students' welfare and support for their efforts—with that of being a friend, which means being a peer, an equal involved in the personal lives of others.

Some student teachers deal with their uncertainty in the class by seeking approval from everybody. If they have a great need to win the students' favor, and if they work toward this goal, they may find themselves unable to manage their class. Gary wrote about his cooperating teacher's warnings:

3/14: . . . I asked her for some feedback about my third-period class. It's my favorite group of kids—I feel like we've really "clicked." But sometimes I feel as though we don't get through as much material. Lewis or Sean tells a joke, and I can't help laughing. Then it's hard to pull the class back together. Mrs. Y. told me that I was getting too close to some of the kids and that the guys might soon treat me more as a friend than as a teacher.

Beth talked with her cooperating teacher about being a friend with the children. Here is how she thought about it and what she did:

1/9: Ms. W. discussed with me the issue of being too much of a "friend" with children. Ms. W.: "If you become too much of a friend, the children will run over you." I agree, but where is the happy medium? I feel she is too extreme.

Later in this journal entry Beth described how being too friendly with a student disadvantaged her as a teacher:

1/9: . . . how do you handle discipline problems? For example: Alice said Donna took her black crayon. Donna denied it. How do you handle this? I responded by saying, "Donna, Alice said you have her crayon. Will you please give it back?" Donna said she didn't have it. I asked her again, very nicely, but Donna continued denying it. When I told her to clean out her desk she immediately returned the crayon. Looking back, I can see that I was too cautious, still talking to Donna as if she was a friend of mine rather than a child. Maybe Ms. W. isn't too far off. I'll have to try her way.

In a society in which adolescents model themselves after the trends of the 20-something population featured on popular television shows and in the media, students may seek to be peers with young student teachers. In this case, clear thinking is again essential. It is quite possible to respect their age and maturity—which they take great pride in—while still clearly delineating the teacher–student role. Consider Janice's journal:

10/28: Today several of my kids asked if they could call me "Janice." I said no. "But it's not fair, you call us by our first names," Taylor protested.

Brittany piped up, "Yeah, so we can call you by your first name."

"No, but would you like me to call you Ms. Smith?" I asked. She smiled and shook her head no. Others joined in, agreeing that *would not* be a comfortable state of affairs. Steve related a really funny story about his Sunday school teacher: "He always says "Mr. Parker" (he imitated a stern voice) unless he's really mad. Then he says PARKER!"

So I thought the point was settled and pretty pleased with myself: I'd treated my students like people, not the little kids some teachers seemed to think they were (one thing I strongly objected to in observations—they were, after all, teenagers). At the same time, I had clearly drawn the line between our roles as teacher and students.

But at the end of homeroom Brian still insisted: "If you call me Brian, I get to call you Janice." On the way out the door, he called: "Bye, Janice." I met his eyes with an unfazed look: "Bye, Mr. Hess."

"Oh, it's no fun if you do that," he whined with disappointment.

Definitely my victory. Lesson learned, and it *was* fun, for all of us.

ANALYZING YOUR CLASSROOM WORK

It is true that teachers are sometimes expected to accomplish the impossible. Take presenting a lesson, for example. Imagine finding material and an approach that will hold the attention of 25 or more youngsters long enough for you to get key points across and have them understood and digested. Teachers have to do that several times daily with children and adolescents and, as Amy reported, it does not always work:

> 3/2: I began a unit on space today by reading the children a short story about a mouse and what happens when she sees the moon's reflection in a puddle of water. I also hung up a skylab poster. I was pleased with the poster because the children took to it right away. The story, however, had its ups and downs. At one point the children seemed really interested in the story. Then a few of the children became very disruptive and the whole class began to lose interest.
>
> I think the whole problem with the lesson, though, was when I stopped to speak to the disruptive ones and when the story was interrupted by an interesting but lengthy point. Some children lost interest then. I also think the interested children began to mimic the behavior of the disruptive ones.
>
> One good aspect of the lesson was that it gave me feedback in the sense that I now know what direction I need to go to hold all the children's attention. To prevent some children from becoming disruptive. . . .

Amy continued her analysis of the situation in her journal, as she explored the many parts of that experience. She approached the problems in a logical way as a rational adult.

You, too, will want to analyze problems you face in your class in this way, using a logical problem-solving approach like COURAGE. You will also want to devote time to understanding your students and to reflecting on the kinds of relationships you have with them, individually and as a group. This is a helpful way to learn about yourself and grow as a professional.

As you examine your work, do not be overly hard on yourself, no matter what flaws or mistakes you discover. No teacher, not even a masterful teacher, has a succession of perfect days, a fact your cooperating teacher will certainly validate.

As you are analyzing your classroom work, bear another fact in mind. If school curriculums were designed mainly around the interests of young learners and if those learners were conditioned to a less authoritarian system, student teachers would not have to be so watchful about maintaining their position of authority. However, student teachers do have to be watchful. Anthony found that out. After a particularly difficult day with his class, he asked his students why they "listened" to Ms. V. and not to him. He raised this question to the whole class. With the frankness that students can be depended on to give, they told him that Ms. V. gets angry and shouts. Anthony wrote:

4/19: I have found it hard to raise my voice and to keep from smiling. But I began to see that I had to try and see what would happen if I did. It worked, I'm glad and sorry to say. It sure made life easier, but it left me with a dilemma. Maybe when I have a class of my own I will be able to condition them to respond to me as the teacher without my having to shout. But it won't work here.

We agree that Anthony's hope is justified. It is possible to teach and control a class in that way. Some teachers do. A teacher can be the complete leader with a smile and without shouting. However, a student teacher may not be able to do so in the class to which he or she was assigned, especially if the children have been trained to respond only to scolds, reprimands, threats, and other forms of intimidation.

We work with an imperfect educational system. That is a fact we must accept. Like it or not, the current educational system is all we have. It is being improved—at a snail's pace—but in the meantime, we must make the best we can of it. That means that we use it as effectively as we know how to help children and adolescents obtain the best possible education they can under the prevailing circumstances.

CRITICAL ISSUES

- Am I seeing students accurately or am I seeing stereotypes?
- What steps can I take to get to know my students better? How will I use what I learn to improve my lessons?
- To what students or types of students am I partial? How can I deal with this partiality?
- How do I think the students see me? What gives me that impression? Will that view work?
- What am I doing to prevent problems with my relationship with students? What else can I do?
- In what ways can I use problem-solving approaches like COURAGE to understand and fine-tune my relationships with students?

6

Building a Good Relationship With Your School's Parents, Principal, Faculty, and Staff

In fantasy and in real life, absent characters sometimes play important roles. Hamlet's father, offstage except for his lone, ephemeral appearance as a ghost, plays a central part in that great Shakespearean drama. In a one-woman play about the poet Emily Dickinson, members of the audience sense that they are witnessing a drama involving many characters. Yet, all the other characters, some of them very central to the story, are offstage.

How much that is true in the classroom! Neither parents nor principals nor department chairs are physically present, but each has a voice as to what goes on in class. Together, they determine some of the important limitations within which we work: the size and composition of our class, the curriculum we teach, the standardized tests we administer, the values we stress, the topics we may or may not discuss, and often even the mood children are in when they arrive at school. Other important absent characters include fellow teachers, vice-principals, the superintendent, and members of the school board.

GETTING TO KNOW THE PARENTS

Most teachers have personal contact with parents under several different circumstances: Parent–teacher meetings and parents' night; individual parent–teacher conferences on "conference day"; parent–teacher conferences for special-needs students; and phone calls or informal parent visits before, during, and after the school day. Selected groups of teachers such as teacher coaches, band directors, drama advisors, and so on, may work closely with parents, particularly when parents provide support groups or run booster clubs for these activities.

Research clearly indicates that children of all ages are more successful in the classroom—as measured by grades, standardized test scores, attendance, motivation, self-esteem, and decreased dropout rates—when parents are involved in their education and in their schools (Burns, 1993; Lazar & Slostad, 1999). Nevertheless, research shows that teachers work to increase parental involvement only infrequently (Burns, 1993). Moreover, teacher education programs rarely emphasize the importance of such involvement and even more rarely provide instruction on how teachers can facilitate parent–teacher partnerships (Chavkin & Williams, 1988; Tichenor, 1998).

The situation is complicated by the fact that parents are not always inclined to contact their child's teachers. In fact, many parents shy away from school. Their reasons are varied: Some feel they are too busy; some feel the teacher would be unhappy to receive them; some feel intimidated by the teacher; some feel that school visits are restricted to problem occasions; and some feel anxious in school because of unhappy or frustrating experiences during their own student days or because of culture barriers or language limitations. As a group, working-class, minority, and immigrant parents are even less likely than others to come to their children's schools. What can teachers do to encourage contact with those parents and reap the benefits that increased parent–teacher contact yields?

The reasons for parental absence suggest potential solutions—measures to persuade parents that they are wanted and welcomed. These can take the form of written invitations, coffee hours, or requests for suggestions and advice. In fact, consider any and all approaches that might reduce parents' hesitancies and stimulate positive attitudes in them.

Despite the many positive benefits of increased teacher–parent contact, some teachers are hesitant to contact parents, either because of busy personal schedules or out of fear of a bad experience. Those in the latter group may be reacting to past episodes in which principals or department heads were upset when an angry parent, perhaps irrationally, accused the school of a perceived injustice to their child or objected to an assigned book. Teachers are also aware that some administrators get disturbed—not simply upset—if the complainer is a powerful figure in the community who threatens to take the problem to a higher authority.

Because one angry parent can injure a teacher's reputation with the principal, perhaps even more than several pleased parents can help it, some teachers steer clear of parents whenever possible. Why risk it, they figure. Of course, there is a fallacy in this logic. Parents who have had initial contact with a teacher are more likely to contact him or her if they perceive a problem rather than complaining directly to the principal. Although Teachers report that they resist seeking parental involvement because they view it as a nonessential task that increases both their work load and stress level, teachers who regularly build relationships with parents say the partnerships *reduce* their level of job-related stress, making work easier and more enjoyable (Lazar & Slostad, 1999).

As a student teacher, you will find one researcher's study of 257 education students' views of parent–teacher contact of particular interest. The researcher (Tichenor, 1998) found that both beginning education students and student teachers felt that it was teachers' lack of knowledge about and experience in building parent–teacher partnerships that was the primary factor behind their reluctance to utilize parental help in students' education.

What does this mean for you, the student teacher? Clearly, building a partnership with parents increases your effectiveness in the classroom. Forging that partnership is easier when you have prior experience working with parents. Therefore, you should do everything in your power to observe your cooperating teacher engaging in teacher–parent interactions during your student-teaching assignment. Moreover, you should work to increase your knowledge of the American family and engage parents in conversation whenever your cooperating teacher deems it appropriate.

The American Family

There is no longer a prototypical American family. According to 1998 data collected by the Center for Law and Social Policy in Washington, DC, more than half of American citizens alive have been, are, or will be in one or more stepfamilies during their lives. One third of all children alive in 1998 were expected to become stepchildren before they reached adulthood; 5.3 million children were already in a stepfamily at the time of the survey (see www.clasp.org). Of course, stepfamilies are not the only nonprototypical family. Many children live with single parents, grandparents, foster parents, adoptive parents, and in any number of other arrangements.

Thus, in the average class you will have students who have experienced the divorce of their parents and the subsequent change in their family unit once or more. You should also expect to have several students whose families are in the midst of this kind of emotional upheaval. In addition, you are likely to have students who have lost a parent or whose biological parents never married.

Some students may come from intact homes where only one parent works outside the household, whereas many others will come from homes where both parents work. Still others may be living with aunts and uncles, grandparents, foster parents, adoptive parents, or same-sex partners; others may shuttle back and forth between households, or live with one parent and regularly or perhaps never visit (or even know the whereabouts of) the other parent.

Whatever familial arrangements you experienced growing up, you now need the knowledge and skills to view the world from multiple perspectives. For example, you may face the challenge of looking through the eyes of a child whose parenting comes from a mother who was 15 at the time of the child's birth; or you may have to cope with an adolescent who spends 3 days a week with one parent and 4 days with another, constantly shuffling school books, sports equipment, and art projects between the two.

A teacher's responsibility is to build awareness and respect of such differences. No matter the age of the students, teachers can contribute much to their appreciation for the diversity of backgrounds and ways of life of all people. This is particularly necessary if textbooks refer to intact, nuclear families and modes of living detached from one or many of the students. When textbooks depict a world in which everyone speaks English at home, women spend time cooking and cleaning, and Christmas is a universal holiday, teachers must supplement the text. Children and adolescents need assurance that their lives are okay, even normal.

Sensitivity to familial differences must be taken into account when planning classroom activities as well. When protocol calls for writing cards or letters to parents or guardians, bear in mind the circumstances of all students. If your art activity is to make Father's Day presents, for example, it would be wise to ask those who do not live with their dads what their preferences are. For one student the solution might be to make two presents—one for her biological father and one for her stepfather. A second student might elect to make a present and give it to a grandfather. In other words, take action that gives you the feeling that you made things right for all your students.

Elementary school teachers, who deal with smaller numbers of students, are more likely to know about the stresses and strains in their children's families. By contrast, secondary school teachers, dealing with many more students in their classes, are unlikely to have that knowledge. They need to be sensitive to the possibility that a marked change in the performance or behavior of students may be due to difficulties at home.

Parents' Open House/Back-to-School Night

In most school systems, parents' night is scheduled once each academic year during the first few months of school. This is the setting in which you are most likely to meet the parents of the children in your class(es). Parents come to this event to learn about the year's curricula, to visit their youngster's classroom(s), and to meet the teachers. The contact you have with parents will probably be brief—perhaps little more than a simple introduction—but it will nonetheless be meaningful, both to you and to the parents.

The introduction at events like these serves an important function for parents. They can now greet the person who has been but a name spoken by their child and perhaps mentioned repeatedly over the dinner table. The events also serve an important function for teachers. Having met the parents once, even briefly, it might be easier to invite them for a conference about their child, should that be necessary, or to solicit their participation in some classroom or extracurricular activity.

Because this might be the one opportunity for teachers to meet with all their students' parents, parents' night calls for careful preparation. If you are fortunate enough to begin student teaching in the fall when most meetings of this nature are scheduled, carefully observe how your cooperating teacher prepares for this event.

At the elementary school level most teachers decorate their room with work produced by the youngsters. Curriculum materials are made available on the children's desks, and the teacher typically presents the curriculum content for the school year as well as the class rules and expectations.

Frequently teachers give an overview of homework guidelines and projects that will be expected during the school year. Many teachers also talk with parents about developmental characteristics of children in their age group (e.g., basic information about interests, bedtimes, and stress, and how to help children develop a positive sense of self).

At the middle school and high school levels, parents are often given the opportunity to follow (in an abbreviated time frame) their children's daily schedule. A teacher may have only 10 minutes to present to each group of parents. During this time, teachers need to describe curriculum goals, outline class expectations, provide information about grading procedures and homework assignments, and explain how parents can best help their children. To state the obvious, teachers (and student teachers) can make the most of this time by preparing well in advance and putting their best foot forward.

Open house night is not the time for individual parent conferences, but it is the time to let parents know you welcome the opportunity to meet with them individually. A brief word to a parent on parents' night may open doors to future opportunities for an in-depth meeting if that becomes necessary or desirable.

Individual Parent–Teacher Conferences

As a student teacher, you may conduct conferences with your cooperating teacher. In most school systems, 1 and frequently 2 days or evenings of the school year are set aside for individual parent–teacher conferences. Parents are encouraged to come and discuss their youngsters' school progress on an individual basis. Often the success of such a day is dependent on how teachers approach this opportunity. Observe carefully how your cooperating teacher notifies parents of this upcoming event and makes preparations for those conferences scheduled.

Although preparing the classroom and collecting work samples representative of recent class work and student progress is important, these tasks are relatively easy to carry out. More difficult, and perhaps more important, is preparing yourself. To speak confidently and accurately about each child, you must carefully consider each student's progress to date. What information is appropriate to share with the parents? What information and insights could the parents provide that might help you help their child? To maximize your learning and avoid embarrassment or harm by saying something that should be left unsaid, share as many of your thoughts with your cooperating teacher as possible before the conference day.

Susi discovered that by reviewing each of the children with her cooperating teacher, she learned a great deal about them, and a great deal about herself.

3/30: Beginning of this week I helped Mrs. C. write out conference slips indicating the strengths and weaknesses for each of the children. I found this to be really enlightening insomuch as I discovered my reactions to the children on a one-to-one basis.

I was hit rather hard by the realization of my own bias regarding each of the children. I discovered in a few cases I have been reacting toward certain children as extremes. One boy, for instance, is a constant discipline problem. I had no trouble listing his numerous weaknesses, so many, in fact, that there wasn't enough room. The surprise part came when I couldn't think of a single strength—not one positive attribute. This was very upsetting to me. I had horrible visions of stereotyping and self-fulfilling prophecies. Not trusting myself to make a mental note, I immediately started an observation sheet on the boy and have listed some positives. Also I have made an effort to provide him with positive experiences.

I also discovered difficulty noting weaknesses for the superlative children. I felt this was also a stagnant attitude inasmuch as it impeded pathways for new exploration. My attitude about them has been something like, they are so fantastic there can't be anything they need to improve on. I think in this case I need to reevaluate just how challenging school is for them.

Consider Susi in a parent conference prior to the insights she reported in this journal entry. Parents would have been misinformed. The parents of the unruly boy would have become defensive ("You just mean you don't like our son?") or worse yet, they would have accepted the version of him as "all bad." The parents of the "superlative children," as Susi called them, would also have been given a distorted portrait of their offspring—one that might have prevented them from further challenging their children. Susi's preparation made a big difference for her and her students.

A good way to prepare for a parent conference is by being empathic. By putting yourself in the parents' shoes you will understand that they want to hear about their child's strengths, weaknesses, progress, and problems. Further, because they want the best for their children, most will be willing—perhaps even delighted—to listen to suggestions you make about homework routines; study skills; supplementary study materials; television, telephone, and Internet monitoring; and so forth.

A difficulty some teachers and student teachers face in preparing for conferences is in mobilizing themselves to overcome their anxieties surrounding meeting parents. Young and inexperienced people in particular sometimes have difficulty presenting themselves as professionals to parents who might be considerably older and well established in the work world.

But if your cooperating teacher provides you with an opportunity to talk with parents, you will see that most parents take you seriously and respect your training. You have something they value: information about their child. They will appreciate your helpful, constructive appraisal. In sharing knowledge with parents remember that you have a right to feel confident—you have been trained as a teacher.

Remember, too, that although you may be somewhat apprehensive about parent–teacher meetings, you are not alone. Many parents also feel stressed about meetings with their child's teachers. Some may have negative feelings about school stemming from their own childhood. Most are concerned that they appear to be good parents, and that teachers know that although circumstances might prevent them from always doing what's best for their child, they are trying to raise him or her the best way they know how. If you have the opportunity to observe your cooperating teacher during a conference, note how he or she works to put parents at ease and assure them that education is a cooperative parent–teacher effort.

If an occasional parent is unjustly critical of you, questions your behavior in the classroom, or even releases anger on you without provocation, put that in perspective. Remember that some adults (parents among them) lead lives of great frustration. They may not be reacting to you personally, but rather to their feelings about school, their struggle in coping with their child, or even their own fear and resentment of authority.

After experiencing your first parent conferences, you, like Laura, will probably be relieved to find that they helped you better understand your students, were easier to conduct than you expected (even if you had to deliver bad news), and boosted your morale when you heard parents mention the positive impact you were having on their children. Laura expressed this in two journal entries:

2/19: The parents I met were concerned about how their children were doing in school. After talking to the parents it became very obvious that the children whose parents worked with them at home were the ones who did best in school.

2/20: There were more parent conferences this afternoon. I had my first and second experience in telling parents that their child was most likely going to have to repeat unless they made tremendous progress by June. Both parents received the news better than I had expected. The conferences have been a very enlightening experience. A few parents complimented me and some said their children had spoken about something I had taught. It made me feel good hearing that.

Active steps can be taken to increase the likelihood that parent–teacher conferences achieve their purposes. First, teachers can seek help from experienced teachers or supervisors in planning how they will conduct such conferences. Asking for assistance is not a sign of weakness, but rather a sign of dedication to one's work. Daher (1994), a bilingual and bicultural specialist and former principal, argued that teachers need help improving communication with parents in general and, we would add, especially with parents whose cultural background is different from their own.

Understanding and respecting differences is a first essential to productive communication. We discussed familial makeup in an earlier section, and this is certainly something that should be kept in mind during parent–teacher conferences. The process of conducting conferences with working parents, parent substitutes, young parents, single parents, and stepparents is no different from that with traditional parents: The teacher listens carefully to get a broader picture of the life of the student and is empathic, showing a genuine interest in the parents' and parent substitutes' hopes, goals, and concerns.

At times, however, difficult situations might arise as a result of familial makeup. When conducting a conference with parents who are separated or divorced, it is best to conduct the meeting as you would with any other parents. If the parents begin to squabble, our best advice is to stay out of their differences, encouraging them to focus on the most important matter at hand, the best interest of their child. If divorced or separated parents request separate conferences, it will likely be in the students' best interest for you to meet that request. This way you can provide both parents with pertinent information, glean insight about both parents' households, and ensure that both guardians build a working partnership with the school.

The specific content of parent–teacher conversations about students from nontraditional types of families may also differ from the specific content of conferences about students from traditional families; that is to be expected because some of the challenges are related to familial status. For example, the son or daughter of a single-parent family is more likely than others to get less after-school supervision and to have available fewer parental hours of help with schoolwork or advice about friends and extracurricular choices in general. There are exceptions, of course, and in some single-parent families the children have more than ample attention. However, the probability of less parental time is greater, and for that reason, teachers should be knowledgeable about resources in the school and community that could be called on for assistance.

If you are student teaching in a school with students who have cultural, racial, ethnic, religious, or language backgrounds different from your own, you would be well advised to expand your knowledge of the differences before assisting your cooperating teacher in conducting conferences. This education will enable you to communicate better, and help your students more effectively.

Another important factor in productive parent–teacher communication is clarity. Daher (1994) proposed five rules as a guide to clear, practical communication. These are presented in Fig. 6.1. Daher also introduced several guides for parents to help make parent–teacher conferences more productive. Inherent in those guides is the idea that conferences are not designed to be one-way dialogues, teacher to parents (see Figs. 6.2, 6.3, and 6.4). The first of Daher's guides, "Let's Talk," provides parents with a tool they can use to obtain information from their child that will enhance the usefulness of the parent–teacher meeting. It also encourages communication between parent and child about school. The second guide, "Before I Go," helps parents prepare for the conference. The third guide, "Letter to My Child," helps parents organize their thoughts in sharing the content of the conference with their child.

These guides can be useful to you as a student teacher. They were developed for the elementary level, but the principles of communication they convey are adaptable for any grade. You may want to use them in their original form or adapt them for use in the years ahead when you have your own classes.

Individual Parent Conferences for Special-Needs Students

There comes a time when a student is so troubled or so troubling in class that a teacher, counselor, or other school or community figure decides a meeting between parent(s) and school personnel is necessary to confer over the best way to educate and manage the child. Sometimes other key players in the student's life (e.g., a psychologist, social worker, religious leader, or speech and language clinician) will also join the meeting. The coming together of the important people from a student's two worlds increases the likelihood that the student will be helped by means of a joint venture.

The motivation for conferring with the parents is often to exchange information—to brainstorm and plan ways to meet the child's educational and other needs. From this joint venture new understandings can develop that might assist both parents and the school, as well as other community professionals, in planning a program to aid the student. Such a meeting is often useful in helping teachers understand what events outside of school could be contributing to problem behavior or recent behavioral changes. For example, an increased need for attention might be related to an imminent divorce of the student's parents. Mo's comment during an interview is relevant:

1. Make it practical.
2. Layperson's language.
3. Use the native language!
4. Be consistent in our communication.
5. Present a consistent message.

FIG. 6.1.   Communication (From Daher, 1994, p. 120).

Parent and child can discuss these questions before the parent–teacher conference.

1. What do you like about school?
2. What is your favorite subject?
3. What would you like to change about school? How would you change it?
4. Name one area that you would like to improve at school. What do you think you could do to improve it?
5. What is one good thing you would like me to tell your teacher about your year so far?

FIG. 6.2.   Let's talk (From Daher, 1994, p. 123).

Take a few minutes to think through these questions before you go to the parent/teacher conference.

1. What do I believe my child does well at school and at home?
2. What concerns do I have about my child's progress?
3. Are there any specific problems or incidents that worry me?
4. What do I need to understand about the way the school or classroom operates?
5. Is there anything the teacher needs to know about my child in order for them both to have a successful year?
6. What is the main thing I would like to communicate to the teacher about my child?

FIG. 6.3.   Before I go: Thoughts before the parent–teacher conference (From Daher, 1994, p. 123).

Your teacher told me that she enjoyed you because . . .
Your teacher says that you were good at . . .
Your teacher says we might work at home on . . .
I promised that we would . . .
The thing I enjoyed most about your teacher was . . .

FIG. 6.4.   Letter to my child (From Daher, 1994, p. 124).

I couldn't believe it. Janet fell asleep during my presentation last week in mythology. She's such a great student. I got so angry. Her head kept nodding and finally she put it down on the desk. I tried raising my voice. Finally, I moved right in front of her as I spoke. Only her mom came for the parents' day appointment. It seems that her parents have been having serious marital problems. So Janet's taken on many domestic tasks as well as a part-time job and has not been able to get her usual amount of sleep. I guess that's why she fell asleep in my class.

So far we have noted how information from the parents can aid teachers, but there is another side of the coin. Teachers may feel they can aid a student by making concrete, practical suggestions to parents and seeking their cooperation. For example, to encourage confidence in reading aloud, they could recommend that parents and students take turns reading portions of a story to each other every evening for a few minutes.

To aid a student hoping to attend college, the student teacher can assess whether the parents are familiar with the process of speaking to the guidance counselor, choosing schools, preparing applications, applying for financial aid, and studying vocabulary and math formulas before taking standardized tests. The family can then be referred to tutors, counselors, or test preparation programs that can help.

The following are some additional examples of student teachers' involvement in parent conferences. Although the cordiality and results of the conferences varied—as did the extent of the student teachers' involvement—in all cases the student teachers acquired new insights into students' behavior. After the conferences, they felt better able to devise strategies to help their students.

In the first example, Ginny was able to use information acquired during a parent–teacher conference to develop a plan aimed at eliminating a child's problem behavior. First, before creating a behavior change strategy, she had to consider how the boy's home and school environments differed and the kind of treatment he might receive in each setting in the future:

2/20: I talked to Mrs. M. about Geoffrey today. She said that when she had a conference with his mother she discovered that his mother devotes all her attention to her children. She said that Geoffrey's family has financial problems and his mom feels that the best thing that she can do for her children is to shower them with constant praise and attention. This helps to explain Geoffrey's attention-seeking behavior. So, with this in mind, I tried to reinforce Geoffrey's positive actions today and ignore the negative ones.

As a result of what I did, he was much more at ease and calmer. However, I'm concerned with the end result—I am giving more attention or praise than he will most probably receive in another classroom situation. Although I noticed a change in his behavior today (he was even more sociable with the other children), I really wonder if it is good to do this. Am I just preparing him to be a behavior problem next year? On the other hand, if I continue as is and then gradually taper off the amount of reinforcements then Geoffrey might adjust. Only time will tell, but this seems reasonable.

Stan, as we see in his journal entries, learned much from a parent conference, but he was not happy with the outcome. His conference with Theresa's mother left him with a greater understanding of a troublesome child's behavior, but also with the knowledge that he would receive little support from the home.

1/10: Mrs. H. told me Theresa has been taught to punch people if they call her a name and that her mother spoils her and stands up for her constantly. Also, Theresa's mother's attitude is belligerent and she lacks warmth and understanding, possibly the understanding and attention Theresa needs.

I saw today that Theresa shows her need for attention by being aggressive, sarcastic, and distracting in the class. I don't know what the best solution would be, whether to ignore her or to keep her busy and make her feel important.

1/14: Today Theresa pushed a book off a boy's desk and cursed. She was also hitting Maria.

1/21: Last week Theresa said she didn't have to answer a teacher "yes" or "no." We had her mom in for a conference today. Her mom didn't smile or extend her hand as I introduced myself. During the conference, she, Mrs. H., and the principal agreed that Theresa should be forced to have respect for her elders. "But I'm still going to tell her, 'If someone kicks you, you kick him back,'" Theresa's mother said at the end. I thought, like mother, like daughter.

Stan looked for civility in Theresa's mother's behavior and found none, except perhaps in the agreement that "Theresa should be forced to have respect for her elders." But that "agreement" solved nothing, as Theresa could not be "forced" to respect others. In assessing the meeting, Stan realized that to enlist this mother to help change Theresa's behavior would take time. It might also require conferences, dealing first with her mother's negative attitude toward the school. If a problem like this should arise next year, Stan thought, he would develop a yearlong plan and enlist the aid of the principal. He would also involve the school counselor in working with the child and the parents.

Gena felt both overwhelmed and excited after attending a conference with her cooperating teacher, Mr. U., and the parents of one of their 10th-grade geometry students, Nick. Her experience in this conference left such a powerful impression on her that at seminar the next day she asked the help of her supervisor and fellow students in sorting out her thoughts:

12/3: Nick's parents called Mr. U. to request a conference after receiving the interim report. It's school policy to send interims to all students whose grades drop an entire letter grade, and Nick fell from a B+ to a C.

Both of Nick's parents arrived for the early morning conference. Nick's mother initiated the conversation. She was apologetic, explaining that Nick had recently been placed on a new medication and that the doctor had been having difficulty adjusting the doses. Consequently, Nick's schoolwork had suffered—he found it difficult to concentrate during class and focus on completing assignments at home. But things seem to be back on track now.

Nick's father asked if Mr. U. would keep them informed about Nick, calling home if he experienced difficulty on tests and quizzes or if several days passed without his completing homework assignments.

It's strange, Nick never struck me as a special needs kid. He pretty much fits in with the class as a whole. His papers are on the messy side, but so are many of the boys'. I guess the only difference I saw were some of his suggestions about how to tackle proofs—they were often quite insightful.

I walked away from the conference with a new appreciation of special needs children and the effects of medications and Nick's parents' efforts to do the best for their child. I wonder how many other kids I don't really know fully.

Alertness at parent conferences pays off. Sometimes the payoff is in the form of valuable information given, as in Gena's case. Sometimes, though, such information is not obvious, not direct, and not out in the open because parents are wary of sharing it with you. For example, they may be carrying around with them the feeling that you blame them for their child's problems, groundless as such a feeling may be. If parents feel "accused," it will be difficult for them to work with school personnel.

Student teachers often experience mixed emotions about calling a parent to set up an appointment to discuss a youngster's difficulties. They want to help the student, but a parent–teacher conference seems too grave a step. The mixed emotions sometimes stem from their own feelings of inadequacy because they have not been able to cope effectively with the student. They might worry that parents will blame them for the problem, insisting that other teachers have not found their child a behavior problem or in academic danger. Sometimes the desire to avoid parent contact comes from the student teachers' amorphous feeling that by calling they are "telling on" their student, an act that might result in the youngster being harshly punished at home.

At other times, student teachers are reluctant to contact parents because such efforts can be temporally and emotionally draining. When student teachers are struggling to keep their heads above water in managing lesson plans, grading papers, and perfecting classroom management, a parent conference represents just one more difficult and time-consuming thing to do. But education works best when parents and teachers work together, and parents can sometimes achieve results teachers could never approximate alone. Moreover, it is educators' responsibility to inform parents of behavior that might prove harmful to a student.

When contacting a parent by phone, carefully prepare your part of the conversation before dialing. By putting the parent at ease and clearly and succinctly explaining the reason for your call, you can improve your chance of success.

With her cooperating teacher's permission, student teacher Denise called Tanya's mother after seeing Tanya smoking a cigarette on school grounds. The telephone call was difficult for Denise because she herself had experimented with cigarettes in school and because, after having trouble with Tanya earlier in the term, Tanya was now responding well to her. After telephoning, Denise felt guilty, but she knew she had taken the right course.

A few days later Tanya began smiling at Denise again. More important, she stopped "hanging out" with peers who smoked at school. This reinforced Denise's conviction that she had acted wisely.

Typically schools have either a formal or informal procedure to be followed when contacting students' parents. They also usually have procedures for completing formal, written discipline reports and for determining whether they are sent to parents. Early in your student-teaching assignment discuss such procedures with your cooperating teacher. You may learn that when a student is involved in a physical dispute, an immediate phone call is placed to the parents in the hope that this early contact will prevent a larger, more complex problem.

Parent Visits During the School Day

Parents visit classrooms both on their own initiative and at the invitation of teachers. They come to meet the teacher, to see the class in operation, and most of all, to watch their son or daughter in action. Visiting parents should be provided with an orientation prior to beginning their observation. Ideally, that orientation, described in the following paragraphs, should take place during a parent–teacher conference preceding the classroom visit. If that is not possible, either the student or cooperating teacher should take the time to welcome an arriving parent and describe the scheduled activities as unobtrusively as possible. A parent's orientation should then include specifics about the content of the lesson, its objectives, and how they fit into broader goals. A copy of the materials the students are using should be provided so parents can follow class activities.

After the lesson is explained, parents could be told that in watching the activities they will find it helpful to note: (a) how attentive their child is, (b) what his or her work habits are, (c) whether the child follows directions, and (d) the extent to which the child relates to classmates. Parents also should be told that their presence might cause their youngster to act a bit differently than usual. For instance, with a parent present, a child may be more or less hesitant to raise his or her hand and answer a teacher's question.

On occasion, you might find yourself presenting a lesson with parents observing. What is that like? Joanna reported what happened to her:

3/2: With three parents in the room I knew that the kids would be distracted, but not to the degree that they were. I was very surprised to see . . . [them] act extremely opposite of what they had ever acted before.

The students were not only inattentive but they could not sit still. At first, Joanna was disturbed by the disruption, but she quickly regained control of the class. She accomplished this by introducing the parents and then immediately setting the students to work, assigning them material that, although not scheduled, generally held their attention. When she saw the slightest sign of disorder, she firmly redirected their attention to the work.

Joanna's reaction to the unexpected disruption—requiring the same disciplined behavior as on any other day—was sensible. Postponing the scheduled activity and substituting another was also wise. The only other deviation she made from regular classroom procedures was to concentrate on giving the students whose parents were visiting ample opportunity to participate actively. Providing such opportunities makes parents feel good and the youngsters happy, all without harm to classmates.

Besides parents, other adults may visit your class, sometimes unexpectedly. Juanita, near the end of her assignment, was scheduled to present a difficult social studies lesson during the last period of the day. As she was about to begin, the principal and several local political officials entered the room and asked if they could observe. Juanita's cooperating teacher said "sure" and privately offered to teach the lesson. Juanita said no, she was prepared. Much to her surprise the students sat, listened, and then participated in discussion. Later, Juanita said, "They behaved like angels." At times students put on their best behavior when unfamiliar adults enter the room, assuming it is they who are being observed. As a student teacher, this certainly works to your advantage.

Parental Reaction to a Student Teacher's Work

From time to time an action by a student teacher, perhaps an expression of warmth or caring toward a child, will be brought to the attention of a parent and will move the parent to react. Most frequently the student teacher gets an oral compliment or a note of thanks. No matter which, it is a much appreciated boost to the ego and should be enjoyed. Charlene reported the following:

2/11: Morris had been a terror at home and at school since his sister was born. That was 4 months ago. I had tried all kinds of ways of dealing with his aggressiveness in class. Taking away privileges failed, the principal's office failed, and behavior modification failed. Then I used role-playing to show him that he had been behaving like a 3-year-old. We role-played for a week and it made a difference at school and at home. Morris' mother called my cooperating teacher and wrote a beautiful, most flattering letter to the principal.

On rare occasions, the note you receive is not one of thanks. Dorothy shared an example of the infrequent critical messages parents occasionally deliver to student teachers. Negative though it was, it set off a chain of events that ended positively:

> 2/12: One of the girls handed me a note from Leona, who was waiting in the coat room at the time. The note to me was from Leona's mother threatening that I "better let Leona have the Valentine party." The reason for the note was that on Wednesday, due to discipline problems, I informed the children that if their name occurred on the board with three marks after it, then there would be no party privileges for them.
>
> Well, Leona would not stop talking, therefore, I put her name on the board. But she had no marks after it and didn't lose her privileges. Leona misunderstood and according to her mother she cried all night because I wasn't going to let her share in the party fun and trade Valentines. Well, I got on the phone and explained what had happened. I told her mother Leona would be at the party as would everyone in the class. I also said "I'm sorry that I upset Leona so much." After talking to my cooperating teacher I reported the incident to Mr. R. (the principal). He said I used a poor means of discipline, but to forget it.

Although criticism from parents is unpleasant to receive, it can nonetheless be instructive. Whether the parent's remarks are justified or not, they are worth considering. Do not allow criticism to drag you down, but do use your journal and COURAGE to reflect on how such differences could be avoided in the future.

THE PRINCIPAL

Your first contact with your school's principal may be the day you visit the school to meet your cooperating teacher. In fact, the principal may show you through the school and introduce you to your cooperating teacher.

As the school's administrator, the principal's role is to maintain the smooth functioning of all aspects of the school. The job includes supervising and evaluating teaching and related services, playing a major role in hiring teachers and staff, and administering all of the operations in the building. Most principals strive to operate their schools in an unobtrusive manner. They prefer to grant teachers freedom within well-defined limits to conduct their classes as they wish, as long as the curriculum is followed. For the most part, principals operate in the background, at least as far as the day-to-day life of the student teacher is concerned. An important exception to this rule, however, is that student teachers are frequently observed and evaluated by the principal, whom they may call on to write a reference letter when they are applying for a full-time position.

As Classroom Observer

Many student teachers quiver at the thought of having the principal as an observer. It is comforting for them to recognize that the principal is a strong advocate of providing the best possible learning experience for all students, including student teachers. That the principal should be concerned about you and your welfare is not surprising. Without his or her support the school would not be involved in a relationship with your college or department of education and offer opportunities for student teachers.

The emotions aroused in some student teachers by an upcoming observation by their principal are not unlike those associated with an observation by their supervisor. You can cope with them by preparing in the same way recommended earlier for a college/university supervisor's first visit.

Jane, whose school had an autocratic principal, found that teaching during an unexpected observation could evoke uncomfortable feelings. Early one morning, late in her student teaching, the principal walked into the class and saw the children out of their seats. Jane wrote:

> 6/5: Mrs. C. [the principal] walked in and said, "What are all of you doing out of your seats?" I explained to her about my "senses table" and how the children recorded what sense they used to guess what was hidden daily in a box. She said, "That's a terrible way to start the day. You kids sit down." Then she walked out. I was so mad. If she had a comment to make she could have said it to me in private and she shouldn't have told the kids to sit down when I said they could be standing.

Although Jane was understandably upset, she wisely avoided a confrontation, responding only with her explanation of the children's activities. She recognized that there was nothing to be gained by an argument. Although Jane's experience was negative, many student teachers have positive ones; that is, their principals provide them with insightful critical evaluation and sometimes with innovative ideas and a fresh perspective.

In an interview, Molly reported:

> The vice-principal had observed me, but not the principal, Mr. C. I had heard about how harsh he was, so I was glad he hadn't come in. Last week, in the middle of my lesson—in he walked—unannounced. Class went OK and afterwards he congratulated me. Turns out he was a science teacher and he gave me several good ideas. I actually told him that I hope he comes back again.

As School Leader

Both as a student teacher and as a beginning teacher, you should find out as much as you can about the principal, including his or her philosophy and mode of school operation. Ask your cooperating teacher about the principal; tactfully ask other teachers, too. If the principal is the kind of person who encourages teachers to talk with him or her, then you should do so. You will enhance your understanding of the school if you find out about the principal's educational beliefs and goals.

It is definitely to your advantage to have a good working relationship with the school principal. For one thing, he or she may be an excellent reference and the source of a letter of recommendation. For another, the principal may have influence in who will be hired by the school system next year or may have friends in other school systems to whom he or she could recommend you.

With your cooperating teacher's approval, invite your school principal to observe when you are doing something that you feel might be of interest. One of us recalls working with a principal who, unlike the cooperating teacher, believed elementary school children should have carefully chosen opportunities to leave their seats. One day, when the students were making silhouette pictures of themselves, the student teacher invited the principal to have his silhouette drawn. His picture was proudly hung with the others on the classroom wall.

Because the school principal is the chief officer in the school and the final authority, he or she is the school's ultimate disciplinarian. A teacher sends a student to the principal's office when the student's presence is disruptive to the class and the teacher has exhausted all possible measures of classroom discipline. As a student teacher you will learn from your cooperating teacher the practices in your school about the use of the principal for this purpose. Occasionally, sending a child to the office may be just the emergency measure you need at a particular moment. If your principal is supportive, do not hesitate to have him or her help you control your class in this way. However, as you may also be told, overuse of this method is likely to lead the principal to believe you have problems controlling the class.

Principals can be tapped for much more than assistance with discipline. It is possible that you will be placed in a school in which the principal is a valuable resource person as well. For example, he or she might have specialized knowledge or skills that can contribute to the development of a lesson or unit. The principal in a school in which one of us taught was noted for his knowledge of the plants and wildlife in a park adjacent to the school property. This otherwise conservative, authoritarian principal could easily and most happily be prodded into conducting fascinating nature walks in the park, providing an excellent foundation for a botany unit.

Sometimes, as in Bob's case, a principal may set a theme for the school. Bob complained, "I'm not happy spending 3 weeks on the town's anniversary, but the principal insists on it." The principal felt strongly that this date was an important one, to be recognized by the students in all grades. He did not indicate how the teachers were to plan their activities, only instructing them to absorb the students in the upcoming event.

During discussion at his student teachers' seminar, Bob came to see that the principal, as school leader, was in his right to set such a theme. In seminar Bob also learned a key lesson—one important to all teachers, but vital to student teachers—educators always operate under constraints of one kind or another in this real world. They must find what those limits are and, working within them, come as close as they can to doing what they feel is best.

As you student teach and when you have your own class next year, sort out your feelings toward your school's principal. You help yourself by not getting caught up in feelings that prevent you from building a useful working relationship with him or her.

THE OTHER TEACHERS

It is true that most of your hours in school will be spent in the presence of your cooperating teacher and students. However, you will encounter other teachers in the faculty lounge, cafeteria, restrooms, and elsewhere. At the elementary school level you may interact with art, music, technology, and physical education teachers who work with your class on a weekly basis or with speech or reading specialists who see some of your children. At the secondary school level you will meet other teachers in your department, as well as some from other departments, especially at grade-level meetings, faculty meetings, and in the faculty lounge.

At all levels, you will have frequent opportunities to build collegiality and learn from others during your short stint as a student teacher. Clearly there are benefits of learning about and experiencing more of the life of your school than you see in one classroom or corner of the building. Try to learn about the educational philosophies and approaches of several of the teachers in your school, perhaps by asking them about their techniques for handling some of the problems you find most difficult. If you teach middle school or high school, remember that many other teachers instruct the same students as you, and they may have helpful hints about lesson presentation and classroom management strategies that have worked for them. If you teach elementary school, other grade-level teachers can prove excellent resources, both for sharing lesson plans and providing information about children's developmental levels.

The other teachers in your cooperating school may also serve as valuable resources when you begin the search for your first teaching position. They may have information that is not yet public, such as one teacher's plan to leave his position to move to another area of the country or another teacher's plan to take a yearlong maternity leave.

One of the greatest benefits of interacting with other teachers is that it helps you develop a professional identity. In the many courses that preceded your student teaching, your life was that of a student; your thoughts were about courses, assignments, and grades. Now that you are a student teacher, however, you discuss matters about students, teaching, and educational philosophy. The more you do so, with your cooperating teachers and others, the more you will begin to feel like a teacher yourself. Developing the feeling that you are a teacher does not happen just because you get your diploma and certification to teach. The certification tells the world you are a teacher, but the deep-seated feeling that you are a teacher is acquired slowly, partly as you teach and partly as you rub elbows with your colleagues.

An interesting paper by Kainan (1994) illustrates how the culture of many schools facilitates this "elbow rubbing." She compared the lunchtime behavior of teachers and university researchers. Whereas the researchers came into the cafeteria, ordered their lunch, and rushed back to their offices, the teachers settled in, joining tables together to spend their lunch talking as a group about students, classes, and other professional matters. Of course, teachers also spend time discussing their families, hobbies, and other interests. If you are able to join in these discussions you will have the opportunity to become better acquainted with the faculty, learn something about their professional views, and feel part of the community of teachers.

THE ADMINISTRATIVE STAFF

Armies, it is said, survive because of the soldiers behind the front lines, and elementary and secondary schools survive, we believe, because of the work of the staff. Although as a student teacher you will probably have infrequent reason to call on the services of the secretaries, it is good to acquaint yourself with them, if for no other reason than to appreciate the totality of the school's operation.

Although the secretaries do the obvious tasks of an office, such as handling correspondence, phone calls, and supplies, some of their work is unique to a school. For example, they schedule rooms and special events, help check teachers' attendance, and make many contacts with parents, both by telephone and mail.

There are at least two reasons to develop good working relationships with the school support staff. First, on this, as on any job, the workday is more satisfying when one has pleasant relations with coworkers. Compared with most other occupations, this point is in some ways even more crucial to teachers, who need good moments with adults because they spend so much time with children or teenagers. Amy, commenting on her experiences as her student teaching was coming to an end, had this to say: "No matter how bad things were going, I could always be sure of a cheery smile from one of the secretaries in the principal's office and somehow that helped make it easier to go back the next day."

The second reason is a more self-serving one. You may have an occasional need for assistance from the staff. For example, you may need to write or phone a parent or a community resource person and will want the help of one of the secretaries. It is much easier to ask for such aid from a friend or acquaintance than from a stranger.

THE CUSTODIAN

Professionals in most fields of endeavor have rare occasion to work with a building custodian. For a teacher, however, the custodian is an important figure. A classroom, even in a high school, is more likely to require extensive cleaning than a lawyer's or doctor's office. When your class leaves the room in disarray, it is reassuring to have confidence that the custodian is friendly and understanding. Custodians often have long tenure on their job and acquire status and influence not usually associated with such a position. Their acquired authority is shown in the following excerpts from Dorothy's journal. First, though, we want to stress that Dorothy's experience is an atypical one. Nevertheless, the report of it shows that the custodian, blue-collar worker though he or she may be, has a quasi-professional standing in the school, and often a sensitivity to the needs of the students as well as the teachers. We also want to stress our consistent point of view that the student-teaching experience is a prologue to your teaching position. This period is a good one in which to practice building relationships with the kinds of workers you are going to want to know on the job next year.

3/7: Today I made another mistake. I used enamel paint in the classroom. Well, the children got it on their hands and just a little on some of the desks. Ms. K. had not been in the room all day so she didn't know what was going on. But when she found out I had used enamel paint she wanted to know why in the world I would use that.

3/8: A good thing did happen today. Mr. G., the janitor, came in the room during lunch and I was cleaning off the desks. He said, "What are you doing?" I replied, "Clearing off paint." Ms. K. then said, "Enamel paint at that!" I explained the whole thing and said, "I know I should have used my head." Mr. G. looked at Ms. K. and said, "What are you for?" She did not reply, so he then said, "I mean isn't it your job to help her learn and give her guidance?"

I must admit he picked up my ego and how thankful I was that someone finally told her what her position was supposed to be. All quarter I've wanted to ask what her job as a cooperating teacher meant to her.

3/9: Well, Ms. K. has been much nicer since Mr. G. made his comment yesterday. In fact, she even said to me today that it was too bad she wasn't in the room when we started the painting.

A NOTE ON NEXT YEAR

In Part II we have devoted space to the people in your student-teaching life, very much in accordance with their significance to you. The students, the cooperating teacher, and the college/university supervisor were each given a separate chapter, and most of this chapter has been devoted to the parents and the principal, with lesser portions to other teachers, the staff, and the custodian. When you become a teacher in your own right, the allocations will change in the following way: By then, you will have incorporated the valuable guidance provided to you by your cooperating teacher and college/university supervisor. It will be part of you. You will therefore focus your energy on direct and more involved relationships with the parents, principal, and staff members at the school in which you will be teaching.

CRITICAL ISSUES

- What role will parents play in my student teaching? How can I get to know and understand my students' parents and home environments?
- How can I best prepare for meetings with parents?
- How will I feel talking to a parent who is much older than I am?
- What do I stand to gain by asking that a parent come in for a conference?
- What can I do to put parents at ease during conferences?
- I'll have no trouble telling parents some positive things about their child. How do I tell them the negatives in a constructive way?
- What suggestions could I pass on to parents about helping their youngsters (a) enjoy learning, (b) develop good study skills, and (c) be disciplined about completing assignments?
- What are the important aspects of my relationship with the school principal?
- What resources can I draw on from other teachers in the school building? The staff? The custodian?

PART III

What and How We Teach

7

Student Diversity and Expectations in the Classroom

Walk through the streets of most U.S. cities and you will find restaurants representing dozens of countries around the world. Walk into U.S. classrooms and you will find children whose families come from and embrace the cultures of those nations and many more.

On those same streets you see differently abled people coping in various ways, some led by guide dogs, some wearing hearing aids, some using electric carts, and still others whose learning disabilities and physical and emotional distress are not readily apparent. Perhaps apparent and perhaps not is the diversity in socioeconomic class, educational level, sexual orientation, and native language of the people you see.

Ours is truly a nation of diverse people, and the challenge of our schools is to educate them all with equality, fairness, and success. Although the diversity among people presents educators with a challenge, it is also a blessing. Having children and teenagers of such different backgrounds and with such different characteristics can bring interest and excitement into our classes.

IMPORTANT TEACHER CHARACTERISTICS

In this chapter we examine several different types of diversity and discuss what they mean to student teachers. First, though, we want to make some general statements about important teacher characteristics that facilitate learning for all students. We start with respect.

Being Respectful

Every teacher must strive to treat all students with dignity and respect. That goal is particularly essential in a society plagued with sexism, racism, ageism, and other prejudices, as the media and everyday experiences continually remind us.

Teachers are models. Because of this, many students pattern themselves after their teachers. If they see these adults behave in friendly and caring ways to all people, they are likely to follow suit. In other words, you teach more than a grade or a subject. You teach attitude and behavior and, if you are good at it, your students will learn to respect you and each other.

Not many years ago school systems isolated and segregated certain students. To give you a sense of what it meant to the isolated students, we give you the words of someone who experienced it. B. Davidson, a disabled individual, wrote about schooling prior to the federal legislation of 1975:

> Socially: We were isolated. Symbolically, and appropriate to the prevailing attitudes, the handicapped and retard classrooms were tucked away in a corner of the school basement. . . . Summing it up, the only contact we had with the normal children was visual. On these occasions I can report my own feelings: Envy. Given the loud, clear message that was daily being delivered to them I feel quite confident that I can also report their feelings: Yuch! (Asch, 1989, p. 190)

"Yuch!" This reaction, we believe, is less common now that fewer students are segregated and that we, as a whole, have become more knowledgeable about those that are differently abled. Nonetheless, the need to help students feel comfortable with each other remains urgent.

One of us was involved in an experiment involving a blind student that had much happier results:

> My principal asked me if I would be willing to be one of two teachers in the state who would take a blind child in my kindergarten. I welcomed the opportunity and welcomed Karen into my class of 22 children. Everything was out in the open. I

explained that she was blind but that she would do just about all the activities. They also learned soon that she was a talented pianist who could play a piece after a single hearing. It wasn't long before Karen was as much a part of the class as any other child. Yes, she was different, but mainly because of her musical talent.

This inclusion experiment with Karen dates back more than three decades. There has been much change since then, but unfortunately, not nearly enough. We could fill this book with quotations from countless published sources about immigrant, African American, Hispanic, Native American, and other children who were made to feel inferior; gay and lesbian teenagers who felt alienated; poor children, some migrant, some homeless, all below the poverty income level, who felt humiliated and unwanted.

Unfortunately, we cannot use only the past tense. Today, too, large numbers of students require special effort on the part of teachers to make them feel welcome, wanted, and respected. Fortunately, we, as teachers, can help them immeasurably. One way we can do that is by being warm and caring people who break down the barriers between students. Another way is by holding high but achievable expectations of all students, to help them attain the academic objectives for which they are capable.

Being a Warm, Caring Person

New teachers, who are focused on establishing routines, gaining students' respect, and maintaining order, might struggle in finding the balance between smiles, sympathy, and stern looks that show they mean business. Although warm, caring, people-persons, they wonder if it is advantageous to show it. Many have heard the age-old teacher adage, "Don't smile until after Christmas."

It is important to remember that children and adolescents recognize and respond to honesty. Assuming one face in front of the class and another in all other aspects of your life does not work well. Allow your natural personality to shine through; allow your students to get to know you. By showing that you are sensitive and caring, you create a classroom in which students feel free to express themselves, enabling true learning to occur.

It helps young teachers to know they can be firm classroom managers and at the same time concerned classroom leaders interested in their students' welfare. Such teachers are sensitive to the hardships many students endure, maybe at home, maybe at school, and maybe between home and school. They manage their classes and use instructional techniques that enable students to enjoy and feel comfortable in the school learning environment. They recognize if students are not at ease and take steps to help them cope with whatever issues—in or out of school—interfere with their comfort and enjoyment in class.

Gabriella, a first-year teacher, described how she handled the evident discomfort of one of her students early in the school year:

9/18: One of the girls new to the school was near tears 1st period. I called on her to read and there was simply no response. I slid on to another person and stopped her after class. Her grandmother (who lives out of state) just had a stroke. She moved from Trinidad just this fall, her father's working in Africa, and she misses all her friends. Too much for a 12-year-old! I was shaken—hard to know what to say. But I stopped by the counselor's office after sending her off to class, and I managed to discreetly walk her down there during recess.

THE IMPACT OF TEACHERS' CLASSROOM EXPECTATIONS

An experienced social worker who had spent her career working with orphaned children always said to her young assistants (including one author at the beginning of her career many years ago), "It's what the children see in your eyes that counts. It's not so much what you say as how you say it that tells them what you think of them—what you think they can do and what they can be. If we really believe they can learn, they will learn." She meant, in her wonderfully insightful way, that youngsters respond to the expectations for them that they sense in others.

She might have added that our expectations of students also shape our behavior with them: If we think they will do well, we tend to do those things that help bring about success. Thus, we help to see that the expectation (or prophecy) becomes fulfilled.

That was the wisdom of a deeply sensitive woman. Her advice is unforgettable to those of us who experienced it personally, but it lacks the controlled observations essential to convince a profession of its significance. Years later researchers began systematically studying teachers' expectations of children. Some have found that these expectations turn into self-fulfilling prophecies.

In a classic study by Rosenthal and Jacobson (1966), about 20% of the children in 18 elementary school classrooms were randomly selected as experimental participants. Their teachers were told that these particular children's scores on an IQ test for intellectual blooming indicated they would show unusual intellectual gains during the academic year. In fact, these children differed from others (control participants) only in that they had been identified to their teachers as "children who would show unusual intellectual gains." And they did! Eight months later all the children were retested, and those in the first and second grades (although not the upper grades) who had been falsely identified as highly promising showed dramatic statistically significant gains in comparison with the other children.

Hundreds of studies have been conducted since that one, and results have been somewhat mixed. Educators who do not put much stock in the phenomenon have seized at these results to argue against expectancy. As vocal as the opponents have been, however, there is too much evidence to discount the impact of expectancy. For instance, Rosenthal (1973) reported that 84 of 242 studies conducted showed that the expectancies of teachers (or participants playing the role) did affect the performance of students (or other participants playing the role). On the basis of this statistic and other literature, by the mid-1970s it seemed safe to conclude that the self-fulfilling prophecy was at work at least in some class-rooms and for some children, and to recommend that teachers be mindful of it.

In being mindful, teachers come to recognize that they base their expectations on students' past performances. They expect much more from students who have records of good grades and high test scores than they do of students with low grades and low test scores. In other words, we expect future performance to be the same as past achievement. Some teachers also come to the realization that they base expectancies on entirely nonacademic factors, including socioeco-nomic status (with the tendency to expect less of lower-class students than middle-class ones), race, and gender.

Some authors have argued that the expectancy effect has little importance be-cause if it does exist, it causes changes that are small in size. Others disagree: "Even though expectancy effects may be relatively small, this does not mean they are unimportant or do not contribute to social problems" (Jussim, 1990, p. 30). Let us be more specific. If the "relatively small" effects were achieved through a change in expectancy, this could amount to a 20% improvement in academic performance. In practical terms—in the lives of the students and the teacher—that is anything but "small" (Rosenthal, 1985)!

One important question has not yet been answered: Suppose that high expec-tations (i.e., higher than past performance, but judged to be realistic for students) were held not just for 1 year or less, as in many studies, but for many years. What would be the result? In other words, suppose a girl who earns Ds in arithmetic receives the message year after year that she could attain Bs instead. It is possi-ble that the quality of her work would improve, because a small effect of self-fulfilling prophecy may accumulate over the years and have a sizable effect on individuals. The negative can happen, too. For example, when a teacher in an early grade indicates in a permanent record (or orally informs the next teacher) that a child is disruptive, that child is earmarked as a disrupter. In expecting that behavior, teacher after teacher could act toward the child in such ways as to en-courage its fulfillment.

Unfortunately, expectations can affect not only the performance of individu-als, but also the performance of entire schools. One author vividly recalls a con-versation with the mother of one of her kindergarten students. The parent was sharing how proud her sister was that her first-grade child—the other's niece—was now reading a second-grade textbook although still in the first grade. The child's teacher had told her that her daughter was doing so well that she was be-ing given advanced work.

The author, expressing interest, asked what the name of the textbook was. The book mentioned was in fact part of the district's first-grade, not second-grade curriculum. When informed of this, the parent of the first grader immediately called her child's teacher. In the end, the incident created a minor uproar as the principal of the first grader's school called complaining to the principal of the kindergartner's school. All agreed, however, that the child was indeed reading a first-grade book, not a second-grade one as the parent had been told.

The principal at the first grader's school thought the book so difficult that it should be taught in the second grade, not the first. Importantly, the principal's urban school served children of lower middle-class working parents. By deciding that second-grade classrooms should use a first-grade book, the principal shortchanged his students. He lowered academic standards, making it extraordinarily difficult, if not impossible, for his students to compete with the other children in the city. He expected less of his students.

As teachers, we can monitor our behavior—and to some extent the behaviors of others—to avoid intentionally or unintentionally perpetuating stereotypes about student abilities based on race, ethnicity, religion, socioeconomic status, and other factors.

To depict how a teacher's expectancy can affect a child's behavior or academic performance, examine Fig. 7.1. It shows that the process begins when a teacher (T) develops an expectation for a male student (S). That expectation could be based on a student's past behavior, academic achievement, reputation in the school, dress, body build, gender, name, ethnicity, or any number of other variables. At Step 4, the student acts on the teacher's message. That could mean he behaves like an angel, assumes a leadership stance with peers, or begins rapid growth in reading skills. It seems easier to understand how, if he is expected to, a student can change his behavior or assume leadership than it is to comprehend how he can "decide to make great progress in reading." Nonetheless, research studies have shown that children may "bloom" academically if they are exposed to that expectation, and in part, they have suggested how the process works.

An ingenious study by Goldenberg (1969), then of Yale University, shows how such unexplainable growth in reading could be fostered. He compared the amount of time, in minutes, the teachers spent with each first-grade reading group, and whether teachers spent prime time (early mornings when both teachers and children were fresh), least prime time (before lunch or dismissal), or neutral time (other times of the day) with the reading groups. The results were unequivocal: Unwittingly, the teachers generally spent more and "better" time with the more advanced reading groups. That is, their expectancy was for higher achievement from these children, and the teachers performed in such ways as to have this prophecy fulfilled.

More than 15 years later, another study of first- and second-grade reading groups in eight schools continued to show how distinct differences in the ways teachers interacted with low versus high reading groups (Grant & Rothenberg, 1986) affected children's learning. Children in the higher groups, but not the lower ones, were helped to acquire the skills, values, and styles of behavior that gave them advantages in school and in life.

For example, Grant and Rothenberg (1986), who were interested in the personal relationships between teachers and children in these groups, found that one important indicator of closeness was evidence of chats between teachers and

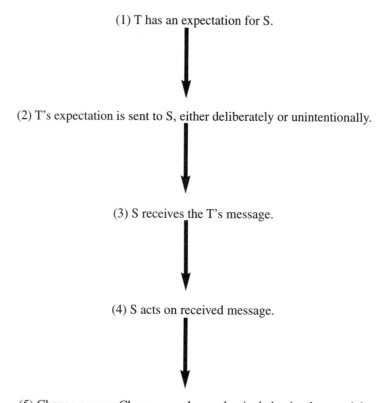

FIG. 7.1.   Teacher (T) expectancy and Student (S) change.

students during lessons. They noted that chats made student–teacher relationships less formal and more relaxed, and they broke down social distance. To illustrate, children in a higher reading group chatted with the teacher about their
homes. The teacher, in turn, talked about national parks and asked if any had
been to one. The students then shared their experiences.

Some of this chatting occurred in the low groups, but to a lesser degree. Further, when a child in a low group wanted to talk about his brother's birthday
party, for example, the teacher was more likely to cut him short, saying that they
had to finish a story and they would talk about his brother's party at another time.
The message embedded in the teacher's interruption "told" the child in the low
reading group that his comment was a diversion. He, of course, may have earlier
observed that when the child in the high reading group described his home, the
teacher listened and responded.

Grant and Rothenberg (1986) explained that the teacher's chats with the students in the higher group contributed to a pleasant, relaxed environment, one that

carried over as the group turned its attention to academic work. The investigators also pointed out that other researchers had similarly reported that teachers tend to create a warmer socioemotional atmosphere for brighter students. Of course, teachers do not deliberately deny children in the lower groups these advantages. For the most part, the teachers are unaware that they are responding to their own expectations about slower and more academically advanced students.

The significance of these studies is clear. As a teacher you have considerable impact on the lives of your students. The influence comes only partly from your effectiveness in helping them master important skills and knowledge. It also comes partly from the fact that when they look at you, often in awe, they see a successful adult figure who has great significance in their lives, and who conveys important information to them about themselves.

Your students look hard at your communications, actively trying to "read" you. They do this by listening to your words, watching your expressions, and noting your body language. You need, therefore, to be conscious of your communications to them, to be as sure as possible that you are conveying a positive outlook and your expectation of their maximum possible development. You need to do this equally for all students, no matter what racial, ethnic, cultural, religious, physical, or learning difference they might have. It is then incumbent on you to help them fulfill that high-achievement prophecy through well-planned activity.

You may be wondering how you can possibly set positive expectations for a student who has not performed well and who seems unmotivated to succeed in school. It is challenging, but doable. Several researchers (Weinstein, Madison, & Kuklinski, 1995) engaged in an ongoing study of a collaborative team (teachers, administrators, and the researchers themselves) to study the process of setting positive expectations for unmotivated students. The team attempted to raise expectations for ninth-grade students in an inner-city high school who were at risk for failure.

To successfully set positive expectations, the researchers concluded that teachers and administrators must counteract low expectations of change that are "ingrained in the culture of the school" (Weinstein et al., 1995, p. 152). The culture needed to be changed so that all personnel in the school challenged the limiting beliefs. The team believed that the best results would come when the change in outlook about expectations was schoolwide. Teachers' own beliefs about their ability to have a positive impact on student learning are vital, and success in a given school is most likely if there is collaborative work among teachers and genuine support from administrators. In the future, you might think about how you can elicit such support from your school administration.

While student teaching, be reflective about your attitudes concerning each student's ability. As a teacher, will you expect your students to perform as they have in the past? Or will you hold the belief that you have the capacity to influence their learning and raise the level of their performance? How will you convey this to your students?

Understanding Differences Between the Genders

Teacher expectancy, of course, can also be played out in relation to gender. When teachers expect girls to outperform boys in acquiring beginning literacy, research suggests they do. When the culture of a school system expects boys to overshadow girls in math and science, upper grade-level math and science courses enroll more male students than female ones.

The gender gap can show up in surprising areas. Who would have expected it to appear in the National Geographic Society's National Geography Bee? Yet, as of 2000, 11 of the 12 national winners since the Bee's beginning in 1989 have been boys, as have nearly all of the state and territorial winners, year after year (see www.nationalgeographic.com). Liben (1995) and her associates found in an ongoing series of studies that the boy–girl differences "reflect students' knowledge of and interest in geography" (p. 9). But most boys and girls sit side by side in the same social studies classes.

Over the course of the past decades, reams of literature have discussed gender inequality in the classroom, particularly in relation to how schools shortchange girls (see, e.g., studies commissioned by the American Association of University Women [1992, 1995, 1999]). Female students' lower achievement in math and science is highlighted and studies point to test scores indicating that the highest scoring boys consistently outperform the highest scoring girls. They also cite evidence showing that teachers devote more of their attention to boys in the classroom and that boys' voices dominate discussion in coed classes.

In recent years, however, there has been a surge of literature on how schools fail boys. Writers often argue that boys perceive schools as girl-friendly, boy-hostile places where young children are expected to sit still for long periods of time and where much learning takes place without the hands-on component many boys crave. Continuing into the middle grades, teachers (who are predominantly female) praise neat handwriting, compliance with directions, and strong organizational skills—all areas in which the average girl tends to excel more than the average boy. Psychologists Kindlon and Thompson (1999), authors of the controversial popular book *Raising Cain: Protecting the Emotional Life of Boys*, wrote:

> The average boy faces a special struggle to meet the developmental and academic expectations of an elementary school curriculum that emphasizes reading, writing, and verbal ability—cognitive skills that normally develop more slowly in boys than in girls. Some boys are ahead of the others on that developmental curve, and some girls lag behind, but when we compare the average boy with the average girl, the average boy is developmentally disadvantaged in the early school environment. (p. 23)

Research and debate on the role of gender equality and sensitivity in schools continues, without substantive conclusions. In a review of the literature, Li (1999) concluded that there are minor differences in how boys and girls are treated in mathematics classes, but that these differences are mitigated by teacher, student, and school culture differences and by teacher gender. Other researchers mention differences across students' age and developmental level (Manning, 1998), indicating that perhaps girls are treated with different expectancies at different ages.

The intellectual debate over this topic is likely to continue for years. At the moment, perhaps the best conclusion for student teachers is that both boys and girls have special needs that may not be adequately met in the classroom. As a teacher, you have a responsibility to design lesson plans that appeal to students of both genders and an obligation to foster a classroom atmosphere that supports the academic, social, and emotional development of both boys and girls. Moreover, you must make a conscious effort to do so.

This is not always easy. Research suggests that both male and female teachers— even ones striving to be gender-blind—treat male and female students differently (American Association of University Women, 1999; Li, 1999; Paechter, 1998; Seiler, Schuelke, & Lieb-Brilhart, 1984). Without even being consciously aware of it, teachers can encourage or discourage, stimulate or numb students' interest in school or an academic field or subject, simply because of the student's gender.

To minimize your contribution to gender stereotypes, we recommend the following strategies, adopted in part from Seiler et al. (1984). Note that the recommendations parallel those of the expectancy literature.

1. Make a serious, ongoing effort to identify your own attitudes about the two genders.
2. For your own use, observe and describe your behavior in mixed-gender groups.
3. Reflect on your attitudes toward students of the two genders in your class.
4. Examine your behavior toward students of the two genders in your class.
5. Use language and voice tone appropriate to the situation, not to the gender of the person addressed.
6. Use praise and disciplinary action in a gender-blind way, basing them only on students' behaviors.
7. In disciplining students, be aware that boys often perceive school to be a girl-friendly, boy-hostile place. For your own benefit, keep a written record of disciplinary actions you have imposed and pay attention to statistics by gender. Are you disciplining children consistently across genders for similar offenses?
8. In assigning roles such as distributing handouts, moving desks, and getting snack, avoid "typical" male and female stereotyping.
9. In class discussions, remember both the teacher tendency to call on boys and the female tendency to be less assertive than boys in getting the teacher's attention.

10. Depending on the grade level in your classrooms, consider how study groups and team projects would benefit—or suffer—from mixed-gender or same-sex organization. Discuss the educational and philosophical factors that might go into such decisions with your cooperating teacher and supervisor.

One useful technique to accomplish many of these goals is to videotape yourself student teaching (be sure to first check with your supervising teacher to ensure there are no school policies against videotaping students in the classroom). In examining the videotape, focus on your interaction with students of the two genders. Becoming more aware of your actions will help you move closer to the ideal of teaching in a gender-neutral way.

RECOGNIZING THE DIVERSITY OF YOUR STUDENTS

Looking at the faces of the children in many U.S. classrooms, one is left with the impression of the United Nations. So many of the world's people are represented here. This raises a significant challenge to the teacher: understanding the cultural differences and their significance in the classroom. If you are student teaching in a school with an ethnically diverse population, a school in which many of the students speak a language other than English at home, or in which many of the students' families recently immigrated to the United States, it behooves you to expand your knowledge of their cultures before beginning your internship. Additionally, if you are student teaching in a school where students' socioeconomic status differs significantly—either because the school draws its population from across the city or county, or in the case of an independent school, because scholarships are provided for children who could otherwise not afford to attend—it will be in your best interest to read and reflect on how differences in socioeconomic status may affect students in the classroom.

Race, Ethnicity, and Linguistic Background

When this book was first published in 1979, the authors chose to direct attention to the differences found in large ethnic groups represented in the United States' urban population. Therefore, earlier editions of this book discussed specific characteristics of major minority groups within the United States at that time. Many student teachers, as well as full-time teachers, were unfamiliar with how cultural differences between home and school impacted a child's academic performance and school comfort level.

Today, however, it is of limited value to make broad generalizations about racial and ethnic groups within the United States. As new waves of immigrants enter the country, the differences among members of ethnic groups are as real a factor as the differences between members of ethnic groups. For example, an assimilated third-generation Chinese American student will experience school quite differently than the child of recent Mainland China immigrants. A new immigrant from Nigeria will read lessons in U.S. history quite differently than an African American who traces his U.S. roots back before the American Revolution.

Moreover, the stereotypes of years past have waned as schools across the country promote multiculturalism and celebrate diversity. That is not to say there are not problems, stereotypes, and generalizations. It is not to say that racism, anti-Semitism, and bigotry have disappeared. But some progress has been made. The current generation of schoolchildren, whatever their race, religion, or ethnicity, are being assimilated to U.S. ways of life through television, music, movies, video games, and other media. Despite their differences, many children and adolescents can and do see similarities.

What does this mean for the teacher? It is important to help students both develop and display pride in their own unique background and recognize the universality of the human experience. When you teach, be open-minded. Be observant of the diversity among your students and be quick to address the issue of differences as they arise. Foster a multicultural classroom. As you teach, you may find it helpful to keep in mind the following "Big Eight Social Identifiers," developed by the Diversity Resource Collaborative in New York City: race, class, gender, religion, sexual orientation, disability (physical and mental challenges), age, and ethnicity (including language and country of origin).

Student teachers must be mindful of ways a student's culture, beliefs, and background could clash with school schedules and activities. The Jehovah Witness elementary school student may be skipping school the day before vacation because her beliefs prevent her from participating in Christmas festivities that focus on non-religious themes. (Similarly, they prevent her from partaking of birthday snacks or dressing up in a Halloween costume.) The Muslim high school student might be avoiding the lunchroom because he is observing the Ramadan days of fasting. The Orthodox Jewish basketball player may tell his coach he cannot compete in Saturday's basketball game, regardless of its importance to the team. In the following journal entries, note how diversity issues faced several student teachers. Janice wrote:

4/17: Interesting exchange in class today. I was introducing a movie clip from the 1920s and talking about the way African-American characters were portrayed. In the middle of my careful explanation of the restrictions Black actors faced—playing primarily the roles of servants, chauffeurs, and entertainers—Melisa (a reflective, albeit blunt, blue-eyed, blonde-haired girl) said, "but Ms. R., you really should say 'African American' instead of 'Black.'" I was a little taken-aback. But it was something I had thought a great deal about, and I was ready with a response. In retrospect, I suppose it was a really good teaching moment.

I explained that terminology has changed a great deal during the course of American history, and that while certain words are clearly no longer acceptable, not all leaders of today's Black community agree on what term should be used. "While 'African American' may be PC," I explained, "not all Black people in the U.S.

consider themselves African American—they might be recent immigrants from Africa, in which case they probably consider themselves, say, Ethiopian, just like recent immigrants from England would probably consider themselves English. Those people that recently emigrated from the Caribbean tend to identify with island culture as much, if not more, than with African culture. It's complicated. Because there is debate about whether 'Black' or 'African American' is the preferred term, I tend to switch back and forth between the two," I said. I scanned the faces for a reaction . . . I wonder what they were thinking, especially the three Black kids in class.

As Janice's example illustrates, it is important to sort through your own thoughts and feelings about multicultural issues before beginning to teach. The process is ongoing, of course, but student teachers must have clear, deliberate notions of how they will present material in such a way that fosters both reflection and respect. As Jake discovered at the end of his student-teaching assignment, multicultural issues are present even when you do not see them or expect them.

6/2: Today was the end-of-the-year honors convocation. Honor roll students are recognized for their achievement and prizes are given to the outstanding student in each subject. Ms. L. and I had discussed her selections for the Latin prize. There are several I felt were deserving in each class, but I understood why she chose Jack and Lori. Besides their solid grade point averages in Latin II and III, they always displayed such enthusiasm in class. But I was most struck when Kako was called up to receive the visual arts award. Kako is Japanese, but I just always viewed her as totally assimilated—she dresses and talks like all the other 10th graders. But as she reached out for her award, she bowed, Japanese fashion, to the principal. It really took me by surprise!

Like Jake, Dorothy was surprised by culturally triggered student behavior she had not anticipated. A White student teacher assigned to an elementary school in a disadvantaged neighborhood, Dorothy taught a second-grade class in which about 25% of the children were African American. One of them, Thomas, concerned Dorothy because she felt he lacked self-confidence and was much more capable than his schoolwork showed. She realized that her expectations were higher than his own. Her problem was how to get Thomas to aim higher. Dorothy's excitement about the possibility of helping Thomas is shown in the first of two journal entries written on consecutive days.

1/10: When Thomas came back from the testing (by the school psychologist) Ms. K. was assigning math to be done before the lunch bell. For the first time Thomas did all the problems. He came up to me saying, "Look, I finished just as the bell rang!" I replied, "Thomas I'm so excited for you—you have the problems all done. May I check them?" Thomas: "Yes." I continued to examine his paper. When I found a problem wrong I would ask him to recheck the problem. Thomas would and then bring it back to me. It appeared that the psychologist showing interest in him motivated Thomas to work. I'm very pleased with the math problems Thomas did.

1/11: Still having a tremendous discipline problem. Felt it's due to the lack of stimulating the children's interest plus the fact of someone new in the classroom and they are testing how far they can go. During reading groups Thomas continued hitting other students, causing confusion and disturbance. I asked Thomas to sit at the experience table to finish the work Ms. K. had assigned the class. It appears that the daily English, spelling, and writing assignments do not hold his attention. Thomas continued jumping up out of his seat, hitting other children, and they then started shouting, "Thomas is bothering me." He got Keith and Horace siding with him, and then when Horace's reading group came back to work with me, Horace refused to do anything. So I moved Keith to a desk by the reading group and he began to do work. I told Horace to read. I did not give him a choice—he read but grumbled. I now had become very upset with Thomas, so I took hold of his arm and told him to sit in his seat. Thomas shook his arm loose and said, "Don't ever grab me again." I replied, "Thomas, I'm wrong for grabbing you, but you must get in your seat and do your work." Thomas did sit down and start working.

The next day in seminar, after being complimented by the other student teachers for the effective way she reacted to Thomas's complaint, Dorothy explained that she was taken aback by his reaction. Because he grabbed and hit other children it seemed so ironic, she said, that kind of complaint should come from him.

An African American student teacher helped Dorothy and the rest of the group understand what it means to many African Americans to be physically restrained or controlled, and how jealously many African American parents restrict the right to use physical means to discipline their children, granting it only to those who they believe have the children's interest at heart. African American students are very conscious of that attitude, having been well trained in it. The African American student teachers were the first to point out that despite her ignorance about that cultural fact, Dorothy had respected the child's feelings while insisting that he do as she demanded.

Schools across the country are developing means to cope with and benefit from the growing ethnic, racial, and cultural diversity of their students and faculty. In some school districts, students of varied backgrounds are predisposed to interact positively due to valuable experiences in their homes and communities. In others, teachers, administrators, parents, community leaders, and students have to work hard to overcome the initial fear and distrust fostered by individuals' early exposure to racism and stereotypes. The battle continues, but many schools have met with success.

Consider these quotations from local newspapers across the country:

Stuart Andrews and Dominique Davis have been inseparable since they met this year. The two first-graders at Central Riverside Elementary School said they are friends because they are both silly and like to tell jokes. But the boys know there are differences between them. "I'm white and he's brown," Stuart said. "But it doesn't matter." "Yeah, it doesn't matter because we are both human," Dominique said. "We have fun together. It is good." (*The Florida Times,* Diamond, 1999)

At its best, Portland High School today is a happy rainbow of colors, where 30 or more languages can be heard. Students of different races and cultures savor the camaraderie of team sports, date one another and share friendships. "This is probably the most diverse school in the state, and I love it," says Joanna Hibbard, a senior who is white. (*Portland Press Herald*, Vegh, 1999)

If you want to time-travel to a future American suburb, turn off your television and walk through this year's Walnut High School prom. Thai American junior Sara Vichit, luminous in a shimmering gown, is slow-dancing with a black senior, Chris Matthews, whose tuxedoed elegance hints at the adult world he is graduating into. There's Jesse Waites, who is white, moving in sync to a hip-hop beat with his African American date, Tiffany Palmer, and a Latino friend, Steven Casado. (*The Los Angeles Times*, O'Connor, 1999)

There is no doubt that diverse student bodies pose challenges. Refugees from Eritrea find themselves sitting next to Ethiopian immigrants in classrooms outside Washington, DC—an ironic situation as the Eritreans rapidly recognize that their Ethiopian classmates are similar in language, culture, and appearance, yet harbor intense resentment toward their classmates because of the injustices Ethiopians committed against Eritreans during the civil war that led the Eritreans to escape to the United States as refugees in the first place.

In some schools, including the Washington-area schools faced with that perplexing situation, ethnic and cultural differences are resolved through thoughtful discussions and faculty-moderated mediation. In others, overt racism and violence emerge. In Maine, for example, Portland High School has struggled with fights between White students and Somali immigrant students. Even in elementary schools, children regularly segregate themselves by race and ethnicity at recess, lunch, and in the classroom. Racial, ethnic, and religious conflict can best be addressed by school- and communitywide initiatives. But as a student teacher, you can help reduce the conflict of differences in your classroom and hallways through several means.

Set an Example. As a teacher, you have your own ethnic and cultural background. Be honest about your cultural heritage and set an example by respecting and understanding the differences of other teachers, students, and staff in the building. Your students will learn from your example.

Develop a Curriculum That Considers Individuals of Diverse Backgrounds. Culture relates to every subject from the fine arts to hard sciences. You can bring culture into your classes by indicating a particular group's contributions to the topic at hand, by directly exploring a cultural group's contributions to the field (e.g., through exploration of their literature, art, and music), and by inviting representatives of cultural groups to share distinctive foods, authentic speech, and unique customs. The aim of doing so is to bring concepts to life and add spice to the classroom experience. The added benefits are equally important: Students of those cultures highlighted can take pride in their background, and students of differing backgrounds can gain the insight necessary to living in a multicultural world.

Model the Desire to Learn.   Remember that you cannot know the distinct meanings of all events for all the cultures in the United States, but you can become aware of the meaning of differences. While you are learning, do not allow ignorance to prevent you from introducing class material from a culture other than your own. It is quite easy to begin a lesson by saying, "I would like to share a portion of this memoir by a Japanese woman with you because it provides a fascinating example of the immigrant experience in the early 1900s. Does anyone speak Japanese? No? Unfortunately, I don't either—I'd like to learn someday. In the meantime, I apologize for my shaky pronunciation of the Japanese words, but we won't let language be a barrier. I want you to hear this woman's powerful story."

Jeff's experience as a social studies student teacher shows that an ethnocentric outlook is counterproductive, if not destructive. Jeff's cooperating teacher, Mr. Y., had asked the 11th-grade students to write a paper about a significant historical character, indicating the reasons for their choice. He gave Jeff the first opportunity to read the papers and write comments on them, which Mr. Y. then reviewed.

During a free period Mr. Y. praised Jeff for the worthwhile questions he posed in his comments and the positive reinforcement he gave to many students. Then he added that he was surprised by comments on two papers. One African American student, who wrote about Malcolm X, agreed with the latter's argument that African Americans must stand strong "as a nation." Jeff's comment was "I thought we were all Americans!" A Hispanic student chose Cesar Chavez, the head of the Farm Workers Union of America who organized a consumer boycott against grapes. Jeff wrote, "Couldn't you find a more significant person than Chavez?" Jeff did not yet understand that by attacking role models he was undermining his students' confidence and their self-expectations. Here is Jeff's delayed reaction:

3/13: A week ago, when Mr. Y. pointed these things out, I knew immediately that I had blundered. I wished the earth would open up under me. But I grew up in the suburbs as an "all-American boy." When I got to college and mixed with other people, I guess I learned about their ideas and values. But I put that knowledge in a separate compartment. I still sort of believe that we're all Americans, who all have the same opportunity, but the other part of me knows it's not 100% true. I must reconcile the two different ones. I owe a lot to Mr. Y.

Socioeconomic Status

In an interview following the end of her internship, one student teacher reported that her students, "all had white faces, but were very, very different." Even in schools where at first glance it appears that students are all alike—in other words, that they share similar backgrounds—one may find substantial socioeconomic differences among them. These differences impact students in various ways in the classroom, on the playground, and anywhere else they interact.

It is important to understand that socioeconomic status is multidimensional; defining elements include the family's economic resources, work roles, access to status and power, and the cultural resources (including education) that control entry into status positions within society (Knapp & Woolverton, 1995). In other words, possession of money alone does not determine socioeconomic status or social class.

This broad definition of socioeconomic status has important implications for education. Before children even set foot in a classroom, their families and communities have taught them how to think, speak, and behave in such a way that facilitates adult success within their social class. But a school classroom has its own culture. Therefore, the socioeconomic lessons children learn play into how they perceive school, relate to the school environment, and behave in response to educational and social stimuli. These perceptions and behaviors, in turn, influence how particular children are perceived by both teachers and peers.

Because lower class students lack the socioeconomic-bound lessons to read the behavioral expectations of middle-class teachers, such students are often perceived as less capable or less cooperative than they probably are (Persell, 1977, 1993). Such perceptions, of course, can prove catastrophic for children. Here we echo the basic premise of this chapter: Hold high but achievable expectations of all students so that you can help them attain the academic objectives of which they are capable. Additionally, be careful not to label linguistic differences such as nonstandard English as "wrong." Instead, explain that they are "different," and although they may be used in casual conversation, they are generally not acceptable in academic settings.

Students Living in Poverty

The reality of the poverty in which some students live confronts student teachers with a form of culture shock. It is one thing to sit on a comfortable chair in the tranquil surroundings of a university library reading about poverty and oppression; it is quite another to come smack up against it and its consequences in real life. Despite courses in sociology and anthropology in which the devastations of poverty were examined, one of us experienced a cultural shock as a student teacher. She wrote in her journal:

> We were returning [to the Bronx, New York City] by bus from an all-day trip to a nature park in Staten Island. The fifth graders were tired but happy after a very enjoyable day of walking the nature trails, visiting the museum, and picnicking and playing outdoors. The children surrounding me on the bus in this happy atmosphere of the day were conversing in a friendly and trusting way. One girl said she hated to think that her cousin was coming to visit for the weekend. I asked her why, whether she didn't like her cousin. She liked her all right, but the cousin, a girl her own age, was coming with her whole family. That meant, she said, "Us children will have to sleep on the floor."
>
> Very naively I asked what was so terrible about that for a few nights? She looked at me, now a little embarrassed, perhaps at my own innocence, and said, "I can't get myself to fall asleep on the floor because I'm afraid of the big rats." Of course, I had read about poverty and rats and malnutrition and brain damage from lead poisoning in hungry little children who eat the peeling paint off the wall, and more, but I had not connected them with my children, with this girl who I had felt was not much different from me only 10 years before.

Another one of the authors remembers an experience in an inner-city teaching assignment early in her professional career. She and her first graders completed a unit of study in nutrition. The teacher was giving herself a pat on the back. What a success her lessons had been—a trip to the local supermarket, a "tasting" day of new and exotic fruits, and an afternoon of making "stone soup" with a variety of vegetables children had brought to school.

On one particular morning the class was reviewing some of the concepts learned. "What vegetable did you have for dinner last night?" Various children responded—french fries, greens, carrots, corn, and so on. Tiffany's response was "tomato soup." How clever—she's really made the connection. For some reason "tomato soup" kept sticking in my mind that day. As the day was coming to a close, I finally remembered why. A day ago Tiffany had said her stove was not working. I took Tiffany aside and asked how her mother had cooked her soup. She hadn't. She had opened the can and Tiffany had cold soup for dinner. Tiffany never returned to school after that chat. Two weeks later I was notified she had moved and her new school was requesting school records. Tucked into her records, I placed a note to her new teacher to keep an eye on Tiffany's home situation.

The transitory lifestyle of many poor families, including those of migrant workers and homeless people, makes life particularly difficult for children. The U.S. Census Bureau reported that in 1998, nearly 13 million children lived below the poverty line in the United States (see http://www.census.gov/ftp/pub/hhes/poverty/poverty98/pv98est1.html). According to that Census, severely impoverished children live in big cities and rural areas, in the coldest parts of Alaska and the hottest parts of the desert Southwest. Moved from school to school and from school district to school district, such children struggle not only with poverty, but also with the lack of stable friendships. Moreover, frequent moves result in a piecemeal education at best. They begin units without finishing them, switch textbooks, and more often than not, fall through the cracks. Such students need all the special attention teachers can give them. Only then can they hope for a more comfortable future.

Unfortunately, poverty is a reality of life for many young people, even in a country as wealthy as the United States. Although student teachers cannot solve their students' problems, they can help alleviate some discomfort and embarrassment. Familiarize yourself with community resources such as organizations that provide food, clothing, and emergency rent checks. Additionally, take care that completion of homework assignments never requires materials some students in your class may not have access to. Whenever possible, work to minimize situations in which social class and material wealth become obvious. If, for example, you request that students dress up as a character in a book when delivering oral book reports, insist that all costumes be homemade. Better yet, have school materials available from which students can fashion costumes in class.

STUDENTS WHO MAY REQUIRE SPECIAL ATTENTION

Besides students of different genders and socioeconomic statuses and those who come from diverse ethnic, racial, and cultural backgrounds, teachers work with students of widely varying physical and mental strengths and weaknesses. In this section we focus on *special-needs* students. This term applies to students with disabilities: physical, behavioral, or cognitive and intellectual, and students who are intellectually gifted. Gifted and talented students are discussed later in the chapter.

The 1975 Individuals with Disabilities Education Act (IDEA), formerly called the Education of All Handicapped Children Act (PL94-142), was implemented in 1977. This federal law mandates that a system be introduced into each school district involving the periodic review of each child with a disability for placement in the least restrictive environment. Unless the review weighs heavily against it, special-needs children are to be placed in regular classes with their nondisabled peers (i.e., mainstreamed or included) to the maximum extent appropriate, and the school provides the necessary specialized personnel, equipment, technology, and services on an individual or group basis.

One major objective of IDEA is to see that students are schooled in the least restrictive environment, but it is important to note that "least restrictive environment" and "mainstreaming" are not synonymous. For many exceptional students, the appropriate least restrictive environment is the regular classroom, but for some, it is not (Schloss, 1992). Under IDEA, school districts must provide for a "continuum of alternative placements." In other words, when a disabled student is harmed by inclusion in a general education class or when other students suffer from the disabled student's inclusion, the school district must provide an

alternative free, public school placement that is most appropriate and least restrictive (Fischer, Schimmel, & Kelly, 1999; Yell & Drasgow, 1999).

More recent legislation, such as the 1990 Americans with Disabilities Act
(ADA), has also impacted school policy. Unlike IDEA, ADA has implications
well beyond education, and it has broader reach within schools. Under IDEA,
students qualify for special services only if a team assembled for their evaluation
determines that special education and related services are needed "because the
difficulty in learning and developing is caused by one or more of the disability
categories specified in the statute." A student qualifies for special services under
ADA if one or more disabilities limit performance of a major life function (e.g.,
walking, hearing, working). To comply with ADA, "services or facilities naturally and routinely available to nondisabled individuals" should be "naturally
and routinely available" to qualified disabled individuals as well. This means,
for example, that school buildings must be fully accessible and usable (Otto,
1998).

Mainstreaming: Inclusion in Practice

More than two decades have passed since the law calling for placement in the
least restrictive environment became fully effective, but many school systems
and educational leaders continue to struggle with the law's implementation.
Polices between school districts and even within schools vary widely (Walther-
Thomas, Korinek, McLaughlin, & Williams, 2000). In fact, Kauffman (1999)
argued that the term *inclusion* has become "virtually meaningless" due to the
fact that certain districts' mainstreaming methods deviate so greatly from the
intent of IDEA and ADA legislation. However, all school systems have made
some efforts to include special-needs students in their regular classrooms. In
doing this, most have moved away from the full-day segregation of most special-
needs students into self-contained classrooms and have instead adopted one of
the following models, or occasionally a combination of two of the models outlined below.

Mainstreaming.   The terminology may differ from state to state or even
district to district, but the premise of mainstreaming is that special-needs students assigned to self-contained special-needs classrooms participate with other,
regular classrooms in whatever areas in which they are capable of doing so. For
instance, some special-needs students join nondisabled classmates for music, art,
physical education, lunch, and recess but spend the rest of their day in a self-
contained classroom. At the elementary level, some join other classrooms for
reading groups and special programs. The extent of an individual student's participation in regular classrooms is based on personal abilities and the individualized education program (IEP) developed by a team assembled to evaluate the individual student's education (discussed later).

Use of a "Resource Room."   In this model, all students—special needs or not—are assigned to a homeroom and, in the middle and upper grade levels, to academic classes. Special-needs students are included in all activities and instruction within their homeroom and assigned classes. Periodically through-out the day, however, they report to the school's resource room where a special education teacher provides them with either one-on-one or small group instruction.

Use of an Aide.   In this third model, special-needs students, like all other students, are assigned to a homeroom and academic classes. They remain with their nondisabled peers throughout the day and a special education teacher comes to them. A student with a physical disability, for example, would be as-signed an aide who could help him or her in the restroom, cafeteria, and in ma-neuvering through the halls. Classroom aides are sometimes assigned to those with visual impairment, neurological deficits, or autism or other developmental disabilities.

All three of these models provide unique challenges for students and teach-ers. Teachers, for example, must accommodate both what and how they teach to meet the needs of special-needs students.

You may have seen materials in your cooperating classroom concerning teaching decisions made to meet the needs of given students as spelled out in their IEP. IEPs are prepared for special-needs student by a team, including a rep-resentative from the school's special education department, the classroom teacher, and other school personnel. Parents and specialists from the community (e.g., physicians or mental health professionals) sometimes provide input as well. Each school year, a student's IEP is revised and a parent conference is held to review the plan.

As you probably observed in your cooperating classroom, when it comes to tests and grading, your cooperating teacher takes into consideration such facts as the poor handwriting of some neurologically or motor-impaired students and the need for extra test-taking time for students with particular learning disabilities. Accommodating students' special-needs in this way can sometimes be a chal-lenge, but when teachers are open-minded and flexible, mainstream and inclu-sion models can work, as Brooke discovered early in her internship.

9/22: I have been having some discussions with Mr. B. about the nature of assess-ment and evaluation. It is an extremely difficult concept for me to sort out in my head. I have been struggling with these ideas since THE320 and still don't know where I stand on the issue. I understand that the world is not fair and that some stu-dents will naturally just seem to do better than other students. But I just don't know what to do about the slightly below average students who are trying very hard but just can't seem to totally grasp what is going on in school.

I am beginning to understand the whole modification concept to help these students feel successful and still challenge them in a regular classroom, but you also can not adapt all work to every given student's individual needs. Mr. B. does a great job varying his assessment between formal tests, written work, and creative activities, but it is still difficult to be fair to all students. There seems to be a catch-22 between wanting all students to be successful and also needing to create some kind of hierarchy where some students do better than others. They are all A-students in one way or another, but every student can't get A's!!!

Brooke's sensitivity and thoughtfulness helped her meet many of her students' varied and numerous needs. Despite some frustrations, she was privy to the magic mainstreaming and a student teacher's open attitude can work. As she described:

11/21: I had originally planned for all the rough drafts to be due today, but because so many students were behind I had to move the rough draft to after vacation if I wanted to get any kind of quality writing. I told the students that if their draft was done before vacation, I would read it and make comments over the holiday.

Yesterday I had given the students time in class to work on their essay writing. One of the Special Education students was doing a really good job and taking the essay seriously. This is a student who didn't even manage to hand in the last essay and came extremely close to failing the first quarter. An ADHD student was sitting quietly writing his essay! I went over to help him and answer a question and at that time I told him I was really proud of him for working so hard on this essay. I could sense that he was about at the end of his concentration and patience. I told him to go get a drink and then come back into class ready to keep working. He sort of looked at me like I had three heads when I told him I was proud of him, but I think he knew I really meant it and he knew he was working hard. Something must have clicked because he came into class today with his rough draft finished!!! It is the little moments like that which make every day worthwhile.

Classifying Special-Needs Students

Students who have special needs but who are typically included within the regular classroom can be divided into five general categories: children with physical disabilities, children with emotional disorders, children with behavioral disorders, children with learning disorders, and gifted children. We briefly discuss each group below, pointing out the primary symptoms or signs to look for in identifying such a child (if records or files do not already indicate a student fits into this group) and some of the techniques you might consider using to more effectively include these students in the classroom. We encourage you to consult with your supervising teacher or library sources for more information in the likely event that you have students with special needs in your cooperating classroom.

Children With Physical Disabilities.   Of all the special-needs children, this group is the most readily noticed. Children in this category often use wheelchairs or crutches, have artificial limbs, or are blind or deaf. Although you will generally be aware of their special needs quickly, this knowledge does not necessarily make inclusion any simpler. Because most of these children look different from other children, they are likely to be treated differently, sometimes in stereotypical or prejudicial manners, by peers and even by teachers and other adults. In most cases, they will not need exceptional accommodations for daily academic activities. However, they may need special accommodations for activities that require motion or movement or that demand physical capabilities they do not possess.

As a student teacher, you will want to be unceasingly aware of such impediments and prepare lesson plans with these issues in mind. As with other special-needs groups, this does not mean you should avoid lesson plans that may, for example, ask students to create Japanese origami figures when you know you have a student with use of only one hand; instead, you should be prepared for an alternate activity (perhaps working with a peer, or building simpler origami figures) for the special-needs child.

Children With Emotional Disorders.   This grouping includes children who have emotional problems, including depression, anxiety, somatization (feeling bodily pain such as stomach aches or headaches in response to stress), eating disorders (e.g., anorexia or bulimia), and other such emotional problems. They may suffer from physical or emotional abuse, be undergoing a stressful time at home (e.g., a parental divorce), or be grieving (e.g., over the loss of a grandparent or pet). Often, emotional distress will be short-lived and will resolve itself in a matter of days or weeks, but at other times the distress will last for several years. When the distress is short-lived, the child or adolescent frequently will not be officially classified as a special-needs child and will not have an IEP but will still benefit from special attention.

Children with emotional disorders may be overly shy or anxious in working with peers, speaking in front of the class, or even communicating individually with teachers. They may frequently be tired during the day, complain of bodily aches and pains, or break into tears. They may also be absent from school much more than usual. From an educational perspective, children with emotional disorders are likely to have trouble paying attention for long periods of time; may not connect well to other students; and may appear sad, withdrawn, and disinterested in schoolwork.

At times, you will be aware that a student is depressed, anxious, or anorexic, or that he or she has another emotional disorder. At other times, however, such disorders will not yet be diagnosed. Often, children and adolescents are reluctant to talk about such problems; they frequently have parents who are detached or who are distressed themselves. For these reasons, when you see symptoms such as the ones just described in a child or adolescent, you may consider asking your cooperating teacher or a school counselor or psychologist to talk to the student. Often short-term counseling can aid students with such distress.

There are few educational techniques that will quickly change emotionally disturbed children or adolescents' lives so that they will immediately succeed in school—other elements of the students' lives are too overwhelming, and often more pressing. Typically, the most effective intervention is for a teacher to help the student obtain the necessary psychological counseling, psychiatric medications, or social support they need. However, there are some small steps you can take in the classroom. Providing some extra attention and help often goes a long way in assisting a distressed student. Helping students overcome social anxiety—by providing structured time with peers—or anxiety about public speaking—by having the child regularly read passages out loud—can be great ways to help an anxious student overcome nerves, and thus make school a less stressful place. Speaking to the student's parents, as discussed in chapter 6, can sometimes help a troubled student regain emotional stability, perhaps by opening the road to professional assistance.

Children With Behavior Disorders.   Many teachers dread the thought of having a behavior-disordered child or adolescent in their classroom. Such children are impulsive, overactive, and frequently disruptive to classroom learning. They are often diagnosed with psychiatric labels such as attention deficit hyperactivity disorder (ADHD) or oppositional defiant disorder (ODD). The symptoms of such special-needs children are readily noticed: rudeness, impulsivity, hyperactivity, inattention, opposition, fighting, breaking rules, cheating, and so on.

Although children with overt behavior problems are diagnosed readily and often treated with psychiatric medications, some children's disorders are not detected until much later. In particular, children who have trouble paying attention but who are not hyperactive or disruptive frequently slip through the cracks. Not until alert teachers (or student teachers) notice problems with inattention are they referred to specialists, who evaluate, treat, and sometimes prescribe medications that prove helpful.

Children with behavior disorders can be effectively educated. Many of the classroom management techniques discussed in chapter 9 prove useful when dealing with behaviorally disturbed students. Briefly, clear, established rules and fair and consistent discipline practices combined with lessons that minimize boredom help maintain students' on-task behavior. Frequent change of activity, hands-on educational techniques, and opportunities for student participation help keep behavior-disordered children involved in the educational process, and therefore less likely to disrupt their education or that of peers.

Children With Learning Disorders.   When one thinks of learning disorders, the first thought is often of the child who is smart but cannot read, or who aces the tests in reading, social studies, and science, but falls flat when it comes to mathematics. In actuality, learning disorders can plague any number of intellectual or cognitive abilities. Deficits in verbal memory, abstract processing, or basic reading ability can all be classified as learning disorders. Generally, a learning disorder is diagnosed when a student's ability in one area of intellectual processing is significantly deficient compared to the student's overall intelligence. In other words, if mathematics ability is significantly worse than overall IQ, that student likely has a mathematics learning disorder.

Many learning disorders are diagnosed when the child progresses through elementary and middle school and encounters academic difficulties in a particular subject or skill area. Sometimes, however, learning disorders are not diagnosed until much later. Consider this example, an abridged discussion one of the authors had with a neuropsychologist:

> Laura was 16 years old and lived in a rural area a few blocks from the Pacific Ocean. She had done above average work in elementary school but was struggling to pass her classes in high school. She had been thrown out of a car in a late-night car crash when she was 8 years old, and her parents were worried that accident may have caused brain damage that was affecting her school performance. They brought her to me for an evaluation. My testing revealed that Laura had a previously unidentified learning disorder that was severely impacting her school performance. It may or may not have been a result of the automobile accident, but no matter what, it was impacting her schoolwork. She was intelligent in nearly all areas of functioning—certainly smart enough to succeed in high school and beyond. But she had extremely poor memory skills. She could not remember words from a list, or shapes that were presented to her. She could not remember numbers or colors that were given to her. All of those memory skills were well within the mental retardation range even though her overall IQ was just above average. Fortunately, Laura had one relative strength—her memory for stories was just below average. I encouraged her parents and her school to help her learn through stories—she should learn history, literature, even science and mathematics through stories as much as possible. Make up stories, create stories out of history and out of scientific invention, whatever it takes—that is the way Laura could be successful in school.

Laura's example is not all that atypical. Unidentified learning disorders can have a major impact on school success, and identification of them—along with learning techniques that may help students adjust for disabilities—can have a tremendous impact on success and happiness in school.

Gifted and Talented Children.   You might be surprised to see gifted and talented children included in a section that has previously focused on children with various disorders. On reflection, however, you might recognize the fact that, just like children with emotional, behavioral, and learning disorders, children who are gifted and talented have special needs in the classroom: Without a proactive teacher who takes precautions, the gifted or talented student may not obtain the education he or she deserves. Surprisingly, it is sometimes the most able students who learn the least in heterogeneous, general education classes.

The features of gifted and talented children, like those with various disorders, take many forms. Some are gifted in all subject areas. More frequently, students are talented; they have exceptional strengths in one or two areas ranging from mathematics and reading to the fine arts and foreign languages. Most gifted and talented students are identified early in their schooling. Their inquisitiveness, advanced vocabulary, higher order thinking, and ability to become completely absorbed in projects often set them apart from their classmates. On occasion, however, a student will have a hidden talent—often something not readily apparent such as ability to memorize facts or ability to think logically with great skill—that is not recognized until an astute educator notes exceptional work and refers the student to a specialist for testing.

As in the recognition of a learning disorder, recognition of a gifted student's talents can help teachers modify their educational approach to maximize student learning. This is especially true in elementary and middle schools where honors and Advanced Placement classes are not available. Because gifted students grasp new concepts more quickly than their peers, they often become bored in mainstream classrooms. To avoid this boredom (and the discipline problems that frequently arise because of it), students might be given the option to work through the same material independently, then proceed on to enrichment activities. The use of pretests also enables teachers to ascertain what skills and information gifted students already possess, allowing them to design work that is sufficiently challenging for those students.

Recommendations for maximizing gifted student learning include deviating from usual procedure in content (through greater depth and elaboration), in process (through independent study and research), and in product (by addressing real-life problems; G. A. Davis & Rimm, 1998; Maker, 1982). Talented students might be given modified assignments in their area of special capability and be encouraged to strengthen areas of weakness—rather than learning a scientific concept verbally, which might be the gifted student's strength, he or she might be encouraged to try to understand the concept visually or pictorally instead.

Evaluation of Mainstreaming

Although school districts have slowly moved forward with inclusion and mainstreaming, the effects of such action are still under debate by academics. MacMillan, Gresham, and Forness (1996), for example, admitted that there is empirical evidence to support inclusion for some students, but questioned the empirical evidence to support inclusion for all children. In particular, they suggested children with severe emotional and behavioral disorders are poorly served in an inclusive environment. Other researchers disagree. In a book designed to help school administrators develop inclusion programs, Walther-Thomas and colleagues (Walther-Thomas et al., 2000) argued that the alternatives to inclusion are ineffective and lead to higher dropout rates.

As academics continue to debate the merits of inclusive practices, classroom teachers continue to search for the best ways to deal with the diverse classroom makeups inclusion has brought. Examples of successful inclusion abound, but in certain cases, particularly in stressful teaching and learning environments, inclusion can become overwhelming for all involved.

For example, while teaching at an urban public school, one of the authors was assigned a second-grade class of 30 that included two children diagnosed with visual impairments, one with a severe behavioral disorder, and one assigned to a self-contained learning-disabled classroom but who joined the others for reading instruction. Early in the year it became clear that several other students had behavioral and learning disabilities that had not yet been diagnosed. None of the special-needs children was provided with an aide. In this situation, meeting the individual needs of special-needs students while still addressing the academic, social, and emotional needs of the class proved an immense challenge.

Some schools limit the number of special-needs students assigned to any one general education classroom to ensure that regular classroom teachers are not overloaded to the point where they cannot meet the needs of either disabled or nondisabled students. In one system, for example, special-needs students are assigned a number indicating the severity of their disruptive influence on the class. Teachers might be assigned three "1-level" students, signifying mild problems, or they might be given a reduced class load and one student with a 3, signifying severe problems. Such practices can greatly increase the effectiveness of mainstreaming, but in most school districts they are not yet implemented. For the multiple reasons already described, teachers and school systems continue to struggle with compliance to the spirit as well as the letter of the IDEA and ADA laws.

What bearing does that have on your work in the classroom? For your purposes as a beginning teacher, we recommend the following:

1. Accept the fact that during your student-teaching assignment and for the foreseeable future, you will have special-needs students in your regular classroom.
2. Remember that teacher expectations can have powerful effects on student performance and that if you expect special-needs students will succeed in your mainstream classroom, they are more likely to do so.

For your benefit and for the benefit of those you teach, it is logical to adopt the philosophy that mainstreaming can work and will work in your classroom.

At various points during your student-teaching experience, and next year when you have your own class, go through your roster and ask yourself about each student. What are your expectations about him or her? Are they realistic and will they promote maximum growth and development? Also think about your behavior toward each individual. Ask whether it conveys your caring, support, and belief in them. Does it lead them to know that you expect them to learn and to grow?

As you ask yourself these questions about individual students, you will be crossing the whole spectrum of group diversity in schools—diversity in gender, race, ethnicity, culture, special-needs, and social class. You will be examining ways to include all children in your educational objectives and plans. You are likely to find this process both difficult and challenging, but you will also find it rewarding.

CRITICAL ISSUES

- Think of three different students in your student-teaching class and decide on the level of performance you expect of each of them. What are your reasons for your decision in each of the three cases?
- What can you do to help students raise their own levels of expectation?
- What steps can you take to help you "see" students as individuals and not as members of particular groups—as male or female, as a particular race or ethnicity, as coming from a particular socioeconomic class, or as a special-needs student?
- Identify some of the benefits of teaching a class in which several or more cultural groups are represented. Are those benefits found in your cooperative classroom?
- Consider a student in your class who has special needs. What aspects of inclusion or mainstreaming benefit him or her and/or his or her classmates? What aspects prove challenging for the student, the class, and you?
- What qualities in a teacher do you consider so fundamental to good teaching that they apply whether the class is mainstreamed or limited to special-needs students?

8

Curriculum and Teaching:
Becoming Competent and
Confident in the Classroom

TOPICS

- Curriculum Guide/Course of Study
- Textbooks and the Curriculum
- Technology and the Curriculum
  Computer-Related Issues in the Cooperating Classroom
- The Arts and the Curriculum
- Observation of the Curriculum at Work
- When You Begin to Teach
  Be Aware of Different Objectives, Affective as Well as Cognitive
  Be Aware That Thinking Ability Changes With Age
  Be Aware of the Importance of Questions in Teaching and Learning
  Be Aware That What You Teach and How You Teach Are Linked to
  Students' Behavior
- Individualization
- Cooperative Learning
- Student Assessment, Student Teacher Assessment
  Assessing Your Students' Progress
  Assessing Your Own Progress
- Teaching the Whole Class the First Time
- Next Year

By the time you begin your student-teaching assignment you will have studied
the principles of curriculum, observed in a classroom, and perhaps participated
in an early field experience program. During your student teaching, your read-

ings and studies will come to life—in your very own hands, so to speak, with you as the central figure. Our objective in this chapter is to examine the curriculum from the point of view of the student teacher.

CURRICULUM GUIDE/COURSE OF STUDY

You may recall from your studies that the word *curriculum* is derived from the Latin verb *currere*, meaning to run. The Latin noun *cursis* means race or course. In essence, we as teachers conduct a group of children or adolescents on a course; we head them down one pathway or another.

Those using a pathway or road generally have a destination. True, we could wander aimlessly, selecting roadways quite randomly. That may be an appropriate choice during a vacation, especially when we want to be totally carefree and can afford to arrive wherever the path leads. Obviously, it is totally unacceptable when we are responsible for the education of students. No dallying? But of course! We can dally, but only after we have chosen our objective (e.g., the basic concepts of decimals or the causes of the American Revolution), made the important decision about the route we will traverse to reach our destination (e.g., readings, chalkboard or Internet demonstrations, drills, worksheets, laboratory experiments, games, drama), and set ourselves a reasonable timetable, taking into consideration all of our destinations during the term or year. Then we will have a clear idea about how much time we have to dally. And dally we must, at least if we mean by that spending some time following the interests that arise quite naturally (and sometimes unexpectedly) out of the planned and scheduled work.

You will not be involved in selecting the curriculum objectives for your student-teaching class. That will already have been accomplished, probably by a team of teachers, administrators, and state officials. Curriculum guidelines may have been developed under the aegis of the school district's curriculum council or perhaps under the direction of the education agencies that develop statewide criteria. Regardless, those outlining objectives look at a curriculum in its totality and build continuity in material from one year to the next. They also ensure that each course's curriculum meets state standards and objectives, possibly as measured by scores on statewide proficiency tests, now administered in many states.

Once you are established as a full-time teacher, you may play an active role in reviewing and revising the curriculum and in selecting textbooks. But for now, as a student teacher, the course of study that you are to be guided by is fixed. Nevertheless, you may still employ considerable imagination as you lead your students through it.

The curriculum objectives you must work toward are usually spelled out in detail in the school's curriculum guide. Typically, these guides explain the significance of a particular subject to the total educational experience of the student, and also detail the specific importance of each particular concept and skill. After specifying the subject's importance, guides move right to the heart of the matter; that is, to the measurable, behavioral objectives, such as the specific skills to be learned in connection with reading poetry (e.g., identifying rhyme schemes, alliteration, and symbolism) or the concepts to be understood in connection with radiation. Those objectives must be clear and concrete if, by the end of a unit's work, we are to reliably determine whether or not our students have mastered them, which is another way of seeing the extent to which our instructional plan has been effective.

To illustrate, one fifth-grade course of study in mathematics includes the following among its 70 plus objectives: reducing fractions to the lowest term, rounding decimal numbers to the nearest whole numbers, 10ths, or 100ths, and defining equilateral triangle and right triangle. In some curriculum guides there may be a cross-reference to the textbook selected for use in the fifth grade. Suggestions for resource aids and materials on the given objectives may also be provided. Videos, audio recordings, instructional kits, instruments, books, computer software, and other educational aids, as well as suggestions for field trips, resources in the community, television programs, and other educational experiences, are listed. Also included is a section on lessons and exercises that the teacher may use to reinforce learning of the concepts.

In some guides there are tests that can be given periodically to evaluate learning during the study of a given unit. Preferably these are tests that are diagnostic in nature, enabling you to pinpoint the particular concept or skill that each student has or has not mastered. In some schools teachers use test questions similar to those appearing on standardized state tests for the same purpose, as a means of evaluating student acquisition of targeted content knowledge and skills outlined in state curriculum objectives.

College students in education, appropriately excited by the prospect of conducting a class as a student teacher, have a large supply of creative ideas. After seeing the school's curriculum guide, some of them become resentful, feeling as if an overwhelming power were at work to force them into a kind of teaching with which they do not agree. This need not be the case. The curriculum guide is intended to be just that, a guide. It will select a road for you to take and provide many helpful signposts and resources to use as you wish. But what you "see" on the road, at what stream or wildflower you pause, what berry you taste, and what hare or fawn you photograph en route is for you and the interest of your students to decide.

We would like to stress an extraordinarily important principle: The curriculum objectives and the methods of instruction are determined by a number of decision makers. These include the public, the media, school boards, political leaders, test publishers, teachers' groups and others. That truism, however, must not obscure another equally important fact: Teachers and their students also create the curriculum (Clandinin & Connelly, 1992).

People outside your classroom decide on the objectives and write the guides, but your cooperating teacher (and you) and the students will determine what learning goes on in the classroom. The teacher is not just a conduit, like a telephone wire, through which a curriculum is piped into the ears of students. To a certain extent this year, and to a large extent next year, your creative ideas and the responses and participation of your students will shape the curriculum. For although the curriculum guide provides the potential for what occurs in the classroom, the teacher plays a major role in determining what that potential becomes. Therefore, when we think about curriculum development, we need to consider the development and preparation of the teacher as much as the development and preparation of materials.

In designing and developing curriculum, is there an overarching aim? According to two educators who have studied the field for many years (Tanner & Tanner, 1995), the curriculum is the means for learners to reconstruct for themselves the accumulated human knowledge and experience, enabling them "to grow in exercising intelligent control of subsequent knowledge and experience" (p. 191). They went on to say:

> Educators have no way of knowing the exact nature of the subsequent experience of the learner in life. But if the process of education and that thing we call curriculum are successful here and now, the learner will be enabled to grow in social power and insight throughout life. (p. 191)

It is not a coincidence that the aim of the curriculum for your students in a basic sense is the same as the aim of student teaching: to enable you "to grow in exercising intelligent control of subsequent knowledge and experience."

TEXTBOOKS AND THE CURRICULUM

If your cooperating teacher has not shown you the teacher's editions and accompanying teacher resource kits for the textbooks your classes use during the first week of your student teaching, ask to see them. Also ask how much your cooperating teacher uses them, refers to them, and deviates from them. You will also want to know the teacher's expectations about your use of them. Request the opportunity to examine the complete set of textbooks used during the year and their accompanying teacher's editions. Take special note of the objectives as you study the volumes. Familiarity with these textbooks will help you become better informed about the program at your school and better prepared to teach.

Teacher's editions include the entire content of the student textbook as well as information similar to that provided in a curriculum guide, but in greater detail. In addition to an overall description of the material and a list of objectives, you will find information on the following: the specific objectives of individual chapters or units, the instructional materials and vocabulary needed for each unit, estimates of how much time should be devoted to each lesson, and suggestions for handling assessments.

Within each lesson of the unit there are detailed suggestions on ways of introducing concepts and instructing students on the material at hand. Frequently, follow-up activities, evaluative tests, remedial measures, enrichment activities, and references for further study are also included.

Considering the need for the large number of lesson preparations during the course of student teaching (not to mention during a full school year), commercially prepared textbooks and the accompanying teachers' editions and teacher resource kits are of great value. With their use you need not devise every single exercise, assignment, and test; you can use some of those they provide, in the original or an adapted form, altered to serve your specific purposes.

TECHNOLOGY AND THE CURRICULUM

As technology becomes central to the worlds of commerce, finance, media, and publishing—in fact, to all parts of life—its importance to teaching becomes clear. Today's students are ill prepared for the world of work if they are not comfortable with and skilled in the use of technology.

"Computer classes" and "computer teachers" became part of many schools during the 1980s and 1990s, but the trend now is to move toward the integration of technology in all areas of the curriculum. Students may use the computer to make data tables in science, interactive presentations in social studies, collages in art, and Web page book reports in English.

Regardless of the age of your students or the discipline you teach, you can be sure that you will have an opportunity to incorporate computer technology in your student teaching. But the question remains, should you? And if so, how?

Unquestionably, the use of technology adds much to classroom teaching. Many of today's students have grown up with keyboards and the World Wide Web, and they like them. Introduce a unit as a computer project and you can be sure of many smiles. As with any teaching aid, however, the decision to use computers should be deliberate. A computer—like a video, storybook, or graphing calculator—should never be used simply because it is there.

Do not fall victim to thinking that material delivered on a brand new CD-ROM or DVD can provide a magical cure for a student's learning problem. You, the teacher, help the child solve the problem, perhaps by deciding to use a machine. In other words, do not let the availability of a new machine or new technology tempt you to wonder, "how can I squeeze this new software into my lesson." Instead ask yourself, "What material should my students be taught, what is the most effective way to deliver it, and can this piece of technology be useful in accomplishing those goals?"

When computers and other technologies are integrated into the curriculum, teachers must be crystal clear about learning objectives. By the end of the project, what discipline-specific skills should the students have gained? What technology skills should they have mastered? How will students learn to see the relation between the two?

As increasing amounts of information become readily available to students for classroom and home use, teachers' roles in regard to knowledge acquisition will shift somewhat, with less emphasis placed on disseminating information and more on facilitating students' ability to acquire, process, and evaluate information. That is no easy task. Although the Web contains myriad resources of great value to students—archival documents, foreign-language newspapers, scientific journals—it also contains much useless, incorrect, and harmful information. Unsuspecting students, for example, may come across Web sites proclaiming the Holocaust a hoax. Teachers must give students the skills necessary to cope with a bewildering and constant influx of information. They must teach students to evaluate the credibility of sources. And they must impress on students their responsibility to properly document all information—graphics and sound as well as print—taken from online sources.

Enormously important, fast-paced changes are occurring in computers and computer technology. Although we cannot predict specific developments, we do know that advances will continue to interest teachers.

Computer-Related Issues in the Cooperating Classroom

Besides their important role in student education, technological advances provide enormous opportunities to aid you, the teacher. During the course of your student teaching internship, you will want to plan how you can best make use of your school and university's technological resources.

Student Teachers Who Believe "I Can't".   Although most student teachers are relatively comfortable with word processing programs, the Internet, and e-mail, many worry that they lack the skills necessary to guide students in the innumerable computer uses reaching beyond those basic areas. They may hold the attitude that they are ill-equipped to help students learn about technology because they are weak and poor learners in that area. This attitude, combined with the knowledge that computers will only grow more powerful and central to school life, makes it easy to feel one is falling behind.

If this is the case for you, it is wise to develop and follow a plan that will increase your mastery of technology skills. On an early visit to your cooperating school, familiarize yourself with the available hardware and software. Ask which computer programs teachers and students utilize. With your cooperating teacher, select a program you would like to master and use with the class.

Teaching the Computer Whiz.   Sometime during your first years of teaching—if not during your student teaching internship—you may have a computer "genius" in class with talent far beyond yours in working with computers. How will you react to this student?

We know how you will want to react. You will want to think of this youngster in the same way as you think of the other students; that is, as a member of the class who, like everybody else, has unique learning needs and strengths. You will want to encourage his or her interest in technology and further the skills already possessed.

But because we recognize that having a remarkably skilled student computer whiz in class can be stressful to student teachers giving their first lessons on the computer, we offer this advice:

1. As always, prepare thoroughly for every lesson. Be aware that technology introduces the possibility of glitches . . . a computer may freeze, the server may go down, and viruses might corrupt your demonstration. Know what you will do if each of these things happens.

2. Monitor the "automatic" thoughts you have as you prepare for the lesson, particularly those that "wander" through your mind. Research shows that these thoughts, called *self-talk,* affect your feelings and your behavior. For example, you might experience self-talk that says, "I'm the teacher. I should know more than the kids." If you do not catch yourself when you have this thought, you will feel bad when asked a question you cannot answer, and not know why you feel that way. You feel bad because, outside of your full awareness, you compared yourself to an arbitrary standard (teacher must know the answers to everything students ask), and found yourself lacking. In actuality, however, it is the standard that is lacking, not you.

3. Remind yourself that eventually you will be asked questions by students for which you do not know the answer but other students in the class do. This might first take place around a computer. Think about how you will respond. You can use this situation to illustrate that learning is a lifelong process. For example, you might say: "I'm so glad you knew the answer! Thank you. I am working every day to improve my knowledge and understanding of technology. One of the joys of learning is that it never ends."

4. Tap the skill and expertise of your student computer whiz by having him or her assist with the lesson. Computer work by nature is self-directed. You may wish to have every member of the class at the same step of a program, but that is easier said than done. An advanced student can unobtrusively help those who fall behind to catch up with the class.

5. If students prove more adept at some parts of a computer lesson than you, celebrate that fact with them. Many children and adolescents spend time wishing they were grown up. Make them aware of times when youth can be advantageous! Whereas they grew up with computers a part of everyday life, many of the adults around them find technology more challenging.

Although mastering new technologies may seem like the last thing you want to do while caught up in the daily struggle of preparing lesson plans, grading assignments, and perfecting classroom management skills, the effort is well worth it. The sooner you learn how to tap the technology resources available, the more time both you and your students will have to benefit from the excitement and clarity they bring to lessons. This is true whether you are teaching prekindergartners or high schoolers, gifted children or those who are developmentally delayed.

THE ARTS AND THE CURRICULUM

Like technology, the arts have special appeal to students. Surely you have noticed the excited buzz when teachers tell their classes they are going to watch a movie. Students of all ages react similarly to hearing a story, listening to music, playing music, putting on a play, dancing, singing, and painting. Of course, at some ages students must be coaxed to participate in what they might deem childish activities, but once they let themselves go, they enjoy the experience immensely.

The arts usually involve attributes that attract young people:

1. Human feelings, as in the play *Romeo and Juliet*, the musical *West Side Story*, the painting *Mona Lisa*, the song "Don't Worry, Be Happy," and the novel *Lord of the Flies*.

2. Activity, such as painting, sculpting, dancing, singing, performing a role, or composing music.

3. Applications, or seeing theoretical topics made more concrete, as when first and second graders learn arithmetic by "going shopping" in a make-believe store; fourth and fifth graders learn about similarities and differences in ethnic cultures by experiencing their dances; and high schoolers learn history through mock conversations between Jefferson and Hamilton, through listening to and comparing the music of Northerners and Southerners in 1860, and by examining the fiction, drama, and poetry produced during the depression of the 1930s.

Role-playing has special merit because it requires no equipment, yet captures the attention of children, teenagers, and adults alike. It can be used in virtually any subject, on any topic. For example, you could set up an imaginary conversation between Pasteur and those who ridiculed his germ theory in 19th-century France or a confrontation between two imaginary friends to show how to peacefully resolve an argument.

Although funding for the arts is often among the first things cut in schools experiencing a budget crunch, research shows that the arts help develop basic competencies in reading, writing, reasoning, studying, mathematics, speaking, and

listening. Yet, Thomas A. Hatfield, executive director of the National Art Education Association, says this is not the primary reason the arts should be studied.
Rather, it is because "the arts disciplines (art, music, theater, and dance) are basic:
as means of communication, as historical components of civilization, and as
providers of unique forms of knowledge. As such, they need no other justification
as essential components of education" (Hatfield, 1998 pp. 11–12). And indeed, the
Goals 2000: Education America Act set national standards in visual art, music,
dance, and theater for all K–12 students—a long-awaited victory for art educators.

Regardless of the subject or age you teach or even the availability of formal
art instruction in your school, you can tap the benefit of the arts for your students, as this history student teacher did:

> 3/12: Classes went well today. I'm so pleased. Image of the day: Kevin Smith
> singing loud, strong, and off-key: "some do think it a misfortune to be christened
> Pat or Dan, but to me it is an honor to be born an Irishman." I got 3rd, 4th, and 7th
> period singing and they LIKED it! (The choir teacher made a piano accompani-
> ment tape for me). Then we had a great discussion about the song ("No Irish Need
> Apply") and the Irish immigrant diary they read last night. I was such an idiot last
> week not to give them questions to go along with the diary entry. They got things
> out of it and enjoyed it this time around. Yea!

OBSERVATION OF THE CURRICULUM AT WORK

Before you begin planning lessons under the guidance of your cooperating
teacher, you will have many opportunities to observe his or her lessons in action.
Observation, as you recall, is more than simply looking or watching. It is purposeful and focused.

There are few skills throughout your career that will be as useful to you as observation. During your internship, observation can enable you to learn your cooperating teacher's implicit objectives in a given lesson, the subject matter he or
she teaches, the methods and techniques he or she employs, and the personal behavior (both initiatory and reactive) he or she displays. Observation can also help
you monitor the reaction of the students and the evidence of a particular lesson's
success or failure.

You will find that using your observation skills outside the classroom is helpful as well. You can learn a great deal about students by observing them in different settings, such as in homeroom before the morning bell, in corridors between
class periods, or at recess playing with friends. Observe with the purpose of understanding students, and therefore being able to teach them more effectively.

Next we provide several examples of observations made by Linda Kozusko, a
full-time secretary who was attending evening college prior to her student-
teaching assignment. Although the quality of the presentation of her observations
is enhanced by her literary talent, you need not be an English major, as she was,
to train yourself to make keen observations.

The first is a report of her observations in the school cafeteria, beginning at 8:30 a.m. We present Linda's journal entry as an example of purposeful observation that leads to a deeper understanding of the students and of the learning environment provided by this school.

5/22: The room was enormous, especially with the added space of external landscape provided by the floor-to-ceiling windows that composed one entire wall of the room.

It was very quiet; students moved to seats and either just sat, or pulled out frazzled looking notebooks and small books to peruse. No one seemed in a hurry, either to talk or to study. The day was beginning for these students who had the pleasant expectation of a soon-to-open kitchen where breakfast would be available.

The students were all white in that room. They were as friendly as half-awake people can be expected to be, and they seemed not unhappy with the fact that it was Wednesday, they were in school and the books in front of them had to be read. This sense of contentment was present throughout my day at Franklin High School.

Lunch hour was more hurried, laughter and calling replaced the silence and shuffling of the morning, but the lack of consternation, the smiling and the eating remained constant. Teachers ate among the students, talking with them, stopping on their way to tables to follow up on plans for some project, basketball news, play problems, etc. The classroom was not a set of walls; teachers and students coexisted on easy terms throughout the day's schedule (even during the fire drill in the afternoon) and in every hall and room that I entered.

It was nice seeing that school could be so open, so cheerful. I went away kind of happy that there are kids lucky enough to be in a free atmosphere in which to learn. I also went away feeling that the school was somewhat unreal—too White, too friendly, too campus-like, too disruptive-free. Perhaps this is an overreaction, but I can't help feeling that Franklin High may be just a little too "West" of cities of hatred, of dirt. All that contentment may not be functional in the future world of these kids. I hope that this feeling is wrong and that the school is not so much an incubator or isolation ward as it appeared in a one-way glance.

This report and those that follow show the quality of observation that penetrates beyond the obvious. It shows what you as a student teacher should look for. One notes physical attributes ("the floor-to-ceiling windows") and moreso the human attributes ("friendly as half-awake people can be expected to be"). Going deeper, Linda generalized about relationships ("teachers and students coexisted on easy terms throughout the day's schedule"). Even further, she weighed what she had seen and speculated about its meaning ("all that contentment may not be functional"). Now after having made these wide-ranging observations, and after checking their validity, she would be in a better position to develop and teach lessons for these students. The same qualities, interpretive as well as descriptive, are evident in the following report.

The cold remains of what was at one time a form of ravioli sat on the cabinet. Next to it, a young man sat with a teacher, Ms. P., to whom he had come for advice on a project for another class. She was very informal with him, her language was that of an adult talking off-handedly with a kid, no pompousness, no "let me tell you how." They were talking about music, about themes present in the songs on a new album of folk music, and she was throwing in some names of appropriate research sources for a paper on one theme. They were involved with one another, eager to talk through the idea, eager to understand each other's feelings about the singers, the theme, music in general. It was good talk, profitable, I felt, for both. I didn't have any sense that Ms. P. had given up her free period to help a kid who was not her own student—all of which, in fact, she had done.

On several occasions during the day, teachers in the department of English identified their goal as being "a Renaissance Person." The creative drama teacher is a musician; he has studied dance. Ms. P.'s off-time activity revealed how thoroughly open to new ideas, new avenues of art and knowledge the teacher should be ready to pursue, how thoroughly open to interruption and brain-picking a teacher must be. I felt so very challenged: my 10 years of staunch secretarial avoidance of questions and interruption hung in the air of that room like tight-lipped gauze that will have to be torn down if I'm ever to teach successfully. All my narrow studies in literature cracked under me—what else do I know, am interested in? Ugh! What a challenge.

Linda's observations brought her face-to-face with a problem many student teachers eventually confront: Even after all my courses, do I know enough to teach a meaningful lesson? Will I be asked a question I cannot answer? These natural doubts are usually soon overcome when student teachers begin interacting with their students. Moving on now to observations more directly related to curriculum, we have Linda's report on the behavior of a teacher in a course on fiction. The course was designed to encourage an interest in and habit of reading.

It is second period of the day and I hurry along a laughter-filled students' corridor toward Room 303 where I am to witness Franklin High's answer to the "uninterested reader disease." On my way, I note a shortish teacher, zooming along with an enormous cart of books, stopping here and there to talk with students. I eavesdrop long enough to learn that the topic of one of his chats is girls' basketball scores. Upon entering Room 303 I find the energetic cart pusher is the man I've come to observe, Mr. W. His zeal for basketball news is immediately redirected into the students in his room, "What book you reading? Who needs a new book? Got a great one on . . . ." I'm reminded of the hospital aide who turns the inertia of illness into active interest through the appeal of a seemingly innocuous Milky Way [candy bar]. It's salesmanship I'm witnessing, high class, very sophisticated, salesmanship.

The buyers are ordinary-looking teens. Males predominate, and I'm told by Mr. W. that the course's appeal is that a free period in which to read is an opportunity valued by the blue-collar sons who spend post-school hours pumping gas or loading supermarket shelves. T.V. has become a drag for most of these guys, and the day's long hours of school and work make a second-period breather for silence and reading a pleasure to be sought. The students are not college bound. The goal for the course, one with which Mr. W. is enormously in tune, is to make reading a free, happy, and worthwhile experience.

He succeeds. A slight girl passes in two index cards (one is required after completion of each book) on which she has written her concise appraisal of the books she has read. Pinned to the cards is a poem, unexpected creative writing from a student moved to write her thoughts on the theme of one work. A huge, young football-type senior rolls over to our section of the room (desks and tables are in wonderful disorder; Mr. W. and I are sharing two seats dead center of the room near the cart) to display with great displeasure a large paperback. "It's boring." "Why?" "Same stuff all the time." "Why not write a parody on it?" "What's that?" "Mock it." Mr. W. uses every student comment and yawn to teach something—and it's so painless, this teaching.

He and I chatted at length. Kids inspire Mr. W. He loves their energy, their zest. I'm afraid it's catching—9 a.m. is a ridiculous hour for zeal. A dedicated teacher, Mr. W. is working on his doctorate in education. His most important task as teacher: Make them write. He expects very little of each student: Read and respect the right of others to read; write a critique of each book, and whenever possible, write some original stuff on the works—a different ending to a novel, a better dialogue within a scene. The course is an elective; within this elective is complete choice of material. His cart is not the world—anything the student chooses to read is acceptable. He sees the writing of the students improving every week. He also brings films to class. *Of Mice and Men* is on the cart, and he will bring the film in soon for the students to see.

All the while that he and I chat, students read, write, approach the cart, bring a problem or thought to Mr. W. for straightening and also at times for simple sharing. Silence and sun prevail. My initial fear that Mr. W.'s zeal might overpower, making him the sole motivator for activity, dissipates as I realize that he's only an arm to the cart. The students are using him.

I'm excited to see this—a human teaching machine—push a button and your next novel is suggested, your misunderstanding of a word is sent to *Roget's* for qualification, your disgust with pornography's repetition is shared. I wonder how this happens. I hated the class I had in high school whose purpose was similar. Perhaps the difference was that silence was mandatory; or perhaps it was the want of choice of material. More likely, though, is the fact that we never "did" anything with our reading. You read *Jane Eyre* and that was that. The requirement to place the reading experience on the page surely is an important character in this course's success. I'm excited by this realization. I share it with Mr. W.—he agrees. My first observation is worth coming here for—I've learned something. Translate an inactive, receiving experience into a communication, out of solitude into sharing, active writing from inactive reading, unconscious reaction to conscious, specified feelings. Read and write.

The final observation took place in an atypical class in that it was composed of only five students. We have included it, however, because of the characterization of the teacher, so different from Mr. W. and yet excellent in achieving the curriculum goals. There is, as you know, no one correct way to be an effective teacher, or to teach content effectively.

By the time I had reached Ms. P.'s room, the heat and newness of the day had won. The class (in home economics) was tiny, five students, I believe, in all. The room was a combination lab and study; this day the students were at desks (large tables shared by more than one student) attempting to plan a menu. They also seemed a bit dried out and tired. Lethargy smacked from each of us in the brightly lit, pink and white cooking lab. All of us, of course, except Ms. P. She was as bright and comfortable-looking as the room. I saw my grandmother in her, so quiet was her way as she moved next to the students to encourage each one's search for recipes. No mean task apparently, since the young girls are terribly diet-conscious and planning meals to be eaten is a struggle against calories.

Of those teachers whom I had observed during the day, Ms. P. seemed the most at ease with her students. The "grandmother" image I think was not peculiar to me. She was genuine in her interest in why I was there, and I felt that sincerity. I'm sure others, for example, these hot, tired kids, also feel that sincerity. She worked the entire period, always aware of what each was doing (not doing), turning her attention to each of them to help. Watching her competent, friendly manner turn a dull period into a nice experience was, in a way, the highlight of my day.

Linda's experiences in the classrooms, lunchroom, and halls of Franklin High yielded profound insights about students and teachers. She especially valued the opportunity to observe teachers using very different styles of teaching to achieve the curriculum objectives of their respective courses.

It is true that some courses are more amenable to certain methods than to others (e.g., the controlled experiment in the physical sciences and role playing in the humanities, rather than vice versa). The differences between the teachers described were not solely due to the subjects they were teaching, however. They were also due to their general styles of relating to their students, their temperaments as people, and the particular teaching strategies they employed—individual reading and critique writing by the first teacher and encouragement and support combined with an individualized research approach by the second.

As we said before, there is no one correct or effective way to implement the curriculum. As you become skillful in observing, you will be able to analyze the styles of different teachers. The best time to start doing that is when you observe your own cooperating teacher.

Answer questions like these in your journal: How does he introduce a new unit? In what ways does she make the topic relate to the lives of the students? What else does she do to make it interesting? What activities does he initiate? How does he get the students involved in activity? What resources does he use?

Diagnostic tests? Follow-up instructional methods? If you were a student in her class would you have found a particular lesson interesting? Would you have learned? If you were the teacher, what would you have done differently? What assessment would you make of the effectiveness of the lesson? After you have answered these questions, list issues you want to discuss with your cooperating teacher to get the fullest benefit from your observations of his or her teaching.

WHEN YOU BEGIN TO TEACH

When you first visit your cooperating teacher's class, locate the points in the course of study/curriculum guide and the textbooks at which the class is working. Scan the prior sections to get sufficient background, then read beyond.

Because your teacher might give you the option of teaching the unit or units of your preference, review the guide and the appropriate textbooks with that in mind. When you begin to prepare for the lessons you will teach, study the relevant sections of the course of study and textbooks. Reflect on the objectives so that you understand beyond a question of doubt what is meant by each of them.

When you, along with your cooperating teacher, decide on the unit or units you will teach, begin carefully preparing yourself to lead the class through that material. Consult a wide array of resources to ensure that you are an expert of sorts on the material you will teach. You certainly want to go beyond the teacher's edition of the student textbook. If you are teaching *Wuthering Heights*, for example, you may want to review your college lecture notes on that novel and reread the most respected published criticisms. You will always teach best when well prepared. Moreover, delving into your own research will ensure that you bring the enthusiasm and freshness of learning in process to your students.

As you review the student textbook and complete your own research and reading, you can begin to set your plans for each learning objective:

- How will you introduce the material in such a way as to capture the interest of the students?
- What activities will you initiate to make the concepts meaningful, given the conceptual level of the students?
- What exercises you will employ to give students experience using the skills connected with the objectives?
- At what point will you begin your assessment of students' mastery of the work?
- What you will do about weak areas diagnosed?
- What will you do (apart from what your cooperating teacher and supervisor do) to personally evaluate the effectiveness of your curriculum unit?

As you think through these issues, remind yourself of five basic principles, discussed next.

Be Aware of Different Objectives, Affective as Well as Cognitive

At any given time a variety of objectives are implicit in the activities of the teacher and the students, not just the explicit one connected with a unit. Although we set our goal, let us say, to raise the reading level of the students in certain specified directions—such as educational objectives in the cognitive domain— we are simultaneously involving the values and feelings of the students— educational objectives in the affective domain (see Bloom, 1956; Krathwohl, Bloom, & Masia, 1964).

To illustrate, as young students are learning through newly acquired phonetic skills to read more difficult words in a story about a family, they are having reactions about the family portrayed in the story. It may give them positive feelings because it is like their family or negative ones because their family (perhaps a single-parent family) seems inferior by comparison. Or, as a result of rapid-paced learning, the able student's self-confidence and satisfaction with school is reinforced, whereas that of a slower child is diminished.

Negative affective outcomes can be averted. The sensitive teacher learns to anticipate them and to take measures to prevent or overcome them. For instance, in the case of the slower learner, diagnostic tests enable the teacher to aid that student by pinpointing areas that require further study. In the case of the child from the single-parent family, the teacher can make certain that such a family is not ignored in discussion of the story but is treated in the positive and constructive way it deserves.

Be Aware That Thinking Ability Changes With Age

The thinking ability of humans of different ages, at least prior to adulthood, varies widely. Piaget (Piaget & Inhelder, 1969) identified four major stages of cognitive development, each of which can be broken down into substages. Although the stage theory is still debated by child psychologists—whether the stages follow strictly in the order given, whether a child can be in more than a single stage at a time, whether the movement from one stage to another can be accelerated, whether these stages are found in all cultures, and even how many stages exist and what is accomplished in each—there is considerable agreement that individuals' minds tend to follow a general pattern of development as they mature intellectually, cognitively, and chronologically.

We briefly mention the Piagetian stages here to refresh your memory or to acquaint you with them if they are not already familiar. In particular, we wish to highlight the qualitative differences in thinking at the different stages.

The sensory-motor stage extends from birth to about age 2, when the child starts to acquire language.

The preoperational stage, which runs from about age 2 to 7, includes preschool and the first years in school. During this stage the child can focus on only one dimension at a time. The classic example used to illustrate this point involves showing a child a round ball of clay. Then right in front of the child, the clay is rolled into a long "sausage." The child thinks the sausage is bigger and therefore is made of more clay. He or she cannot coordinate the two dimensions of thickness and length. Because it is longer it is bigger to the child—he or she does not consider the fact that the sausage is also thinner.

The meaning for the teacher is that this child should not be expected to be able to work out problems that require simultaneous manipulation of two or more dimensions. When one encounters a child in this age group who is unable to understand (and most are unable) that a mother, at one and the same time, is also someone's daughter (two different dimensions), this child is not backward or dull, but simply at the preoperational stage of development.

The stage of concrete operations extends from about age 7 to 11. Although students in this age group are noticeably different from their younger counterparts in their mental abilities, they still have limitations in their thinking when compared with adults. They are rigid and dependent on a concrete form of thinking—thinking that is tied to what they know through their senses or through manipulation. This means that they are unable to work out problems that require them to consider systematically a variety of possible solutions to problems. They are not yet capable of thinking in terms of hypotheses.

In teaching children through the age of 11 or 12, working with concrete materials is of great value. Symbols, whether words or numbers, get their meaning from the world of concrete objects. One way to reduce the number of vacant stares during lessons and failing scores during tests is to give concrete examples. For instance, help the children learn the concept of subtraction by letting them see the result of "taking away" sticks or marbles or pennies.

The stage of formal operations typically begins at about age 12. It is at this stage (which not all people achieve) that individuals acquire the ability to conduct the most advanced form of thinking. They can engage in hypothetical thinking; that is, they can consider a variety of solutions to problems, including those that are not available to their senses.

Having general knowledge about cognitive development and being sensitive to the cognitive level of your students will help you plan and teach your lessons. If you have a student who, despite repeated explanations, seems unable to grasp a lesson, you might recognize that it is perhaps the student's immature cognitive development that is causing the difficulty. If this is the case, you can reframe your teaching technique to make use of concrete examples, enabling the student to comprehend.

Still another advantage in knowing how humans develop learning and thinking abilities is that it can help us, as teachers, accelerate the growth of those abilities in our students. Although there has been considerable controversy about the possibility of accelerating growth, it appears that the kind of teaching that encourages active thinking (and not just memorizing and drill) does facilitate that development (M. Schwebel, Maher, & Fagley, 1990; Vygotsky, 1934/1986).

Be Aware of the Importance of Questions in Teaching and Learning

As you know from countless life experiences, questions lie at the heart of learning. Research is conducted because you pose questions you cannot answer (why are my eyes blue and my brother's brown?). Discoveries are made because you question established beliefs (how can Santa Claus travel all over the world in one night?). Inventions are born because you ask yourself "how can this be done better?" As a young learner, you may think that answers are better than questions. In college, however, you learn that perspicacious questions are as important as brilliant answers. As a teacher, you will, of course, both ask and answer questions. You want your students to do the same.

Questions serve many purposes in the classroom. They stimulate thinking, initiate discussion, encourage creative thinking, and review material studied. As a teacher, it is important to know that there are distinctly different types of questions, and that the question you pose should match the purpose you wish to achieve. An excellent question intended to stimulate thinking (e.g., In what way is life for a child living in the Southwestern part of the country different from that of a child living in the Northeast?) may be entirely inappropriate as a review of material studied.

Questions can be thought of as being at different levels in a hierarchy (Bloom, 1956). Students must be able to answer questions at a lower level before they are able to deal with those at the next higher level.

At the *knowledge (or information) level* we seek to know if the student has possession of essential facts; let us say, whether the student can identify what a state legislature is. Next, we are interested in the student's *comprehension level*; that is, whether the student can explain in a meaningful way, in his or her own words, what a state legislature is. At the *application level*, the student is asked to explain the services that a legislature performs and the products that emanate from it.

The *analysis level* may be assessed by questions that break down material into its component parts and show relation among the parts, such as questions that get at committee structure, party control, and lobbies. The *synthesis level*—the ability to put it all together—is tapped by asking for a description of the situation in the state if there were no legislature. Finally, at the *evaluation level*, students use their own standards and values to critically assess state legislatures, maybe considering such standards as efficiency or speed and such values as fairness to all constituents and the influence of lobbies. Here, the questions are clearly not designed to get "right" answers, but to elicit the students' own thinking and reasoning.

→As teachers, our aim is to raise the level of questions so students will have practice thinking and reasoning at the highest levels of their capability. For your purposes while student teaching, however, it is enough for you to be aware of the differences and simply ask questions that challenge each of your students.

In virtually all situations you will want to use questions that tap the knowledge and comprehension levels of students (Do they know and do they understand?). Raising questions that draw on the application level is important not only because it provides further evidence that students understand what they are studying, but also because students are more likely to be interested in class when they see the usefulness of what they are learning.

Posing questions at the analysis and synthesis levels challenges students to take material apart in order to understand each part, then put it back together again, achieving a deeper understanding of the whole. Teachers enable students to grasp deeper meaning by asking—orally and in writing—questions at the analysis and synthesis level.

In the long run, the aim of our education system is to help students develop to the point at which they can field any level of question. As you prepare a unit for your student teaching, remember that the evaluative process is essential to life. Students need practice establishing a set of values (e.g., democracy) and determining how closely the set of ideas associated with them (e.g., the Constitution) comes to actualizing those values. Therefore, if possible, you will want to develop questions at the evaluation level. You will find that students enjoy the challenge of trying to answer probing questions, provided that they are compatible with the approximate stage of their conceptual development.

One other interesting way to think of questioning is to break it down into two types: convergent and divergent. Convergent questions have answers on which most people generally agree; that is, they converge. These questions can be as simple as, "What is the capital of the United States?" or as complex as, "What is the derivation of Einstein's theory of relativity?"

Divergent questions, as you would expect, have answers on which people differ or diverge. Here is one: "Supposing we were choosing a new capital for our nation, what would you choose and why?" As you can see, such questions—and you can introduce comparable ones even for young children—force us to think. Many students enjoy the discussions that follow such questions.

One important fact to keep in mind is that although there is great value in teachers asking thought-provoking questions, studies show that teachers tend to ask students too many questions (e.g., 40–150 in a 40-minute class) and students rarely ask any—about 2 (Sarason, 1990). Tim shows that it does not have to be that way:

4/19: I made a discovery today! Well, it wasn't a real discovery because Pat (university supervisor) has talked about it a lot lately. For me, it was a great step. First, instead of asking a whole slew of little questions, like "How does the blood stream handle oxygen?" I asked, "Supposing you didn't have a heart, what would be missing?" At first they laughed and said, "Your life." Then they started thinking and debating. I had them hooked. With this one question we got into more than half the reading assignment. And before class was over one boy asked what smoking did to the heart. I felt good.

Tim's experience gave him confidence. Children and teenagers do not want to be bored any more than college students do. They respond to a teacher who respects and encourages their thinking ability, and who is not afraid to have them ask questions.

Be Aware That What You Teach and How You Teach Are Linked to Students' Behavior

Curriculum and the maintenance of discipline in the classroom are finely intertwined. The fact that an appropriate, well-executed curriculum can have a great impact on students' in-class behavior is discussed in chapter 9. Here we only want to say that the planning of a lesson can be thought of as a combined logical and psychological process.

Your thoughts may include these: The students in my class, no matter how homogeneous they may seem, are bound to be different in their past experiences, current state of knowledge, interests, and inclination to attend to class activities. I am not a psychologist and my job is not to "analyze" them, but I will be a more effective instructor if I keep particular students in mind as I plan my lessons. By consciously thinking of individuals in class, my lesson plans will be directed to the faster as well as the slower students, the quieter as well as the more vocal, the girls as well as the boys, the educationally disadvantaged as well as the advantaged, the children of racial and ethnic minority groups as well as of the majority. My questions, my illustrations—yes, even my physical positions in the classroom when I teach—will be attuned to these differences and will enable me to capture most of the students' attention for most of the time.

You may be asking yourself, how in the world am I going to keep all these ideas in my head while I am teaching? Answer: Do not try. The suggestions we have given are intended for your use primarily while you are planning lessons. By incorporating these ideas into your plans you increase the likelihood of teaching a good lesson. We pass these ideas on to you in the same spirit that coaches advise their players to "remember the fundamentals" before a big game. When you have solid fundamentals, the rest follows. For teachers, the fundamentals mean thorough knowledge of the substance of our unit, solid lesson plans, and a clear link between our plans and the composition of our class.

Another question we are sensitive to: How can I be prepared for the unexpected? Answer: No matter how well you plan, the unexpected could arise in any given lesson. Although you cannot control the laws of chance, you can lower the probability of an encounter by anticipating the unexpected.

Consider the questions students might ask. Answer them now, in advance. If a new one arises during class and you do not know or are not sure how to answer it, be straightforward. Explain that you will find the solution by the next day. On the next day, explain just what steps you took to obtain the answer, for you will be sharing invaluable knowledge about the process of investigating and problem solving. An alternative approach to that difficult question would be to make the search for a solution a joint one. Whichever you choose, it need not in any way detract from your status as teacher.

We have a final point in connection with this section on teaching and the curriculum. Many student and beginning teachers have a tendency to prepare lengthy lesson plans. That can be a valuable exercise. However, it is no substitute for a concise plan with which you are so familiar that you hardly need to consult it during class. Effective teachers proceed through their lessons smoothly, keeping an open eye on student attentiveness and response and shifting emphasis as needed.

INDIVIDUALIZATION

Part of the process of lesson planning involves raising the important question of individualization. How much time will you devote to individual needs and how much to addressing the needs of the group as a whole? In college or university training, student teachers learn that recognizing and addressing the needs of individuals is the mark of a good teacher, and it is. Good teachers engage all of their students all of the time—or as close to it as humanly possible. The problem is that these two important instructional principles—individualization and whole-group engagement—collide. With 20 to 30 children or teenagers in a room, it is difficult to work with one individual or group of four and at the same time monitor the rest of the class (Copeland, 1987).

This dilemma has led some educators to characterize teachers as decision makers. According to this model, teachers carry out routines, watchful for cues about how instruction is proceeding. If a cue tells you it is not going as planned, you decide whether the situation is beyond your tolerance. If so, you decide what move to make (Shavelson & Stern, 1981).

For example, you ask a question about Tom Sawyer's behavior with his aunt. Several students make comments. As you are listening to one student—Rachel—answer thoughtfully, a group of boys in the back of the room start their own conversation, laughing loudly. That behavior is beyond tolerance, so you interrupt the general discussion and tell the disruptive boys that they are missing the important points Rachel is making. They may talk in their turn, and their comments would be welcome.

Every day, every class period presents challenges like these and you must react almost instantaneously. For example, in the lower grades, one child is crying, another must go to the bathroom, and a third is pushing a fourth. In a ninth-grade class, one is cursing another, a third has her head on the desk, and a fourth is passing notes to a fifth. As Doyle (1986) said, teachers face complicated sets of cues of different kinds, many of which come at the same time.

When you individualize, you focus your attention in one direction and not in other directions. As much as you can help those students you are working with, you lose touch with the others. The fact that you cannot monitor the behavior of everyone explains why individualized instruction is so difficult.

COOPERATIVE LEARNING

Chances are you will be doing your student teaching in a traditionally oriented class. If that is so, we are not proposing that you experiment with another approach or try to persuade the cooperating teacher to choose another way. Nevertheless, knowing the principles of cooperative education can be helpful even in a traditional class.

Cooperative learning is a fundamentally different approach to learning. Instead of a teacher verbally imparting information to the class for long periods of time, students ask questions and work together to answer the questions and solve the problems they pose by drawing on many resources. In one sense, they are young researchers and scholars investigating problems while working together for a common purpose.

The arguments in favor of cooperative learning are that it stimulates and involves students, encourages them to learn, and inspires a spirit of cooperation and community. It fosters academic achievement and positive interactions among students, two primary purposes of education.

The argument against cooperative learning is that it may produce fewer academic benefits than other alternatives, such as grouping students by ability, for certain groups of students. In particular, it is argued, gifted students might suffer in a cooperative learning atmosphere. Although it may serve gifted students well in terms of development of social skills, research suggests that their intellectual and academic needs would be better served by an accelerated pace or individual study projects (G. A. Davis & Rimm, 1998; Winebrenner, 1992).

One of the best known and most extensively researched cooperative learning methods is that created by Slavin (1994; Slavin & Shaw, 1992). Known as the Student Teams–Achievement Divisions (STAD), it has been used in Grades 2 through college, and adapted for science, social studies, English, math, and numerous other subjects.

The idea is a simple one. As Slavin (1994) described it, you, as the teacher, present a lesson. Your students will be attentive because their individual scores and team scores depend on their listening carefully. Then, all the four-member learning teams already organized in your class—each made up of a student mix in gender, ethnicity, and performance level—get to work. Their job is to see to it that all team members master the lesson. They help each other in the interest of the team by studying worksheets, discussing problems, comparing answers, and correcting misconceptions and mistakes. Then they take individual tests during which students are strictly on their own. Individuals win points if they equal or exceed their own past averages. They are not compared with other students.

You have probably played on some team or participated in a musical, drama, or dance group. If so, you know how important it is to do your best for the team, and also how much the team is helpful and supportive because your doing well is so important to everyone else. Who wants to see a teammate strike out all the time, or play a note during a rest period, or take a misstep during a dance performance? Slavin (1994) said:

> The team provides the peer support for academic performance that is important for effects on learning, but it also provides the mutual concern and respect that are important for effects on such outcomes as intergroup relations, self-esteem, and acceptance of mainstreamed students. (pp. 6–7)

STAD is one of many forms of cooperative instruction. Some, like STAD, and the Learning Together approach developed by Johnson and Johnson (1989), are curriculum free and meant to be applicable to many subjects and grade levels. Others, like Team Assisted Individualization in Mathematics and Cooperative Integrated Reading and Composition (CIRC), were developed to apply the principles of cooperative learning to domain-specific (i.e., different subject) learning (Slavin, 1994). The use of these methods shows that achievement could be increased in all students in heterogeneous classes. In fact, CIRC proved very effective for students with learning disabilities who were mainstreamed. They achieved at significantly higher levels than their nonmainstreamed counterparts who did not have the advantage of this cooperative learning approach (Stevens & Slavin, 1995).

The basic elements of cooperative learning have been defined by Johnson and Johnson (1991):

1. Positive interdependence: Students realize that they depend on each other to complete the group's assigned task.
2. Face-to-face promotive interaction: Students help, encourage, and teach each other and they share resources.
3. Individual accountability: The teacher assesses the performance of each student and shares the results with the student and the group.

4. Collaborative skills: Teachers instruct students in essential skills such as trust building, communication, leadership, decision making, and conflict management.
5. Group processing: Groups spend some time discussing their progress in achieving goals. Teachers also give feedback on the groups' performance to the groups and the whole class.

What can student teachers learn from the cooperative learning movement? Among other things, they can learn that student involvement makes learning more exciting; that student teamwork, or cooperation in any form, brings students closer together; and, particularly important, that teamwork leads to higher achievement for some students.

STUDENT ASSESSMENT, STUDENT TEACHER ASSESSMENT

Let us suppose that you have now completed your first unit of instruction. You come to a salient feature of student teaching or, to be more accurate, of teaching in general—assessment of progress made during the course of the unit. This is not the easiest or most comfortable process.

But as you and your students complete a unit, it is vital to assess what was learned. In other words, you must both measure students' progress (through tests, quizzes, papers, projects, or other forms of assessment) and conduct a self-assessment (through critique) of your work. In this section we first discuss student assessments, then student teacher assessments.

Assessing Your Students' Progress

Psychology has given us methods to assess many human characteristics, among them personality, intelligence, sensory acuity, oral language and perceptual-motor skills. Of special interest to teachers, however, are the achievement tests that assess progress in reading, mathematics, and written language, among other areas. Some of these are standardized tests, sold commercially, in given subjects like algebra, geometry, and German, that can be used to compare the performance of your students with that of a national sample of students. Other achievement tests are constructed for use in connection with particular textbooks. Still others are state-mandated exams testing all students in the state on achievement in particular subject areas and skills.

The most common of all achievement measures, however, are those that teachers themselves construct, like quizzes, tests, and final examinations. For your purposes, teacher-made tests have advantages over commercial tests. Why? Because you know exactly what your instructional objectives are. Your tests are designed to ascertain whether those objectives were met.

Teachers assess their students regularly and for a variety of reasons. In particular, teachers want to know how much and how well their students have learned the content covered in class. This knowledge enables them to make important decisions such as whether the teaching approach should be maintained or modified; whether the objectives should be maintained or modified; how students should be grouped within the class (e.g., either for special assistance or enrichment and an accelerated pace of instruction); and finally, whether referring particular students to a specialist is advisable.

Let us say you want to know if Jane and John have learned last week's lesson. On a commercial achievement test your last week's lesson might be covered by only a single item. That is not enough. You will use 10, 20, or more items to more precisely pinpoint what they learned and what they did not. With that information, you can prepare experiences that will help them fill the gaps in their learning. After all, your purpose is to assess the instructional needs of each student.

Teacher-Made Tests. From your own experience as a student you know there are different types of teacher-made tests. Now that you are the one designing and administering the tests, however, you will want to know more details about the two major test formats, select and supply.

Select formats are those in which the answer is among the possible responses presented to the test taker, who is asked to select one response. The select format includes three primary types of tests: true–false, matching, and multiple choice. The last of the three is the most useful and the true–false is the least useful because, by chance, students will make the correct choice 50% of the time, even if they do not know the information or concept you taught. Select formats are used to assess knowledge, comprehension, and the application of skills.

Supply formats do not present the answer. The student must supply it in a written (or oral) response. Two types of such tests are fill-in (e.g., The capital of France is _____) and extended response (e.g., Explain the benefits of student participation in class discussion). The supply format, especially the extended response, is the preferred mode when assessing more than knowledge, and in particular, when assessing the ability to analyze, synthesize, and evaluate knowledge.

In developing tests, teachers need to make them dependable. In the language of test makers, the tests should be reliable. An important characteristic of reliable tests is that they are so clearly written and thoughtfully constructed that students taking them again tomorrow would get about the same scores they obtained today.

To be dependable the tests must also be valid. Valid tests accurately measure what you intended them to measure (e.g., verb tenses, division of fractions, or the main themes in *Julius Caesar*). For purposes of classroom use, the tests should have what is called content validity. To determine whether your test has content validity, ask yourself these questions: Do these test items really measure what we have been studying? Are these items broad enough to cover the area studied? Do the items cover the material at the level of comprehension that was my objective?

As schools across the nation place increasing emphasis on meeting state standards in student performance—perhaps as measured by scores on state proficiency tests—some teachers are turning to state proficiency tests as models for creation of their own classroom assessments. Research consistently shows that when students are familiar with the format of test questions, they tend to perform better.

Of course, there are some negative consequences to "teaching to the test." One is that the state test may or may not measure specific objectives of the classroom teacher. Whereas some state proficiency tests emphasize critical thinking and analysis skills, others stress content mastery. As you student teach this year and develop assessments for your own classroom next year, carefully consider the purpose of classroom assessments and the best way to achieve your objectives and meet state standards.

Regardless of what kind of classroom assessments you ultimately choose to administer, the reality is that both you and many of your students will feel tremendous pressure to succeed. Brooke expressed this sentiment in her student-teaching log:

10/27: I was really upset all day because the 7-2 class (the one I started teaching first) did a lot worse [on the test] than the 7-1 class (the class average was 10 points lower). I was really bothered by this and couldn't understand why and started thinking that I hadn't taught them right and felt like an ultimate loser. I was really worried about handing the kids back their tests and had been internalizing their grades much more than I think I should have been. Finally, at the end of the day I discussed this with Mr. B. and we looked at the class lists together and he tried to explain to me that there are just very different kids in each of the classes and that he would expect one class to do much better. I still feel pretty bad about the kids but I don't really think it is my fault anymore.

I still think it is amazing and really scary that their education is in my hands. I am petrified that some lesson is just totally going to flop and they are not going to learn anything. I need to get over this fear but . . . there is so much pressure from so many outside sources on having students succeed and be successful that I don't know where to focus my energies.

As a student teacher, you cannot expect or hope to change the realities of national and state educational policy. You can, however, model learning for learning's sake—the great pleasure that comes from knowing and understanding, not from scoring well on standardized tests. You can also challenge students to think beyond the knowledge and comprehension level to apply, analyze, and synthesize information. Asking probing questions, both in class and on your tests and quizzes, will help accomplish these goals.

For further assistance in constructing and using teacher-made tests, see Salvia and Ysseldyke's (2001), *Assessment*. Pay special attention to the chapter on teacher-made tests of achievement.

Alternative Forms of Assessment. Of course, student progress can be measured in ways other than formal testing. In science, students might conduct a laboratory experiment and submit a written lab report, which would then be graded. In modern foreign languages, students might script a television commercial and perform it—in the target language—for their class. In English students might turn in a journal in which they have written responses to their reading of various literary works. In history students might research and write a term paper and then present it to the class through a multimedia technology presentation. The possibilities are nearly endless.

Critical essays, research papers, and oral presentations have long been a part of U.S. education. In recent years, these and other forms of alternative assessments have gained favor. In some schools, students create portfolios, collections of their best work during the course of a quarter, semester, or academic year, and turn these in for their term grade. Some educators have argued that alternative forms of assessment provide a more accurate, well-rounded reflection of student ability and work than do tests. In particular, many have recognized alternative assessment as a useful way to measure the academic growth of special-needs students.

When determining how to best assess student work at the conclusion of a unit, carefully consider your objectives and the purpose of your assessments. In many cases, teachers find that a combination of traditional pen-and-paper tests, written work (essays, reports, and papers), and creative projects provides the best measure of students' progress.

Assessing Your Own Progress

After completing a unit of instruction, it is important that student teachers—and full-time teachers—assess not only their students, but also themselves. This is not easy because in retrospect, we are bound to find some flaws in our lesson plan, mode of instruction, interaction with students, and so forth. For this reason, we tend to put off criticism and self-criticism until tomorrow. Yet when things are fresh, it is of extraordinary value to review the entire process of planning and conducting the class through the unit, recognizing what parts went well, what activities, experiments, readings, drills, performances, and the like were and were not effective, and with what kinds of students.

Consider the interactions with and between students and your handling of the unexpected. Next, consider the findings from your interim diagnosis of progress, your change in plans resulting from that, and finally your end-of-unit evaluation of student progress. How well did your students fare?

Ideally, you should do this type of critique prior to receiving an evaluation from your cooperating teacher or college supervisor so you have practice doing this independently. Even if circumstances do not permit that, you will find it to your professional advantage to engage in self-criticism.

Another essential step is to ask yourself about the future: Next time, what will you do differently and what the same? To what extent will you change the proportion of whole-class to small-group teaching? Will there be more or less student participation? Will you again use the same reading materials, exercises, workbooks, illustrations, poetry, role playing, experiments, instruments, and outside consultants? Will you plan to use the same kinds of questions? Were the questions posed representative of more than one level of questioning appropriate to the cognitive development of your students?

If you record the critiques, yours and others, in your journal or elsewhere, you will be able to evaluate your professional growth as you progress through student teaching and your first years as a regular teacher. You will also have a record of the resources, aids, techniques, methods, questions, and personal styles that worked for you.

There is still another useful way to evaluate your professional development, now and in the future. With the help of a guide introduced by Tanner and Tanner (1995), you can determine at what level of curriculum development you are functioning and work toward functioning at a higher level. You may find that your current mode of teaching is reflected by one of the following (taken from Tanner & Tanner, 1995, pp. 630–631):

1. Level I, Imitative–Maintenance: Teachers at this level slavishly follow the curriculum guide, using only ready-made materials, like workbooks and textbooks, without evaluation of their appropriateness or effectiveness. They show no imagination and seem to feel no freedom to introduce activities or create materials that would strengthen the curriculum.

2. Level II, Mediative: Teachers at this level "are aware of the need to integrate the curriculum and deal with emergent conditions" (p. 630), like students' questions about things that concern and interest them. They are aware of the need for a curriculum that integrates and does not fragment knowledge, and they evaluate the materials they use, not using them blindly. However, for the most part, they remain "at the level of refining existing practice" (p. 630).

3. Level III, Creative–Generative: At this level teachers act collaboratively with other teachers to create and generate an improved version of the curriculum and ongoing assessments and revisions of it. At the same time they are engaged in their own classroom in evaluating and improving their teaching. They identify their teaching problems and use problem-solving methods to overcome them. They experiment with different teaching modes and share their experiences with other teachers.

As Tanner and Tanner (1995) pointed out, one does not have to pass through the first two levels to reach the third. Level III does not require years of experience. Teachers can attain that level early in their careers, depending, in all probability, on the professional role models they have studied and on their personal and professional values. The more teachers that function at Level III, the greater the likelihood that the curriculum will be a living experience, responsive to changes in knowledge and society.

TEACHING THE WHOLE CLASS THE FIRST TIME

The bulk of this book is meant to help you prepare to teach. Because the first time one teaches the whole class is very much on the minds of student teachers, we set out some general guidelines for your consideration.

- Begin to plan the lesson at least a week before the assigned date.
- Be clear about the objectives of the lesson (as spelled out in the curriculum guide or given by your cooperating teacher).
- Thoroughly master the content of the lesson.
- Prepare print, audio, or audiovisual material well in advance.
- Check that material is in the sequence you will use it, and that all equipment is in good working order.
- Consider ways of engaging students ("getting them hooked"), maybe by having them involved in activity.
- Prepare "filler" material and activity to be used in the event that the lesson is completed earlier than expected.
- In your mind, picture the class before you, with the cooperating teacher sitting in the back row.
- Direct your attention to each part of the classroom, looking at each student at some point during the lesson.
- Picture the lesson going along well.
- Prepare for the possibility that students who are occasionally disruptive will disturb the class.
- Picture yourself talking to the class and leading a discussion.
- Encourage many students to participate; do not be controlled by the wild hand-wavers.
- Prepare an interesting closure to the lesson.
- Picture your satisfaction at a well-taught lesson.
- Start rehearsing the lesson, from beginning to end, a few days before you teach.
- Having prepared so well, go to class that day feeling competent and confident.
- Afterward, evaluate the extent to which the objectives were achieved.

- Evaluate the quality of your teaching, looking at strengths and areas that need improvement.
- Welcome and be open to the cooperating teacher's critique, and use it to improve your teaching.

When you plan extensively, as just described, the result will bring you an incredible feeling of satisfaction. Sure, there will be plenty of room for improvement, but just look at what you accomplished! Arlene described the satisfaction she felt at the end of her first lesson:

10/19: This was the week where I finally taught. When Angela (my mentor teacher) told me that I would be teaching *Sir Gawain and the Green Knight* first, I was a little freaked out. I have always felt that it is really important for a teacher to know and appreciate his or her subject matter and, although I took a course on *The Pearl*, which scholars believe to be by the same poet, I did not feel comfortable with *Sir Gawain and the Green Knight*. I used all of my nervous energy to read anything and everything I could find about this poem. I quickly grew to enjoy and appreciate it and felt that I knew enough to come up with the unit plan based loosely on Angela's unit plan from last year (mine is twice as long because she said that she felt rushed with it last year).

The period before my first class I nervously looked from my notes to the clock to my notes and to the clock again. Finally I went down to the classroom and taught my first real lesson, which flew by and left me in the classroom with a sort of paralyzed excitement. I will never be teaching for the first time again. I knew that I made a lot of mistakes, but I could not help being happy . . .

Once you have celebrated your considerable accomplishment, you should begin evaluating your work, as Arlene did. Her journal entry continues:

Aside from the emotional rushes that follow each class, I have been left with a number of questions. I really believe in discussions where the teacher's role is very small, however, I am afraid to let that happen in my classroom because I am afraid that we will not cover something that I put on their guided notes. Would that be the end of the world? I really want students to learn about how to read a poem like this—how to decide what parts are significant and what parts are not—how to support their arguments if they believe that something is significant and someone else disagrees—why people find this poem worth studying. I intend to ask students to point out passages that support their points, but I end up feeding them passages and trying to get them to find specific points that I feel are important.

I had been so careful to notice each student when I was observing, but when I started to teach all of my thoughts were tangled up in the material I was trying to cover, the time, and the students who were raising their hands. I managed to refer back to what students said, which I think they really appreciated, but I didn't do much for the students who were saying nothing.

On the first day I put a lot of effort into explaining some people's fascination with this poem. I explained the work that goes into reading the handwritten manuscript and talked with them about what it means that the text is translated. I spoke too quickly and brushed over parts that I should have been emphasizing. Angela reminded me afterward that I could always go back to something I said the previous day. In teaching there are very few mistakes in terms of content that cannot be fixed. Teachers often go over the amount of time they plan to spend on a subject. I do realize, however, that part of this flexibility is because this is a private school and that many schools have requirements for the length of units that are much more strict.

The next day I went over some of what I had rushed through the day before. I pointed more clearly and directly to the study guide and explained how I would use it if I was in their place. The third day I led a discussion that was more student-directed than before, but then I pushed a subject that had been exhausted and became a little flustered.

I also have the problem that I often phrase questions badly. I am trying to remember to let 3 seconds pass before assuming my question was poorly worded, but isn't it worse to let a bad question sit than to assume it is a good question and that students need time to come up with an answer? I am trying to think of group work that I can do in class to involve more students. I am also trying to think of good discussion questions that will allow me to have less involvement in the discussions. I need to write on the board more often.

It has only been three days and I am already feeling more comfortable teaching. My main worries are that I am teaching the wrong things the wrong ways and not so much that I will have trouble in front of the classroom. I am trying to put more creativity into my lesson plans and return to what I was taught in my methods class.

The kind of careful, critical self-reflection Arlene engaged in enabled her to continue to improve her teaching. Using COURAGE, you too can use your first whole-class lesson as a stepping stone to success.

NEXT YEAR

Lo and behold, your student-teaching experience will be behind you and the new school year will be upon you—much more quickly than you anticipated. The summer is a time for preparation.

Get acquainted with the neighborhoods in the school district and the student composition that is likely to be represented in your class or classes. With that information and the curriculum guide and textbooks, you will be in a good position to prepare for your work next year.

Outline the units you plan to introduce and the approximate time frame for each. Then, build a collection of resources for your units, at least those scheduled for the first part of the school year. Remember to think widely: What materials are available at school? In the community? In your personal collection? Review other possible sources of materials: your former cooperating teacher and college supervisor, other teachers in the school where you student taught, your student teacher peers, and so on.

Extend and expand your mastery of all material covered in the student curriculum. You will want to conduct as much of your own reading and research over the summer as possible. What college-level books, texts, and reference material will support the background reading necessary for writing lectures, designing experiments, and setting up demonstrations? What supplemental material will help you answer challenging student questions? Are there reliable Web sites that might provide supplemental information accurately and efficiently? Remember that many of your college professors can also be of service here. Are they willing to discuss lesson plan ideas with you? Do you know how to contact them over the summer months?

This is a time, too, to collect a set of materials that interest and excite students of the age group you will be teaching. These could take the form of quiz-show questions, comics, TV commercials, anecdotes, games, music, experiments, and how-to activities (e.g., repairing cars or baking cakes). High school students will welcome illustrations and materials representative of teenage culture.

Finally, join an educators' listserv and develop the habit of reading one or two professional periodicals in which you are likely to find timely and practical suggestions about curriculum and the use of various resources.

We conclude this chapter by noting that beginning next year, you will possess the power to plan your role as a teacher. You will not be dependent on others to tell you how to teach and manage the class or what materials to use. You will find it useful to receive advice and may even seek it out. But you will be free to choose what of it you consider helpful and what not, incorporating suggestions as you see fit.

CRITICAL ISSUES

- In what ways can the curriculum guide be helpful to you? The teacher's edition of classroom texts?
- How can technology and the arts be used to enliven class and accelerate learning?
- What aspects of using technology in the classroom are potentially problematic? How can you cope with this?
- What have you learned about the class curriculum so far that will help you in your student teaching? In your teaching career?
- How can you use questions to achieve your goals in the classroom?
- How will you weigh the benefits and drawbacks of individualization and cooperative learning?
- What techniques will you use to assess your students' learning? Your own learning?

9

Classroom Management and Discipline

"Discipline!" The word captures every teacher's attention. Everyone knows that keeping order is top priority in today's schools.

We take it for granted that discipline is very much on the minds of student teachers, but what about "old hands" in teaching? Discipline problems can be so difficult that they are on the minds of even the most experienced teachers, as you can see in the following words, reported by Clapp (1989):

> Discipline and classroom management were my biggest fears as I entered teaching. After 19 years of teaching (though I am considered by others to have very good classroom management—my principal always recommends that visitors observe my classroom), each summer before school starts I still have nightmares featuring my class in an out-of-control situation. (p. 32)

This teacher was one of 1,388 respondents to a questionnaire study of 10 educational issues of concern by the education magazine *Instructor* in 1989. Discipline was ranked first of the 10 issues by 69% of the teachers who responded. It ranked ahead of such issues as teacher salaries, teacher preparation, and teacher empowerment, and continues to do so in recent surveys of teachers and the general public (Tauber, 1999).

Two findings are worth considering. First, the teachers in the 1989 study did not blame themselves or the children. They saw discipline problems as the result of larger social issues. For example, 38% attributed class disruption and the other assorted discipline concerns to changes in the American family. One teacher said, "It's hard to punish a child for misbehaving . . . the breakdown of families causes poor self-esteem and results in discipline problems" (p. 32). Another teacher explained that hunger, neglect, and abuse (physical and sexual) were problems in her suburban school. The behavioral problems, these teachers say, are evident in the children but they were caused by social problems over which teachers have no control. What does this mean to the student teacher struggling with discipline issues? It is important not to blame yourself unfairly. You may not be able to prevent all discipline problems, although you can learn to cope with some of them more effectively.

The second key finding from the *Instructor* study is that teachers try very hard to be more effective in coping with problems of classroom management. Most of them seek help from other teachers. The survey indicated that teachers also sought help from school administrators, college professors, supervisors or mentor teachers, and support staff. Student teachers got help from their cooperating teachers and their college supervisors.

THE DIFFERENT MEANINGS OF "DISCIPLINE"

The word *discipline* has several connotations. Often the first to come to mind in connection with education is the punishing of students for the sake of maintaining order. Less common, but of greater importance, is discipline as a positive approach to education: the state of order that enables a class to achieve its objectives. Used in that way, discipline means good classroom management.

In general, we speak of a disciplined way of life as one that follows a consistent pattern. People organize their lives that way because it helps them accomplish their professional and personal goals. The same may be said about a disciplined way of teaching; that is, it allows teachers to accomplish their objectives.

The perfect marriage of teacher and students comes when class members experience you as a person interested in helping them learn and grow. If they recognize you as such, they will accept as appropriate almost any form of classroom management you adopt. They will accept as required whatever measures you consider necessary to maintain a disciplined class.

Order

A disciplined class can be more or less structured, and more or less permissive. Your crucial objective is to be consistent and keep the kind of order needed for your method of instruction. Order is as necessary in a classroom as it is in a family, and in both settings, children prefer orderly situations and orderly lives, even if circumstances lead some of them to behave as if they did not. They like it, want it, and need it, as much in a permissive or open classroom as in a traditional one.

Without some order there can be no teaching and very little learning. Consequently, the student teacher's priority is to maintain his or her kind of order. Many psychotherapists believe that resistance to therapy must be dealt with before anything else: If the client persists in fending off the therapist, the two engage in a struggle of wills and nothing worthwhile is accomplished. The same struggle can take place in the classroom, and it is the teacher's role to circumvent it and build order in the classroom environment. Here is an example, taken from Steve's journal, reporting on the problems of his cooperating teacher, whom he regarded as a good teacher.

> 1/15: The children do not listen to the teacher when she is presenting a lesson. They are doing a thousand other things. Some children were playing tic-tac-toe, others were playing cards, some were coloring, while still others were doing homework. She is a good teacher, but none of the children were listening, so they don't even realize that she is a good teacher. While Mrs. S. was giving the language arts lesson, only about 7 or 8 students out of 30 were listening.

> What have I learned from this observation? I have learned that I must have the children's complete attention in order to really teach. It doesn't matter if I'm a good teacher if nobody is listening. One of the things that I am going to demand from my students is that their desks be cleared off—as many distractions as possible must be eliminated. That is not to say that I will have their complete attention, but at least it will be a start.

By no stretch of the imagination could Mrs. S. be classified as a good teacher on the basis of this observation. Perhaps what Steve was reacting to was a well-organized presentation of valuable language arts material. However, that is of no value whatsoever if, as Steve himself wrote, "nobody is listening." Facing this kind of situation, teachers must give up their present method of classroom management and experiment with others until they discover one suitable to the students in their classes.

With other students who have been conditioned—from experiences at home or in school—to listen, this teacher might be well received. Mrs. S.'s mode of teaching might even be workable with her current students at a later point in the year. If she is to be able to use this method successfully, however, her students must first be taught through experience that when the teacher presents a lesson to the class, it is time to listen, watch, and raise one's hand for permission to participate. As Steve came to see, when Mrs. S. "finally exploded and scolded all over the place," it silenced and focused the students temporarily, but "hollering" and scolding are not usually effective as long-term solutions.

When a teacher relies on loud reprimands to curb disorder, disruptions will inevitably recur and escalate, and the class will not come under control again until the teacher once again scolds loudly. It is better by far to introduce the ultimate means of control when your voice and demeanor, although firm, have not reached your upper decibel limit. For your sake and that of your students, condition the class to expect that discipline will follow immediately after a third disruption. Two warnings are more than enough.

Bear in mind that you have double responsibility to function this way. First, you owe it to the class to lead (after all, you are its leader) in such a way that they will get a disciplined education, one that perfects and strengthens them. They deserve your help in gaining mastery over the skills and content in the curriculum. Second, by responding to disruptions in a fair, consistent way, you teach students the habits of good citizenship. The most effective way for children and adolescents to learn good citizenship is by living it, not by reading or hearing lectures about it.

How can you, as a student teacher, maintain order and manage disruptive students? We propose seven important principles for successful discipline and classroom management. Note that these principles depend on action you take both inside and outside the classroom.

SEVEN PRINCIPLES OF SUCCESSFUL MANAGEMENT

#1 Functioning as the Adult Leader

The first important step you can take toward being an effective classroom manager and disciplinarian is to accept the fact that you are on the other side of the desk. You must adopt the role of an adult leader.

As teachers, we are responsible for establishing an environment conducive to learning. We are not complete adults in class, and thus cannot manage effectively, if in a corner of our brain there still lurks the consciousness of being one of "them," or the desire to want to be one of them. If you discover such outdated notions, clearly explain to yourself why they must be banished.

Amy, in telling of her problem with Randy, explained her "shock" that the child followed her instructions. Amy had not yet thought of herself as an adult leader, a necessary step for being effective with discipline.

4/25: I have noticed that I have to be firm with some of the children and I definitely have to follow through with what I say. Although I always knew this was true, seeing the children react to my behavior provided evidence of my beliefs.

Amy reported in her journal that when she had a few of the children outside, Randy was disobedient, threw stones, and refused to go inside as she had directed. She warned him that if he did not go inside as ordered, he would not be allowed to go out later in the day. Randy disobeyed Amy, and so she told him he had lost his afternoon recess privileges. That afternoon, Amy was on the playground with the other children and Randy wandered out of the building. Amy reminded Randy of his loss of privileges and Randy returned to the classroom quietly and without protest. In her journal, Amy wrote, "He followed my instructions. I was really shocked!"

Remember that all the Randys in your classroom view you differently from the way you view yourself. Although Amy may think of herself as somebody just a few years out of adolescence and as a learner in the classroom, to Randy she is an adult and teacher.

If you are an undergraduate student teaching in a high school, older students might not automatically perceive you as an adult. They probably recognize that you are only 4 to 5 years older than they are; they realize you have grown up watching the same movies, listening to the same music, and adopting the same slang. Nevertheless, if you act like a teacher, they will learn to respect and obey you as one. You can do much to speed this process by ensuring that your dress, speech, and demeanor are that of a teacher, not of a college student, when you set foot on school grounds. Most important, be confident that your superior knowledge of the subject matter and deeper understanding of the learning process qualifies you to instruct your students, regardless of their age. If you are confident of yourself and your abilities, students will sense it immediately.

At various points during your student-teaching experience, assess how you think students perceive you. Make recordings in your journal. Then check your perceptions by noting how students actually react to you.

In sum, functioning as the adult leader means asserting oneself as a teacher, being strong and effective. This can often be done in thoughtful and quiet ways. As discussed in chapter 5, problems can be avoided by minimizing students' boredom, keeping class lively, listening attentively as students express concerns, and rewarding good behavior, usually by praise. Using COURAGE to disentangle the causes of ongoing discipline problems is also a "quiet" approach.

#2 Managing Time—Managing Ourselves

People are paying more attention to time management these days, largely because so many of us feel overwhelmed by the demands of our jobs and personal lives. During your student teaching stint you, too, will likely feel pressured by the responsibilities of your student teaching assignment, college/university coursework, and desire for a social life. In coping with such a heavy schedule, it helps to realize that the idea of time management, although catchy, is misdirected. It sounds as if we have to manage time when in fact we have to manage ourselves. Managing our time really calls for self-management.

Our aim here is to briefly present ways to help you (a) become aware of how you use time and (b) learn to develop schedules that designate time in ways consistent with your goals.

Tess was faced with a self-management problem. She liked her student-teaching assignment in chemistry and physics at a high school that had recently won the state championship in girls' tennis. Besides student teaching, she volunteered to be an assistant tennis coach. She thought that the coaching would make her more competitive in the job market.

Two weeks into the term she found that she was overloaded. She spent after-school hours with the tennis team and used her evenings to prepare for her science classes. Bedtime was routinely well after midnight. Her friends began calling Tess "the shadow" because she was there one moment and gone the next.

Fortunately for Tess, a speaker at a faculty meeting discussed the topic of efficiency. Three related points the speaker made hit home for Tess and led her to take action:

1.   Identify, in writing, all the tasks you need to accomplish for the time period under consideration. That could be tomorrow's classes, the full week ahead, or the remainder of the semester. (The speaker humorously suggested that once they are on paper, the brain cells in our heads that were working to remember those tasks are freed for other uses.)

2.   Rank each item according to its importance. Use three categories: must do, tasks that have direct impact on you and your teaching; important but not essential, tasks that may offer indirect or lesser benefits; and useful but not essential, tasks that have potentially desirable benefits, but fewer than the previous categories.

3.   Within rankings, prioritize your tasks, giving yourself a push to do the least pleasing tasks first. Doing them first reduces your tension about having to face those unpleasant tasks later.

Most of us resist applying this advice. We are accustomed to tackling the simplest, quickest tasks first and then, with pleasure, crossing "to do" items off the list. For maximum payoff and minimum headache, we should be crossing out the most essential and most difficult tasks first.

Applying these guidelines to your student-teaching experience, here are some questions to consider:

1.   In the coming week, what are my most important tasks? Rank order them.

2.   Considering each one, what must I do to prepare for it, and how much time is needed for that preparation?

3.   Taking into account the time slotted for class(es) at my college/university, the time for essential personal appointments or tasks (including sleep and

recreation), and the time that might be filled by unexpected emergencies (e.g., car servicing or an unresistable invitation to a friend's party), how many hours are available for preparation?

• If those hours are not sufficient, what can I cut out this week to give me more time? What tasks can I—or must I—complete more efficiently? For example, if you find yourself spending an unreasonable amount of time grading a stack of student papers, consider setting a timer and committing to spend no more than your predetermined time limit on each student's essay.

Time management and self-management are subjects you could discuss with your cooperating teacher. How does he or she manage time? How does he or she cope with the feeling of being overwhelmed? The same topic is an appropriate one to raise with your supervisor and other student teachers.

Because full-time teachers with rich and satisfying personal lives are always busy, there is no better time than during student teaching to develop the habit of monitoring and regulating your use of time.

#3 Planning

Time and self-management are of particular importance in connection with lesson planning. The third factor in effective classroom management and discipline includes thoroughly planning a day, preparing for contingencies, and being mindful of the needs and interests of your students.

Sheryl's journals reveal that she was developing into a pro at thoroughly planning school days. By combining intellectually stimulating activity with firm control in her classes, she was able to create a balanced program. In the following journal entry she described how she gave students opportunities to work out problems and receive appropriate rewards.

> 1/27: I had the kids by myself the whole day. I had a chart on liquid measurement, and I asked them very simple questions and we went from cups into quarts, and pints into gallons. Then they did board work and had an exercise in math, which for the most part they did very well. I would check their answers with the book and check the wrong ones and let them try again. When they got it wrong the second time, I would write in the answer and tell them to figure out why it was right. When they could explain it to me, I gave them a "100" and many were eager to explain why the answers were right. After math, we had health. Our health discussion was excellent. It was very mature. Everyone participated, and many interesting questions were raised. There are a lot of things to learn about bacteria, and we discussed the topic until 10:20 . . . .

Besides content, Sheryl had thought about the kind of behavior necessary for the children to profit from the activities planned. She then demanded that behavior.

But, as the journal shows, her careful planning also provided for flexibility as students' moods, attention, and energy levels changed:

> 1/27 [continued]: . . . Then we had a film strip, and the children were so talkative and inattentive that I turned off the machine. I told them they didn't want to watch it, so they could watch a blank wall if they didn't want to pay attention. They got quiet after 5 minutes, and I told them they could make it up . . . . They had been working pretty hard, so in the afternoon all I had planned for them was music and then working on their masks. There was no scheduled recess and I let them vote if they wanted an early recess or get to work on their masks. They voted to work on their masks.
>
> Since they got restless, I took them down to the rest room about 25 minutes early. We took 20 minutes because they cannot behave in the halls and we started all over every time I heard them talk. I plan on doing this every time, no matter how long it takes. I keep insisting that they can talk quietly in class but not in the halls. Of all the kids, mine are by far the worst. In a way, I think they appreciated it because they knew I was tired too and wanted perfection. For the rest of the afternoon, I let them work on their masks and they played records. At 3:00 they began clean-up and had it done in about 8 minutes, which was quite an improvement. I read *Charlotte's Web* and the kids really listened. That was a good day for me.

Sheryl's day was successful because she planned well. All the children participated in the health discussion and mask making. She reacted immediately to disruptions and required orderliness both in the class and in the hallway. One senses in reading her report that the children felt she was setting requirements as much in their interest as in her own. Most children respond favorably to rational authority; that is, to a leader whose demands make sense to them.

Sheryl's next reports were positive: Most of her plans worked perfectly and the class was becoming a cohesive group enjoying the exercises, activities, and discussion. However, Sheryl's journal entries also contained the inevitable ups and downs. A few days later Sheryl wrote she was "just miserable," because she had yet to find a way to cope with the few disruptive children. She did not have a solution, but would not surrender to the situation. Sheryl was a determined and proactive problem solver who learned from her successes and mistakes and those of her cooperating teacher. She learned to plan activities that appealed to the class as a whole. She developed the self-control necessary to avoid becoming angry and being drawn into bitter battles with students who had serious problems. Being mindful of her goals and what it took to reach them, Sheryl never yielded to the easy temptation simply to blame the children. She liked them, struggled to understand them, and sought to plan school days in ways that made lessons more interesting for them. Here is her final report.

> 3/18: This will be the last time I write. My class is getting better and they are controlling themselves more. They still are fighting and arguing, but it's more verbal,

more reasonable and less physical. Frances and Mindy will have trouble for the rest of their lives. Things frustrate them so easily. Steve is a pain but a smart one and is a leader and salesman.

The kids still get away with more with me than with Mrs. R., but when it counts, they are with me. It will be sad leaving.

Discipline and curriculum are inseparable in some very important respects and most noticeably so when most of the class is unruly. Any time such disruptiveness occurs, the effective teacher asks, "What is wrong with my objectives or my plans to carry them out?"

In many cases, the students have no personal interest in the content being presented. This problem sometimes can be dealt with by combining unappealing subject matter with appealing illustrations. For instance, fractions can be taught using pies, football fields, and coins; geography by following the road trips of professional basketball teams; literature by referring to popular music favored by teenagers.

The choice of content and method (what and how we teach) is important in preventing and correcting discipline problems. In planning specific class material, one can do much to enhance the likelihood of order simply by taking into account the needs and preferences of the learners. The effects of the choice of content cannot be underestimated, as illustrated by the case presented here.

One of the authors taught a ninth-grade English class for boys in which the behavior of the teenagers was almost uncontrollable. This was the lowest rated section in a tracked system. The students had diverse interests, but tended not to count reading or writing among them. With the consent of the chair of the department, the teacher brought in books that he thought would interest the students—sports, adventure, mystery, mechanics, and science fiction. He encouraged the students to bring in anything they preferred.

Many class periods were devoted to silent reading of a book or magazine of the student's choice. This was followed by discussion about the reading or about a personal experience that the reading brought to mind. Sometimes small groups of three or four would be organized for reading aloud and small-group discussion. When this approach was well established and all students were participating (most of them eagerly), they were then asked to write a few sentences, then a few paragraphs, and later still a few pages about their readings.

Was this a mysterious, almost miraculous transformation in behavior? Not at all. The students had viewed school as a place where they were forced to go to study topics that did not interest them.

It is easier to compel children to attend school than to compel them to study. Real learning is an active process, and no one can force anybody into it. These ninth-grade English students resisted not because they were mean or recalcitrant, but because education had no meaning to them and made no sense. The teacher said, "Look, you have to be in school. I'm not requiring it, but the state does. As long as you are here you can either waste your time, get into trouble, or make the best possible use of it. I'll help you find whatever you'd like to read—whatever you'll enjoy reading—whatever you'd want to read to learn something for your use—not my use, but yours."

When they heard that, not once but repeatedly in words and actions, they came to believe it and they made better use of the time. Instead of pen throwing, foot tapping, and outright fist fighting, they were reading, discussing, and writing about repairing cars, hitting baseballs, and finishing a basement with recycled materials.

As the weeks passed, they took to discussing characters in some stories, and even the way these characters dealt with problems not unlike some of theirs. These students learned, perhaps for the first time in their lives, that reading could be enjoyable and useful and that school could be in their interest and for their benefit.

Although national, state, and school standards do not always allow you a choice in what content you cover, you do have a choice in the ways you present it. Planning lessons that are instructive yet interesting, productive yet playful will increase the likelihood that what discipline problems you do have are greatly minimized.

#4 Developing a Personal Theory of Management and Discipline

In your education courses you probably became familiar with several different approaches that would allow you to manage a class effectively. It is good to get acquainted with a variety of approaches while you are still developing your own theory of management and discipline.

Two educators (Tompkins & Tompkins-McGill, 1993) proposed a variety of methods to manage students' behavior. They told about one boy, Eddie, whose humorous antics started a painful cycle: He joked, other students laughed, the teacher (a series of them!) got furious, he joked more, then the teacher became angrier, and so on. Finally, one teacher reacted by enjoying Eddie's humor and joining in the laughter with Eddie and his classmates. It did not take Eddie long to learn that it was all right to be funny once in a while, at appropriate times. The practice used by this teacher is called *tension decontamination through humor.* In the following journal entry, note how Arlene trusted her instincts, and therefore avoided making a student's humorous story into a discipline problem:

10/19: There were more students who spoke up during this class period, but it was also almost Homecoming and all of the students in all of the classes were completely wired all day. The class was not out of control, but just excited and chatty. When we began to discuss the boar hunt [in the poem we are reading], Mike had a story about his uncle who hunted boar. Everyone laughed, but I told Mike to continue and he ended up making a very relevant point. So far I was not thrown—if I had to guess ahead of class which student would have a boar hunt story, I would have guessed Mike. As we began to discuss the relevant question of why hunters hunt boar (Mike said that it did not taste good and that hunters hunt boar to show their strength), Brandon also had a story about boar and he said it tasted good. Then Jake, who rarely talks, started talking about someone he knew who hunted boar. At this point my mentor teacher was laughing and asked, "Where are all of these people hunting wild boar?!" Half the class was laughing and half the class was seriously considering the question and answering her. It was a very fun class, although not a good way to have class regularly. At first I was concerned that I had made a disciplinary mistake that I could not go back on, but the next day the students were much more calm . . .

Among many other techniques proposed by Tompkins and Tompkins-McGill (1993) are the following: planned ignoring (useful if you believe that by not giving attention to it the unacceptable behavior will stop), signaling unacceptability of behavior (a useful first step by making eye contact with the student and giving a stern look), and time out (useful when the student is out of control or stirring up a group, or when there are physical dangers to self or others).

Time out is most productive when teachers can calm down students and speak to them for this purpose: to help them "learn about themselves, see how they contributed to their difficulty, and how they might have done something differently" (Tompkins & Tompkins-McGill, 1993, p. 58). In an elementary school, time out can take place in a part of the classroom itself. In middle and high schools, students might be sent into a special room set aside for that purpose.

Discipline practices come in and out of favor as a response to societal changes and educational trends. Undoubtedly you have studied many theories of discipline in your educational courses, discussing the relative merits of each. Although we do not review those here, we would like to emphasize that the principles of good classroom management are both universal and timeless. Theories come and go, but rational problem solving and sound thinking always serve you well.

Seeman (1988) argued that the best classroom management policy incorporates a variety of management approaches. We think the questions he raises are noteworthy:

1. When does a situation or a problem deserve to be called a "disciplinary problem?" Because teachers differ among themselves, and even within themselves from time to time, this question is not easy to answer. Sometimes teachers transform a nonproblem (like a joke a student cracks) into a disciplinary problem. Sometimes, Seeman (1988) wrote, a mishandled difference about a grade or about a student's motivation unnecessarily turns into a discipline problem. In his definition of a discipline problem, note especially what he placed in parentheses: A behavior (not merely the expression of a feeling) that disrupts (or is potentially disruptive to) the learning of the rest of the class (not just the learning of the

disrupter), or disrupts the role responsibilities of the teacher (not just the personal feelings of the teacher). (p. 42)

2. To prevent discipline problems, we ask, what are the sources of them and what events precipitate them? In a study he conducted, Seeman found, for example, that some problems originate outside the school, some inside the school (but not in the classroom), and some inside the classroom. Those in the last group could be due to classroom climate, student interactions with each other or teacher–student interactions. There is a big payoff for teachers who, early in their careers, learn to classify the origins of problems and introduce ways to prevent them. In some instances, teachers must recognize that certain things are beyond their control. For example, if several students continually arrive late to your class because another teacher—whose classroom is at the other end of the school—refuses to dismiss them until the last second, you might have to accept that you will have to start class without them.

3. Why does one technique work for one teacher yet not for another who is in virtually the same situation? Ms. Doe calls for order and the class is silent; Ms. Roe does the same and you would think no one had heard her. Seeman's study revealed the important concept of congruence: How students react to directions, assignments, and reprimands depends on how believable they evaluate the teacher to be. If they regard the teacher as credible, they respect and obey him or her. If they see the teacher as a "phony," they do not. *Sincere* and *genuine* are apt terms to describe the way students perceive teachers who command respect.

4. Why limit oneself to a reward and punishment system? That could result in ignoring the sources of the problems as well as the feelings of the students. In Seeman's view, classroom discipline should be based on a good relationship between student and teacher as well as on the teacher's power, and not just on the latter.

5. Why limit oneself solely to nurturing and empathic relationships or to the use only of reason? Such limited approaches neglect the value of reward and punishment (hopefully exercised by a respected and respecting teacher). They will also fail with students unable to think empathetically and with those lacking abstract reasoning skills. Moreover, these techniques tend to be applied to the needs of the individual at a cost to the class as a whole.

An eclectic approach, one that draws on whatever strategies you find useful, seems most desirable. An effective approach must fit with your values and personality—you should feel comfortable with it. Besides suiting you, the approach should give your students the feeling that you mean what you say, whether you are talking in caring and supportive or demanding and critical ways.

When you confront a difficult discipline problem during your internship, use your journal to write down what happened and record the way you handled it. Were you happy with the end result? Could you have handled the situation better? When you see your cooperating teacher effectively handle a discipline issue, record that, too.

Think about your own theory of management and discipline. Try to define it. Compare it with those theories you have studied and with the techniques modeled by your cooperating teacher. Be open to change as a result of learning other theories and approaches and your ongoing experience.

#5 Problem Solving

A third important principle for successful classroom management and discipline is to routinely use a logical problem-solving process, such as the COURAGE method described in chapter 2. Even for the experienced teacher, effective management practices and procedures for handling disruptive situations come with careful thought. After reviewing and analyzing the day's events, a teacher is in a better position to handle whatever difficulties might develop tomorrow. The next two sections illustrate how much better student teachers fare when they use effective problem-solving approaches while student teaching instead of using an approach marked by impulsive problem solving and inconsistent behavior.

Effective Problem Solving.   The entries here, written by Janet, show how she used her journal to actively analyze what was happening in her class and to plan for the days ahead. Although her wrestling with problems was sometimes frantic, Janet battled ardently, determined to master her craft.

3/11: Some days are good and some days are just awful. Today was awful. When it comes to a group activity I lose so many of them and I don't think it's me; it seems to be because a couple of children disturb the rest, and when I'm trying to take care of them the others start talking and I can't blame them. When I say some children disturb the others, it's a physical disturbance that has to be dealt with. I guess I have to try and keep things going at a faster pace to try and eliminate any "time" for them to hit. Even though the rest of the day went fine, that small part discourages me.

Janet engaged in an important problem-solving process: She diagnosed the onset of problems as resulting from a couple of children who, by drawing her attention, led her to neglect the rest of the class. Further, she proposed a way to deal with the problem; that is, by keeping the students involved in the learning activity. A few days later Janet was pleased to see some signs of progress.

3/15: Things went better today, I had my head together and things went a lot more smoothly. I still have trouble keeping everyone's attention, but I think it's because I don't use Andrea's techniques; as a result they keep testing me. I don't mind, because I know they don't mean it personally and it's not taken as such. We started a new subject today, the circus. I'm excited and am looking forward to it.

Janet had one of those good days, the kind that make you feel you are gaining mastery. As she put it, "I had my head together." Having our heads together while teaching means not getting rattled (essential to good problem solving) and remembering that we are teacher and adult in the presence of student and child or student and adolescent. A month later Janet wrote:

4/15: The day was crazy. Talking about it in seminar made it sound worse than it was. It's just an incredible feeling of frustration—having so much I want to accomplish and have the children do, that I get hung up in "management" problems. It's more than that. It's that I'm getting hung up in my idealism and how things seem to be. I know I'm making progress, but it's so slow; maybe I just need more positive rewards by immediately seeing what I'm trying to accomplish. I don't know. It's hard to be your own teacher when you're constantly in someone else's shadow.

Something else bothers me: my supervisor's idealism—I guess it holds for the seminar leaders too. All of you come up with good suggestions, but most of the time it's impossible to implement them to the fullest. I come up with so many ideas and suggestions, activities, etc., but I'm only one person with a class full of active children so I can't always be with all of them, meeting every need all of the time.

By the next day, especially after the seminar, Janet was again allowing herself to feel overwhelmed by the work. She sensed that she was imaginative like her supervisor and seminar leaders, but she compared herself with them, a beginner with three pros, and she found herself wanting. She did not compare herself with them as they were or could have been as beginners, which might have been more valid and reassuring. At least, however, she was near recognizing that it was not they who were setting inordinate demands on her, but she herself, and that those demands were creating some of her problems in managing the class.

4/17: The day went a lot better. Things went smoother and the children were somewhat more responsive. I'm trying to get them to pick out "worthwhile" activities by making suggestions. It just takes time, I guess. I also seem to plan more than I can accomplish. My mistake, I guess, was trying to pack in too much, like two days work in one.

In the 4/15 journal entry, Janet wrote that her frustration was due to her wanting to accomplish so much that she got caught up in management problems. However, management is part of a disciplined class and the hallmark of a master teacher. Good management calls for setting realizable goals and organizing the day in such a way as to be sure the goals are met.

In her 4/17 journal entry Janet showed recognition that she defeated herself by trying to accomplish too much. She had now gotten a clearer idea of her role as teacher. If she learned nothing more in her student teaching, she learned one of the vital lessons: The classroom is no place for superwomen (or supermen). Real people do much better. They do not demand of themselves or of their students more than humans can accomplish.

Janet developed as a teacher because, as we noted, she regarded her difficulties as problems and she worked through them in a thoughtful, problem-solving way. On a nightly basis she used COURAGE techniques to define problems, understand her relation to them, and test out different hypotheses. She dealt with her own problems, the kind she called "hang-ups," with courage. Her reward was success as a student teacher.

Impulsive Problem Solving and Inconsistent Behavior.   Joyce, by comparison, was not functioning as a good problem solver. Instead of using her journal for systematic problem solving, she simply recorded the day's events.

Because Joyce did not think ahead, when she had difficulties with her class she had to make important decisions on the spot. As a result, she behaved impulsively: She acted first and thought about it only after she had recognized that her actions had not worked. Obviously, such an approach tends to be ineffective, as her journal entries suggest.

1/19: I sat Frankie next to Michael to see what effect Michael would have on Frankie. Michael is a bully and he started punching out Frankie. He defies any type of authority. I kept him after school to talk to him, and he sat there and looked at me as if I were crazy. This has really upset me. I've got to reach him somehow, but nothing seems to work.

1/20: Susan was a real problem. But some of the fault lies with me. I changed seating arrangements. [I put] Susan . . . next to Eva. Major mistake. She talked, talked, talked.

Within 2 days, Joyce had rearranged the seating of two difficult students and in each instance, almost immediately after doing so, realized her mistake. Joyce became very disturbed over her inability to cope with the situation, and no wonder.

Joyce was distressed by the behavior of her class and wanted to understand the students better. However, instead of analyzing the situation, defining the problem, and developing a plan of action, Joyce behaved like the proverbial chicken with its head cut off. Her difficulties were not due to a lack of talent, as she began to think they were, or to a lack of concern for the children. Rather, her problems were largely a result of what she was not doing outside of the classroom: logical problem solving.

George, like Joyce, had a difficult student-teaching assignment. His was by choice, however. He wanted to teach science in an urban high school. In his words, "The first week was a disaster." Mr. L. had him work with a group of six behind-grade-level students. To George's dismay, after listening to his lesson for a few minutes, they just ignored him. They conversed among themselves, or fiddled with a pencil, or just sat there turned off. By the end of the week George was in crisis: "Do I ask for a transfer to a nice well-behaved suburban school? Do I change my career? Or do I follow my fantasy and flee to a sunny beach?"

Although he fumbled during the first week, trying this and trying that, a talk with his supervisor on Friday afternoon helped him get back on track. She warned him about impulsive and inconsistent behavior and encouraged him to spend the weekend thinking about the situation critically and logically. He concluded that he had been too idealistic in expecting the teenagers to "bloom" in the hands of a caring, permissive teacher. He decided he could only maintain his sanity and his commitment to urban schools by setting realistic expectations and experimenting with different structured approaches. He remembered a phrase he had learned in class earlier that year and told himself he needed to follow the "three mores": more structure in my lessons, more patience, and more realistic expectations. After 3 weeks of "mores" and several conversations with his supervisor, he had this to say:

> 2/12: I feel that some of the kids see me as being on their side—that I'm really interested in them. They're listening a little more and some of them know I mean it when I say, "Let's get down to business." Most important, they're beginning to see that what we are studying does have something to do with their lives. I've got to keep reminding myself to be patient.

George's experience reflects the principle that a teacher's style of management has to be adapted to the circumstances in the school, and doing that calls for effective problem solving. Children and teenagers who see little if any connection between school and their lives are different in their classroom attitudes and behavior from those who see a close connection.

#6 Preventing Problems

Teachers often end the school day saying, "If only I had done so-and-so," by which they mean "If I had done so-and-so, I would have prevented the awful problem I'm faced with now."

It is impossible to overstress the importance of prevention. That is why, in one sense, this entire book is devoted to prevention: Preparing for Student Teaching, Building a Good Relationship With Students, and Becoming Confident and Competent, to cite a few chapter titles, are all about prevention. In this section, we approach it head on and by name.

Establishing open lines of communication with each of your students is one key to preventing problems. Communication lies at the heart of teaching. How and with whom you communicate has considerable bearing on the classroom climate and the attitude of students. Fair and equal treatment is important to students, and so is a teacher's respectful attitude toward them.

There are countless ways you can foster a healthy classroom climate and positive teacher–student relationships. Recognizing each student by name, for example, builds morale. It tells the class you are aware of each one of them as an individual. This could be done at any point during a lesson, even in saying "hello" or "goodbye" as students enter and exit. Consistently saying such a simple and polite word as "please" shows you are treating students with the respect they deserve.

Whenever possible, show students through word and deed that you are interested in them as people. Recognize the important events and milestones in their lives—birthdays, the loss of a tooth, the earning of a driver's license—and celebrate with them. Note how Brooke showed her students she cared:

> 11/13: I was really unhappy with something I did today. I did what I had always hoped a teacher would never do when I was a student. I assigned homework on the night of a school concert!!! I know it is not really a huge problem and teachers do it all the time, and part of me knows the kids will live through it, but it is something that I really wish I was more conscious of. I always felt as a student that my teachers never really cared about extracurricular activities. Over half the class is involved in band or chorus and they worked hard for that concert and I really did not intend to give them homework to do that night, but at the same time, I needed them to read the next section of the chapter if I was going to do anything constructive in class.
>
> To combat that apathy I felt teachers frequently had about students' activities outside the classroom, I decided to GO to the concert. Before I went I had those feeling like I shouldn't go, I was going to feel stupid when I was there, etc. After I got there I was so happy that I had gone. The kids were great! Of course, it was your typical school concert with the chorus being a little off-key and the clarinets coming in at the wrong time, but there was so much more going on. The kids all looked great, dressed up and excited for their concert, and they all did a fantastic job. You could tell many of them were proud at the end of the concert. And I was happy I went—now I can truthfully tell them in school [tomorrow] that I enjoyed their concert.

How teachers make their students feel is crucial to student behavior and success. To take an extreme example, a longitudinal study of more than 1,200 students from first grade into high school concluded that students' perceptions of whether their teachers thought they were doing well academically was among the characteristics significantly related to the students' subsequent dropout rate (Ensminger & Slusarcick, 1992). A second longitudinal study that followed about 1,200 students from seventh grade into young adulthood found similar results: Perceived teacher rejection resulted indirectly in a higher dropout rate (Kaplan, Peck, & Kaplan, 1997). Remember what the literature says about expectations: What you think about your students is typically what gets communicated to them through your attitudes and behaviors. Those communications, in turn, affect your students' attitudes about themselves, and also how they behave in your classroom.

In classrooms in which learners know they will be respected as students, valued as individuals, and treated fairly and consistently in all situations, a healthy classroom climate forms. Students have few reasons to act out in anger or frustration with a teacher in such an environment. That does not mean students will not be disruptive and difficult at times—problems stem from many other causes—but discipline issues will be minimized.

In working to establish the kind of healthy classroom climate and productive teacher–student relationships that minimize problems, student teachers should be aware of the concept of *student brinkmanship,* defined as behavior that students engage in to resist school authority (or in other words, to resist you, the teacher).

The concept of brinkmanship, of being on the brink or on the edge, is used because the behavior involved (e.g., chalk squeaking, book dropping, chair tipping, pen tapping, note passing, and enthusiastic hand waving) is done at a level not really punishable. Students know they can get away with this brinkmanship level of behavior and, in doing it, they express and release some of their hostility to authority.

Newman and Licata (1986–1987) studied the relation between such behavior and teacher and classroom climate. Their participants were students and teachers in 122 classes in a large, urban–suburban school district in the Midwest. The findings of this carefully designed study suggest the following useful hypotheses:

1. Students are less likely to use brinkmanship if they feel positive about the teacher as a considerate person and about the classroom climate in general. In other words, if they find the teacher is considerate (friendly, respecting, warm, and trusting), and if they find the classroom climate favorable (cohesive, students interact and feel friendly with each other; satisfying, students like their class and work), then they tend to be less hostile and not engage in brinkmanship.

2. The frequency of student brinkmanship is inversely related to classroom routinization. Teachers can reduce the incidence of brinkmanship by increasing the amount of time given to following well-established, orderly routines. Initially, to establish routines, the teacher sees to it that students know what work is to be done and when it is to be done.

Implicit in Newman and Licata's (1986–1987) study and their discussion of their findings is this advice to student teachers: While you are developing a positive teacher–student relationship based on consideration of student needs, rely heavily on routinization. Once the relationship is established to your satisfaction, you can then give routinization its proper place and use it consistently with your own teaching philosophy and approach.

In sum, you can prevent problems by developing good relationships with your students, which in turn helps build a positive classroom climate. Clear, meaningful, and frequent communication with all students helps make them feel valued and respected, and therefore less likely to engage in disruptive behavior. Make sure that communication goes two ways—listen as well as talk.

As discussed in chapter 5, you can prevent problems by ensuring that lessons are interesting, allow for student interaction, and relate to students' lives. This, too, helps build a positive classroom climate. Moreover, it prevents problems stemming from boredom.

You can also prevent problems by acting with consistency and fairness when handling all discipline matters that emerge despite your best preventative efforts; this makes students feel you are an adult leader who can be trusted.

#7 Maintaining Vitality

Somewhere down the road in your career you may begin thinking about how to maintain vitality in the classroom. You might, in fact, find yourself thinking about it now as you compare your enthusiasm, excitement, and joy with the more subdued attitude of your experienced colleagues. You might even detect a tired, worn-out look and demeanor in one or two colleagues who although teaching, are really only waiting for retirement. You might find yourself saying: I never want to lose my enjoyment of teaching; I never want to stop finding students amazing and lovable, funny, and fun.

You are exactly right. But after years of teaching, some find they have to exert a bit of effort to prevent boredom or indifference from creeping into class. The good news is that many, many teachers spend decades in the classroom, finding each new group of students a fresh challenge and unsavored delight. What is their secret?

An article written to help college teachers of psychology maintain vitality in their classes can be helpful to other teachers as well. Here are some points made by Lloyd (1994):

1. Be willing to experiment. Do something different. Maybe include more demonstrations and activities, improve your discussion leadership skills (we are not born with them), or consider using cooperative learning strategies.
2. Keep a written record of what works and what does not. Write notes to yourself as you get new ideas.
3. Look for new ideas about teaching from your teacher publications, from conferences and workshops, and books.
4. Watch yourself in action. Have a class videotaped and get a unique perspective on your teaching.
5. Stay in touch with your students. You are of a different generation from them. If you refer to some TV programs you enjoyed as a child, you might get a vacant stare because they never heard of them. As you get older, work at knowing the culture of the younger generations.
6. Cultivate a positive attitude. Maintain your enthusiasm. Your enthusiasm and your interest in reading, studying, and thinking may infect them.

Another practice sure to be helpful in maintaining vitality is establishing a file in which you keep cards and letters from students; transcribed thank-you phone messages from parents; and scraps of paper with scribbled notes of kind words, insightful responses, and funny expressions uttered by your students. Whenever you doubt your work in the classroom or effect on students, all you have to do is reach your hand into the file and pull out one of many treasures.

CRITICAL ISSUES

- What do you have in mind when you think of discipline?
- How do you feel about assuming the role of adult leader?
- What strategies will you use to effectively manage yourself and your time while student teaching?
- How can planning be helpful for successful classroom management?
- What is your theory of classroom management? How does it provide optimal conditions for learning?
- What classroom management problems have you faced in the past and how did you deal with them? Would you act differently now? Why?
- How will you maintain your vitality as your teaching career unfolds?

10

Coping With Tough Problems

During your classroom observations you probably noticed the teacher's attention turn from whole class to individuals to whole class, or perhaps whole class to groups to individuals or vice versa. As teachers, we relate to each of these entities: class as a whole, small working groups, and individual students. We also find ourselves in the position many times a day of having to decide to which entity to attend.

How we divide our attention among these entities is worth considering. Of course, the welfare of the whole class is our first priority. For this reason we guard against the demands of some one student distracting us from this prime responsibility and leading us to give him or her so much attention that the class suffers as a result. On the other hand, we want to maximize each student's learning and sometimes, to do that, individual attention is a benefit. As you can see, teaching is a balancing act.

As we examine some of the tough problems that teachers find in relation to individual students, let us keep the class as a whole always in the foreground.

MEETING BOTH INDIVIDUAL AND CLASS NEEDS

This section focuses on behavioral problems of individual students and methods teachers can use to resolve them. We begin with Kate, who discussed discipline with a substitute teacher and gained new insights.

> 2/9: As I thought about it later, I decided that I need to learn to be a little firmer with the children. At times I tend to sacrifice the needs of the group for individuals because I am afraid of hurting their feelings. Consequently, when a child begins a monologue completely sidetracking us from the group's discussion, I will usually let the child continue his/her story. But meanwhile, the rest of the class becomes bored and fidgety. As I get to know the children better I am beginning to realize that children's feelings do not bruise that easily. For example, today I asked Glenn to go on an errand for me. Cindy asked to accompany him, but I told Cindy that I only needed one person for this job. Much to my surprise I got a cheerful "OK" and she went back to what she was doing.

Kate had the good experience of being an effective leader for the children. More important was her recognition that concern about the feelings of a particular child should not stand in the way of what is important to the welfare of the class. Kate was correct about the principle involved, even if her example was a very tame one compared to many reported in the journals. Before we turn to the more difficult ones, let us read how Julie dealt with a student who frequently spoke out in class, this time during the vice-principal's observation visit.

> 3/15: Mr. R., the vice-principal, came in to observe me this morning. I was surprised that I wasn't more nervous. As a matter of fact I was very calm, I thought. I was in the middle of a lesson on the concept of "more and less." The children were all attending to what was going on—their participation helped to keep them all interested. Mr. R. told me later that he thought I did a fine job so I was glad it worked out well.
>
> As I was doing my lesson, Crystal began blurting out all kinds of things, including asking me why I wore glasses. This is not unusual for Crystal: Her attention span is not as long as that of some of the other kids. Of course when you're being observed, you want everything to run smoothly, but when my patience was wearing thin concerning Crystal's outbursts I stopped momentarily and asked myself, "Are you trying to look good in front of the vice-principal and forget Crystal, or are you trying to do a good job of teaching?" I knew instantly that I had to stop Crystal from disturbing the class. I did, and I feel good about it.

The day before the scheduled observation, Julie had discussed Crystal with her cooperating teacher and had planned how she would handle her. Julie, knowing that Crystal was an impulsive child who had not yet internalized the social controls necessary for concentrating on a lesson, provided the control externally. She accomplished this by walking close to Crystal and saying something like: "Crystal, I want you to listen—to listen very carefully—and I don't want you to talk again until I call on you. Do you understand?" Crystal responded both to Julie's words and to the tone of her voice.

After Julie had called on several of the children to answer questions or to give an example to help illustrate the lesson, she called on Crystal. That step is an important one in the process of helping a child incorporate controls. It rewards the children for the control they have exercised, no matter how briefly, and informs them that with such self-control they will still get attention from the teacher and have their turn.

THE DEFIANT STUDENT

Steve recognized very early in his assignment that the students were undisciplined and that the cooperating teacher's practices contributed to their behavior. For example, Mrs. S. would pass out two worksheets at once, with the result that as she was giving directions on the second, the students were working on the first. She would also tell the class which worksheets would not be collected and graded, a strong incentive to resistive students to ignore them.

Steve was not thrown by the situation. In his third day as a student teacher, "several of the boys were chewing grape gum. I would ask them to throw it away and they would fake throwing it away. I finally ended up taking a piece of paper and telling them to put it on the paper and then throwing it away myself. They have no self-discipline."

His statement was not that of a teacher in panic. He knew that the "gum" misbehavior was directed at him, a test of the new teacher, and he took it in stride. When his first attempt did not work he shifted gears and succeeded in passing the test: He maintained his authority as teacher and enabled the group to do the work of the day. Thereafter, with the same spirit, Steve searched successfully for activities and larger projects that won the active participation of all students some days and most of them on other days.

Steve did not have an easy time with John, who is typical of a type of student who challenges teaching professionalism. Sometimes youngsters arouse the animosity of the teacher, a situation that often leads to a battle for power and an almost total preoccupation with how to subdue the student. Such a reaction, although understandable under provocative circumstances, denies the teacher the chance to understand and resolve the problem. The preoccupation with this struggle also gradually erodes the teacher's effectiveness with the class.

If the student teacher gets caught up in such a contest, he or she will have less time and energy to concentrate on the class as a whole. Steve's experiences, reported in his journal entries, give examples of what a student teacher must do to avoid getting caught up in such problems.

> 1/28: Today John was totally obnoxious. It is spelling test day. I gave the children about 10 minutes to study. John just sat there and wrote about five words on a little piece of paper—a cheat sheet. Right before the test I took it away. Then I gave the first spelling word—he spelled it out loud—I ignored it. I, however, reminded the whole class that they must be silent. John shouted out the spelling of the next word. I crushed his paper. Then when we were in line to go to the rest room, he pushed a girl down. Mrs. S. saw it and scolded him harshly. He had been performing for Mrs. S. all week too. He then acted like the scolding was the greatest thing that ever happened to him.

Steve recognized that John's actions were not directed against him personally, for Mrs. S. had trouble with John earlier in the week. For whatever reasons in his personal life, John, at this point in the school year, had a need to get attention and defy adult authority. We may not know what provoked him. Nevertheless, as effective teachers we must convey to John, at a level he can understand, what knowledge we do have:

- You have your reasons for doing what you are doing.
- You are doing this not because you want to but because some undetermined need is driving your behavior.
- That undetermined need might be conflict in your family and household environment, anxiety about failing in school, immature attempts to impress the attractive girl sitting next to you, or any number of other things.
- Whatever is driving your behavior, it is disruptive to others and to yourself, and it is unacceptable and will not be permitted.
- As your teacher, I will use every means available to me to prevent your behavior, starting with the most humane and least humiliating and progressing as necessary.
- Although I recognize that external factors may be driving your behavior, that recognition will not cause me to be "easier" on you. In your interest, I must act decisively to prevent you from further damaging your self-concept and from further alienating yourself from members of the class.

Steve handled the cheating encounter relatively well. When John defied him by spelling the first word given on the test aloud, however, Steve might have said, "I know that you are looking for attention. I can't allow you to get it this way because you are disrupting the class." He then could have made the consequences of further misbehavior clear. For example, "If you disrupt this testing process again, you will be removed from the classroom and a parent will be called." Then, of course, he would have to be prepared to follow through with these consequences. Although the wording of the warning sentence is flexible, note the phrase "if you disrupt this testing process again." Some students will continually test limits, interpreting your words—when in their interest—to the letter of the law. If Steve said, "if you spell a word out loud again . . ." the student would know that in fairness, humming loudly could not result in the consequences spelled out by the teacher.

When managing defiant students, it is essential to consider them as individuals. The actual discipline threatened might depend on the student. For some, the discipline awaiting them at home might be much worse than that issued at school, and a promise that misbehavior would result in a phone call home would work well. For others, being denied recess privileges and the opportunity to join friends in a pick-up basketball game would be a much more effective discipline tool. Each child is different—be flexible and observant to learn what works best. At the same time, be careful that you are always a fair disciplinarian; disruptions of equal weight should result in discipline of equal severity.

Student teachers often ask about effective measures to cope with the disruptive behavior of one or two students who use too much of their time and energy, leaving too little for the rest of the class. It is a good question. Fortunately, studies have shown that teachers have a great deal of power to influence the disruptive behavior of students.

It is common for teachers to ignore students who are working steadily, while being occupied and sometimes entirely preoccupied with the pupil who is disruptive; or to ignore that same pupil when he or she is actually beginning to do classwork. Unfortunately, the whole class gets the message: "If you want to be noticed, stop working or, better yet, cause trouble."

Beginning in the late 1960s, educators developed the concept "catch them being good"; in other words, praise students for positive behavior to reinforce it. A study by Madsen, Becker, Thomas, Kosen, and Plager (1972) suggests that emphasizing the positive may be more effective than criticizing the negative. The strategy is still useful today.

The investigators sought an effective way for teachers to correct the behavior of first-grade children who were standing when they should have been working. Typically, the teacher directs the offender to sit down and get on with the work. The researchers found that when teachers concentrated on children's violation of rules by telling them to sit down (their voices sometimes increasing in intensity), the misbehavior continued; when they increased the commands to sit down, standing up behaviors actually increased. However, when the teachers turned their attention to praising behavior that was incompatible with standing up (i.e., sitting and working properly), the standing up declined.

The teachers caught the child being good, giving praise, attention, or a smile when a child was seated and at work. When teachers saw a child standing and walking unnecessarily, they ignored the child and instead went to a neighboring child and praised him or her for being seated and working.

The success of this approach may be seen in this finding: In a class of 45 children and 2 teachers, there was a decline of 100 incidents of standing up per 20 minutes, a substantial difference in the functioning of any class.

Anna tried various techniques in an effort to stop a group of several adolescent girls from talking and giggling when she was presenting material. Anna explained:

> 11/4: I reprimanded the girls since Day 1. It didn't work, so Ms. C. suggested our putting some teeth into my discipline. I had them stay after, write lines, clean the chalkboard. Nothing worked. Then I gave a quiz after one lesson. They all failed— but that didn't seem to change them. Then Ms. C. and I re-thought things. I lecture. The girls talk or giggle. I yell at them. The boys think it's great—I'm yelling at the girls, and so on. This week I stopped yelling at them and let them talk. Instead I praised kids that answered my questions. The girls came around. They are defi- nitely listening longer now—last time there were no flare-ups.

We become accustomed from our experiences growing up at home and in school to focus primarily on misbehavior. Shifting gears to a new way of func- tioning is not easy, but it is worth accomplishing because it enables us to be more effective teachers.

No one should be left with the impression that this procedure means being "soft" on students who violate rules, disrupt classroom activities, and seek to un- dermine our authority. On the contrary, the objective of using methods that mod- ify behavior is precisely to eliminate or at least greatly reduce the incidence of such kinds of unacceptable behavior. In doing this, of course, you must strive to praise all students when they are behaving appropriately. In other words, you should not continually single out the same students as models of proper behav- ior. You should also praise a student who is making an effort to improve his or her behavior. When you select that student to pass out papers and the job is well done, make sure the child is commended.

A useful tactic when you first encounter hostile behavior is to remember that it might have its roots outside the classroom in problems people have about feel- ing in control of their lives. For example, students vary on how much control they feel they have in social situations. A study of junior and senior high school students has shown that those who feel they have some degree of control over what happens to them tended to exhibit prosocial behavior in the classroom; that is, they were rated by teachers as being task-oriented and considerate in contrast to distractible and hostile (Bradley & Teeter, 1977).

What is the practical value of such a finding? If disruptive students believe that luck almost totally controls how they make out in school and other social situations, then changing this belief may modify their behavior. How could a teacher change this belief? Would setting up a contract that rewarded them for their own successful performance help the students learn that they can have some control over the outcome of situations? Would involving the students in deci- sions about their discipline help them develop a feeling of control and decrease misbehavior? These are effective measures although they do not always succeed in changing every student's behavior. Only by trying them can you know whether they will work for your students.

THE INTIMIDATING STUDENT

Ruby had a different and more serious problem than any we have yet examined. About 6 weeks into her student teaching she began to understand that she, as a teacher, was afraid of one of her second graders.

> 2/28: I didn't realize until this morning that my feelings about one child in particular, George, are becoming terrible. George is the one who gets and keeps the class out of hand, and when he isn't there, things go so smoothly. I can do extra things with the class which are a flop when George is there. This morning I found myself hoping that George would be absent. I think that I'm afraid of him.

To begin with, Ruby's assigned class was hardly the most conducive to good teaching. Her cooperating teacher had been given all the "problem children" in the grade. Ruby silently disapproved of some of the cooperating teacher's practices, especially her frequent shouting. The cooperating teacher openly disapproved of Ruby's quiet manner, insisting she must shout at the children. The cooperating teacher was absent frequently, and there was a turnover of substitutes. These circumstances made life difficult for Ruby; her experiences are instructive, however, because even with better conditions, student teachers (and experienced teachers, too) often find themselves at similar loggerheads with one student or another.

Next we analyze the reasons for Ruby's development of fear, an emotion that can immobilize a teacher, making him or her an ineffectual classroom manager. In doing so, we refer to journal entries made earlier than the one just cited. About 7 weeks before that entry, Ruby made her first reference to George in the journal and made her first series of mistakes.

> 1/11: George is testing me to see how far he can push me. I don't quite know how to handle it. Today he and Matt were having an argument over who Mrs. W. had said could take the ball out. Matt had the ball and George walked up and hit him in his stomach. I separated them and George said, "I'm going to kick his butt after school on the way home." I said, "No, you're not." He said, "Yes, I am too." I said, "Do you want to stay in for recess?" He said, "I'm not staying in nowhere." I didn't really want to make him stay in and I didn't want him to fight with Matt, but because of other encounters that we have had I felt that I should do something. Just as this happened, Mrs. W. came in and told everyone to go outside. I didn't say anything.

Ruby interpreted George's behavior in a personal way—that he was testing her. She was being tested as a teacher, but not by design; George was behaving in his characteristic manner. She got enmeshed with George as much as Matt did, responding to George's threats to Matt in an unrealistic way (a teacher cannot police children on their walk home from school). She then threatened punishment (staying in for recess) and did not carry it out. Ruby, it should be noted, gave him a choice: to cease being belligerent or stay in during recess. When she failed to carry out the disciplinary action, he learned that she wilted under his domination. Nothing so quickly undermines the authority of a teacher than failure to carry out the consequences of unacceptable behavior.

> 1/20: Today I had my first crisis in the classroom. George started about three little battles in the classroom. After I settled the third one down (between George and Raymond), George hit Raymond with his fist on the side of his face. Raymond was crying and George was threatening to beat him up after school. While this was going on, the class was getting completely out of hand. I had no idea where Mrs. W. was, and all I could think of was to take George up to the office and come back to quiet the rest of the class. Raymond was still crying when I came back down. I quieted the class and tried to talk to Raymond. He wouldn't talk, but the side of his face was swelling pretty badly. I took him to the office.

> 1/23: I had problems with George today. He was disturbing the class, running about the room, talking and constantly out of his seat. I finally had to take his recess away. He said he wouldn't stay in. I talked to Mrs. W. about it, and she said I couldn't handle George the way I handled other kids. (This was obvious.) Authority turns him off. Mrs. W. suggested that I talk privately with him, discuss what he'd been doing, and let him choose his punishment. I couldn't let him go out after that, so I told him that I wanted to talk to him during recess. He waited without much fuss. We decided that he was talking and that he should stay in. I turned my back to talk with a reading group and he left. When he returned we talked again and decided that he had to give up half his recess tomorrow. I was afraid that it might look to the rest of the class as if I were favoring him, but Mrs. W. said that they didn't pay that much attention and this is the best way to handle George.

> 1/24: George didn't come this morning and afternoon recess was only 5 minutes long, so I ended up letting him go to recess.

Ruby "taught" George that he could manipulate the classroom situation. On 1/23, Ruby took her cooperating teacher's advice and gave him his choice of punishment. She then failed to carry it out both on that day and the following day. So, 2 days in a row George's earlier lesson was reinforced—the new teacher (Ruby) doesn't enforce discipline.

Two weeks later (2/7) Ruby recognized again that George was the key to the problems she was having with the few children who were disruptive, but she continued to show her hesitancy about being the adult teacher, the rational authority in the classroom. The next day (2/8) she was "amazed" to find that this child behaves like a child when the authority figure behaves like an authority figure.

> 2/7: Today was about the same as most days except for an unusual number of problems with George, Chad, Alex, and Stewart. George seems to incite the problems and the others follow. Once this happens it is almost impossible to get things run-

ning smoothly. George was really bad today, but I can't tell how far to let him go before stopping him.

2/8: Today was a very short day, but George was disturbing the class again. I decided that I had to stop it early today. I took him by the hand and took him outside of the classroom and talked to him and he agreed to stop. I was amazed. He was completely submissive to being taken out, reasonable and honest in the discussion, and much better behaved in the classroom. The class behaved much better too.

Students like George, who have learned to behave disruptively for attention, do not change as a result of one good experience with a teacher or even after several good experiences. Their behavior typically fluctuates from day to day. Of course, so does the behavior of the teacher who is inconsistent in acting the part of the adult leader.

About 3 weeks later, Ruby realized that fear was at the root of her relationship with George, as she had written in her 2/28 journal entry, quoted earlier. He was absent for several days, during which time Ruby reported good and enjoyable hours in the classroom. The first day he returned, the first sentence in her journal entry was, "George came back today and everything eventually went back to the usual upset." In Ruby's 3/3 journal, the last on George, you can see how her cooperating teacher had put George in an exceptional position in the classroom, and how that handicapped Ruby in dealing with him effectively. With her cooperating teacher absent, Ruby asserted herself:

3/3: George was here again, but things went much better. He didn't want me to do my unit and he insisted on running all over the room and talking until the kids couldn't possibly remember anything I said because every sentence was broken by my having to correct him. Finally, I just told him to get into the coat room until we were finished. He will have to do his unit work at recess on Monday. If the substitute hadn't been there, I wouldn't have been able to do the lesson smoothly for the rest of the class because George would not have let us. She sat near him and watched to make sure that he was doing as I said. George is afraid of only one thing, going to the office, but I'm not even allowed to send him because Mrs. W. thinks that he should be allowed to do more than the other kids are allowed to do.

George needed help, much more than Ruby could provide. An investigation of his health and family histories, as well as a careful review of his school records, could give us clearer notions about his behavior. But most student teachers have neither the time nor the competencies to do that. If student teachers are to survive and develop as educators, they must learn to cope with the Georges they encounter. Often this is difficult, particularly when the Georges may be bigger, stronger, or have access to dangerous weapons outside of school. However, student teachers can and must overcome fear when it arises; they must be the adult to the child.

At several points when Ruby had more pleasant exchanges with George, largely through her own solicitousness, she thought she had won him over. But those were acts of appeasing someone who was feared, a kind of behavior just as ineffectual in the classroom as anywhere else. George's behavior must be dealt with rationally and consistently. Such action requires careful and systematic thought, the kind associated with problem-solving methods like COURAGE.

Using COURAGE With the Intimidating Student

If Ruby had used COURAGE in planning her work with George, it would have very likely led her to:

1. Conduct private talks with George explaining that nonparticipation is acceptable if it does not disrupt the class, but his teacher likes him and wants him to participate so that he can become smarter and more successful in school.

2. Begin a concerted effort to catch him being good. When George is seen behaving appropriately he should be praised, and perhaps rewarded. For example, George could be given some special tasks such as handing out materials to classmates.

3. Deal with disruptive acts firmly and consistently. The method used should end the disruption immediately but set the stage for George's reentry into the group. For a young student like George, it might be helpful to have something "quiet" ready to give him at his desk—a favorite picture book, for example. While he prepares himself emotionally to rejoin class activities, he is occupied rather than disruptive.

4. Remember that George is a child and a victim of some unhappy experiences. We do not need to delve into his history, although knowing it will help us understand him better.

5. Remember that sometimes a teacher's "fear" is really a fear of releasing anger on a student who has made classroom life unbearable. Students are not hurt by the appropriate expression of anger by a teacher who is trying to help them control their self-defeating behavior. They will generally respect such an expression of feeling and learn from it.

6. Remember that in 10 to 15 weeks or so she should not expect to accomplish what regular teachers are unable to do with children like George in a year.

7. Remember that seating arrangements have some profound effects on the activities and behavior of students. A study of the impact of various seating arrangements on behavior, attention span, and teacher's attitude showed that being assigned seats in the first rows (closest to the teacher) led to better student work and gave the students the most teacher attention (A. I. Schwebel & Cherlin, 1972). Comparable results would very likely be obtained in a study of seating in less traditionally arranged classrooms.

Although it is clear that 8-year-olds like George can be intimidating through their behavior, deliberate evaluation of the circumstances and rational decision making with a method like COURAGE enable a teacher to reassert control, thereby helping both the disruptive student and class benefit from a sane learning environment. But what of the student who towers over you, the star quarterback or 6'7" basketball center? Clearly, you cannot lead them out of the classroom by the hand when they begin to act up

An important factor to keep in mind is that children and adolescents mature at different rates, and sometimes physical maturity outpaces intellectual and emotional growth; a student may look like a 20-year-old adult but still act like the 14-year-old adolescent he or she is. A learning disabled 7-year-old may be taller and heavier than his peers, but still think like a 4-year-old in particular domains (areas of thinking). Remind yourself of that, and speak to the child or adolescent within rather than reacting to the more adult body without. Even when teaching or supervising students a mere 3 or 4 years younger than you, remember that in almost all instances you have both superior knowledge and experience within the school domain. More important, you have the responsibility to act in the best interest of the class and uphold the rules of the school. Behave as the adult authority and in most cases, the high schooler, just like the second grader, will play his or her student role.

THE STUDENT WITH LOW SELF-ESTEEM

Many students with low self-esteem go unnoticed because they are not troublemakers. For example, only after student teachers manage to deal with the aggressive students do they become aware of the passive, withdrawn ones. Recognizing this, a student teacher brought up the issue in seminar class and asked advice about handling a particular boy who was in both his homeroom and geography class: "He never raises his hand, talks almost in a whisper so that I can't hear him, and has no friends. Except in geography, he barely has passing grades. What can I do, especially to get him to learn more?" This is the advice he received:

This student has a many-faceted problem and you, as his teacher, have to understand and treat it accordingly. First apply a systematic problem-solving procedure like COURAGE to develop a list of options. Possibilities might include:

1. In geography: (a) You can use the student's strength to build his self-confidence through positive reinforcement. You can call on him to answer questions and praise his responses immediately after they are given. (b) You can have him make a special presentation to the class on some aspect of geography. If he should speak too softly when delivering his speech (or at any other time), you could say, "I like your comments very much and I want to be

sure everyone in the class can hear them. Please speak up." Then praise him for even the smallest increase in volume.

2. With peers: (a) You could enlist an outgoing student to befriend him and include him at the lunch table or in some physical activities. (b) You could arrange to have him do peer teaching in geography or be tutored by another student in other subjects.

3. After school: (a) You could encourage both him and his parents to explore extracurricular activities. For example, although he is afraid to speak up under ordinary circumstances, he may be able to do this behind a puppet stage or as an actor with a small part in a drama club play. (b) You could explain to his parents that while he seems to have difficulty making friends in school, he might find it easier to relate to peers in a small group, especially if those peers share common interests.

4. With a counselor: You could refer him to the school counselor and work with him or her to monitor the student's progress

With imagination and COURAGE, you can delineate dozens of other possibilities. Because there is no one correct way to help this boy, you should experiment until you find one or several that work. Remember that student teachers (or regular teachers for that matter) are not magicians. Work toward your goal with patience, but do not expect to transform a highly withdrawn student into a highly gregarious one in 3 months or even a year's time.

Another question that stimulated extensive discussion arose in one of our student-teacher seminars. An English teacher said that a major problem she faced was that a few of her students were learning disabled, especially dyslexic. The result for them has been poor grades and low self-esteem. "What do you think I ought to do about that? Do I work on their self-esteem? Work on their reading ability? Or what?"

Her set of questions brought forth many ideas. Following is a summary of the conclusions: Because self-concept can affect academic success, it makes sense for teachers (and student teachers) to informally assess their students' self-concept and its development over time, just as they do—although more systematically—their students' academic achievement.

Individuals' self-concepts play crucial roles in at least three areas that can affect classroom performance:

1. Behavior: Students who do not see themselves as able are not likely to act competently. Instead they will function in ways consistent with their self-view.

2. Expectations: Students who view themselves as poor performers expect to fail exams. Thus, they are less motivated to prepare and more likely to fail.

3. Interpretation of performance: If students have trouble mastering a technique, and their self-concepts are low, they will likely blame themselves and perhaps give up.

One's self-concept is important at all ages. Because adolescents go through profound personal changes, however, they inevitably struggle more with theirs than their younger or older counterparts. Adolescents can be helped in bolstering their self-views. A teacher's first step toward providing such help requires an informal assessment of the students' self-views. If, on the basis of the information collected, the teacher determines that self-esteem is a problem, the next steps could include the following:

1. Try to identify the basic skill deficiencies that may be contributing to individuals' low self-esteem. Find or develop training materials to help them overcome the deficits. When skill deficiencies are great, consider eliciting parents' help in strengthening skills. You might also recommend a peer or professional tutor or refer students to the resource room or learning center.
2. Teach students to evaluate their performance realistically, identifying what they have and have not learned, what they are strong in (for which they deserve praise), and what they are weak in (for which they need help). Teaching students to accurately self-evaluate their performance takes time.
3. Teach students to set realistic goals. Some individuals with low self-views make excessively high demands of themselves. Setting attainable goals that they must work hard to achieve is more suitable to the building of a positive self-view.
4. Praise is a great tonic. Give it to students when they deserve it; teach them to praise each other and to compliment themselves for work that merits it. Praise is unlike money in that our supplies are unlimited. Teach students that they can benefit others and themselves by spending it freely.

Having said all this, however, we must add a caveat. Remember that self-concept is a deeply engrained aspect of one's psyche, and as such, it does not change quickly. Nevertheless, progress and improvement can occur. It may be slow, but the actions of striving for it can transform the classroom atmosphere, benefit your students, and make your work more satisfying.

THE ABUSED AND NEGLECTED STUDENT

Abuse can be emotional, mental, physical, or sexual in character, or a combination of these. Neglect includes failure of parents to properly feed, house, clothe, emotionally support, or supervise their child. Laws in all 50 states require teachers to report suspected cases of child abuse to appropriate authorities.

Teachers are in a unique position in students' lives. They are often the only adult outside the immediate family to whom a student can turn for help. Teachers have an enormous responsibility in this area—to be alert to students in need. The physical signs of youngsters in need of help may be obvious: burns, bruises, cuts, or inadequate clothing during cold winter months. The behavioral signs, such as listlessness, fearfulness, aggressiveness, and emotional instability, however, may be symptoms of problems other than abuse and neglect, so one must be cautious about coming to premature conclusions. In any event, if you have suspicions, share them with your cooperating teacher, who, in turn, will in all likelihood discuss them with the school nurse, counselor, principal, or social worker before a decision is made to report abuse or neglect to the proper authorities.

Teachers who become familiar with community resources and maintain good relationships with parents can be helpful in many ways. As a student teacher it would be wise for you to find out as much as possible about the resources available in your school's community: food banks for the hungry; sources of free or low-cost clothing; community resources that might provide after-school tutoring or supervised activities for needy children; community resources that can provide emergency help with transportation, utility and rent bills, and other necessities; housing shelters for homeless families or for battered parents and their children; public health clinics for pregnant teens or adolescents struggling with eating disorders; and so on.

Often a student is unable to concentrate in school because of overwhelming problems at home, such as the unemployment of a parent, a sibling's serious illness, or parental marital conflict. Although a student teacher cannot change a student's life, it may be possible at times to ease some of the burden. Parents generally welcome any offer to help them with their child's well-being, but some are too afraid or ashamed to ask.

SEXUAL ISSUES

Problems in class concerning sex often shake the confidence and comfort levels of even experienced teachers. Chances are most student teachers receive little instruction, if any, in coping with sex-related problems, such as the kinds of difficulties Sheryl, Carla, and Lori faced. Sheryl, who was student teaching in a first-grade classroom, wrote the following in her journal:

> 2/15: I really had a teaching problem. Frances wrote a note that said "Steve's in Meg's pussy," and Steve got hold of it and brought it to me. I really wasn't sure what to do. I took Frances outside and asked her if she wrote it and she said she wrote some and Steve wrote some. Steve denied it (I only asked him if he wrote it), and then I spoke to Frances again. She admitted writing it. I asked her what she thought I should do. She said that she should apologize, which she did to Steve very nicely. She was crying and I told her I knew her mother would be upset and that I was disappointed. I told her to rip it up, which she did. I know harsher punishment would not have helped and it would have ruined anything that I had going with her.

The best that can be said about this report is that Sheryl did not evade the situation. Although she thought that she had spared Frances, she was unaware of the fact that she had greatly magnified this young child's little note and aroused consider-able guilt about sex. Yet she had not even asked Frances why she wrote it. Compare Sheryl's behavior about this sex matter with her actions the following day.

> 2/16: Many of the boys were clowning around, and I ended up putting four names on the board to stay in for afternoon recess. Steve immediately erased it and I chose to ignore his doing that. However, when it was time to go out, Mrs. R. reminded him. He put on another fit and said, crying, he was going to be bad for the rest of the time I'd be here and punishing him like this would not do any good. I ended up letting him write something 50 times and hand it in the next day.

The boys clowned. Steve erased the names Sheryl put on the board, put on a fit, and threatened "to be bad" for days. For all of that, Sheryl had him write "something" 50 times. Surely by any standards of what disrupts a class, Steve's far outstripped Frances's. By any standards of what kind of behavior must be dis-couraged, Steve's was more self-destructive and disruptive than Frances's. Why, then, did Sheryl react as she did?

Carla's experience helps us answer that question. Carla's cooperating teacher, Sylvia, informed the class that there was going to be a "good" and a "bad" list on the board. Carla, she told them, was in charge of whom went on which list. Those on the bad list would not get one of the freshly baked Valentine cookies. Carla described what happened:

> 2/11: The children would run up to me and ask me to put them on the good list. I don't know if I like labeling kids good and bad, and I don't want to be seen just as the disciplinarian—somebody who can dispense rewards and punishment—and that's all.

> In circle, Kelly wouldn't put a book away after consistently being told to, so Sylvia put him on the bad list (I didn't want to put anyone on bad—they were either good, or weren't on at all). Then Josh pinched me hard and he went on the bad side. Later I crossed them both off, but Sylvia said they had to stay on bad. So they got no cookie—and did they ever cry! Sylvia said there was no excuse for Josh's pinching me, and I guess I agree, but Kelly with the book? Well, I guess he'd never do what we say if our "threats" (no cookie) don't come true.

> Later Josh jumped on me and started lifting up my shirt and pressing at my breasts (and I know he meant to—it wasn't that he just happened to touch there—because of the way he looked at me as he did it). I read an article on "Sex in the Classroom" and how to discuss it, but it didn't go into a situation like that. I looked at Josh meaningfully (I hope) and moved his hands. I didn't know what else to do.

We would agree with Carla that Sylvia's lists were hardly suited to aid Carla or any student teacher. We have no knowledge about the part the lists played in Josh's behavior. We do know, however, that Carla did not raise the slightest ques-tion about Josh's first attack on her.

Does it not seem surprising that apparently without provocation he should pinch her? (She did not say where she was pinched.) Would not any student teacher be perplexed and interested in seeing an explanation? The first aggression was so overshadowed by the sexual aspect of the second one, though, that she seemed oblivious to the cause of the first. Yet, the first was much more mysterious than the second, which was "provoked" by Josh being put on the "bad list."

Quite understandably, Carla was startled and frightened by Josh's behavior. Her description suggests some of her bewilderment. We do not know how he jumped on her or how he looked at her (e.g., was it in anger or did she see sexual passion) or what her facial expression was like when she looked "meaningfully" at him. Did she show anger or humiliation or embarrassment?

These questions are not meant to belittle Carla's responses to a difficult interaction. They are meant to indicate the special problem we adults have over sexual acts. Carla halted the behavior and thereafter made no issue of it. We are left without knowing whether the pinch was "sexual," even whether Carla's perception of the pressure on her breasts was sexual, whether these were Josh's nonsexual reactions to a frustrating mother substitute, or whether other factors were at work. We do learn from Carla's next journal entry that Josh is socially backward for his age and "acts out" rather than "talks out" his anger.

> 2/12: Josh and Tammy and Megan all wanted to be the engineer and Josh was pushing and biting the two girls because he wanted to sit in the front chair. Sylvia put two other chairs there and said now we'll have three engineers. (Would I have thought of that? I think so.) I just wish that Josh could verbalize instead of constantly hitting and pushing and kicking and then crying when he gets hit back. I keep telling him to "tell me or tell them," but he runs over and hits.

Josh acts out his emotions. He pushed and bit because he was angry. Probably his touching Carla was also motivated by anger (rather than sex impulse), and part of helping such a child is in letting him or her know that he or she may not express emotions physically that way, with teachers or students. The child must, in fact, never be rewarded for such action as Josh was by Sylvia, the cooperating teacher, who provided extra chairs so that he and the two girls could all be engineers. Coming as that action did immediately after "pushing and biting," she simply reinforced inappropriate behavior.

Although adolescents are generally more sexually knowledgeable (or experienced) than Josh and his classmates, student teachers should respond to sex-related issues in much the same way. Lori's encounter provides an example:

> 1/20: Something unusual happened to me today, and I'm not sure I responded to it in the best way or not. I was walking down the hall between 4th and 5th periods, and Janita told me I better get into the girls' bathroom right away. She wouldn't tell me why, but I opened the door. I figured someone was probably throwing up, or

maybe there was a plumbing problem. I went in and heard some funny sounds, and then some laughter. I couldn't tell what it was. I knocked on the stall door and asked, "Are you OK?" More laughter. Then a male voice—I recognized it, Joe! What was he doing in the girls' bathroom? I told him to open the door. He said he didn't want to. I requested again, in a firmer tone, and he did. He was there with Ashley. Hard to know what they were doing, they said they were just "messing around," but I heard sounds that seemed, in retrospect, to be zippers going up and down and snaps being fastened. I delivered them straight to the principal's office, and they went willingly. What a shock! I figured the kids were pretty advanced sexually but never guessed they'd try to get away with hooking up in the girls' bathroom. I'll have to be ready for things like that, or more, when I chaperone the school dance next weekend.

Lori left the disciplining to the principal rather than tackling it herself, which, given the severity of the transgression, was probably a wise decision. However, because teachers normally engage students who have broken major school rules in conversation immediately after the event—even if students will ultimately be sent to the principal's office—it might have been worthwhile for Lori to first explore the issue with Joe and Ashley. Lori could have asked the students why they decided to engage in these sexual behaviors at school, and why in a girls' bathroom. Many would argue that it is neither abnormal nor problematic for adolescents to explore their sexuality by kissing and touching. Lori was unable to determine if Joe and Ashley had crossed the boundary of appropriate sexual behavior for their age group, however that boundary might be defined. Regardless, it is clearly unacceptable for teenagers to engage in sexual behavior at school. Moreover, it is unacceptable for people of any age to sneak into opposite-sex bathrooms. Lori could have approached this as the behavior to focus on in her discussion rather than the sexualized behaviors that were more of an unknown entity. She could have then conveyed this information to the principal and perhaps the school guidance counselor.

Some student teachers who work with older adolescents find themselves in the distressing position of being the target of students' sexual harassment. In a study about the gender issues embedded in the student-teaching experience, Miller (1997) found that half of the 16 female student teachers she interviewed who were completing their assignment in New England high schools spoke of being "demeaned and objectified" by male high school students. Examples ranged from whistles and catcalls to a student teacher being asked out on a date by one of her students to direct challenges in class: "Excuse me. There's one thing I'm confused about, Ms. Kaley. Can you clarify it? Ms. Kaley, are you engaging in premarital sex?"

Unfortunately, harassment is still a reality of life in this country. For a variety of reasons, including the fact that some adolescents feel powerless in many aspects of their lives, students might engage in it. Although victims cannot be blamed for its occurrence, student teachers are well advised to think about the way they present themselves both in the classroom and in other areas of school life. Maintaining the adult presence necessary for effective leadership also helps delineate a line between teacher (adult) and student (child). This is not a fool-proof method for avoiding harassment, but it certainly cannot hurt. Additionally, student teachers should remember that good teaching empowers students, allowing them to exercise control over their futures in more productive ways.

Overall, in dealing with sexual problems, we recommend the following:

1. Avoid impulsive reactions to sexual talk and behavior. What each of us has learned about acceptable references to sex varies from individual to individual, family to family, and culture to culture. What is acceptable to you may be frowned on in some communities, whereas what you disapprove of or are even shocked by may be acceptable in the school district to which you are assigned. Furthermore, the code of acceptable speech and behavior that you learned in elementary and high school may have changed drastically in the intervening years.

   Needless to say, we are not arguing for a do-as-you-may policy in regard to the use of sexual expressions. However, we are arguing against a teacher reacting impulsively with self-righteousness or outrage. To guard against that kind of response we advise you to curb any tendency to act based on your emotional reaction alone, and instead to be thoughtful about coping with the use of sex language and behavior that disrupts the class or upsets you.

2. In this area, as in others, preparation is a key to effective classroom management. Talk to your cooperating teacher and to fellow teachers to learn what their practices, preferences, and rules are. Ask them about what problems have come up this year and in past ones. Think about how you would handle different situations that might arise.

3. When a student uses sexualized language that disrupts the class, treat the behavior as you would any other. You will want to stop the disturbance, which is sometimes best achieved by ignoring the provocation. You will, in any event, want to pursue two steps in dealing with a student who makes regular use of sex language that deviates from the mores of the school. The first step is to consider the reasons for the behavior. For example, does this student come from a family very different in culture or social class from the rest? Alternatively, has this student learned that sex language gives him or her attention and relationships not otherwise attainable with his or her repertoire of social skills?

   The second step is to develop a plan of action. If it turns out that the student is employing home-bred vocabulary, a discussion with him or her (and with the parents) is in order, not to express disapproval of the family's language, but to explain the difference between acceptable language usage at home and at school. In the more likely event that the student uses sexual expressions to gain attention (sometimes by provoking the teacher), your plan should involve the same steps you would use to eliminate any other disruptive behavior.

The subject of sex has become more public and prominent during the past several decades. Complex social forces led to more open discussion of the topic and to the infusion of highly sexualized content in films, television, and popular music. Naturally, school atmosphere and class discussions are bound to be affected by these societal changes and by the fact that children are getting a good deal of exposure to sexual issues at young ages. During the 1980s, with the rise in the incidence of AIDS, the nature and prevention of this disease became subjects for discussion in many high schools, and in some, condoms were, and continue to be, freely distributed.

As you know, there are no easy answers to the enormous social and health problems related to child and adolescent sexuality. Teachers can only do their best to help students, in age-appropriate ways, to understand and cope with the effects of living in a sexually charged society.

THE DISRUPTIVE STUDENT

Disruptive students leave the student teacher frustrated. The experience of working with them can be instructive, however, and in some instances and to some extent, the students can be helped. However, we do not minimize the difficulty of working with such students or even having them in class. It is not easy to contend with students like Donna, who shouts at her second-grade teacher, "Don't tell me what to do, you bitch you."

Not only do such students drain teachers' time and patience, but if appropriate steps are not taken, they can also leave too little time for teachers to attend to other students in need. A study of 1,013 fourth-grade students revealed just that: When investigators (Finn, Pannozzo, & Voelkl, 1995) examined the relation between achievement and teachers' ratings of behavior, they found that disruptive students' achievement scores were significantly lower than the compliant students' scores; they also found that the inattentive and withdrawn students scored even lower. Teachers tend to ignore the inattentive and withdrawn while giving much attention to the disruptive. However, teachers who are aware of such dangers can use logical problem-solving techniques like COURAGE to develop strategies to deal with this problem.

In an earlier journal entry Julie had referred to Lucas as "the kid who's had me climbing the walls." Let us examine how she dealt with this disruptive student:

3/3: Lucas was back to some of his tricks today—banging his feet on the floor during show-and-tell. When asked to stop he replied, "I don't care—I don't want to see anyone's show-and-tell. . . . I don't have a show-and-tell anyway."

On the other days I had answered angrily and tried to out-shout him. I knew that didn't work and I'd better try something else. I tried to handle his statement in the best way, a considerate way. I explained that show-and-tell was a time to listen and that the class members have something they want to share with us. It is important that we are polite and listen together. I also invited him to bring in something for show-and-tell. I reminded him that show-and-tell objects can be lots of things—an interesting rock you find on the way to school, pine cones—things that he may be able to find.

A few days later Julie had the kind of poignant experience in her relationship with Lucas that represents some of the rewards in the difficult profession of teaching. However, Julie also showed that she is a realist and does not expect that a few constructive interactions with a child can counteract all that is destructive. She also demonstrated how positive a force a student teacher can be, whether or not that experience elicits a permanent change in the child's behavior.

3/8: Today Lucas again was disruptive (singing, stomping his feet, pounding his hands) during show-and-tell. When I asked him to stop, he continued, saying, "I don't want to listen." I got to the point where I just tried ignoring his behavior, knowing that attention was only reinforcing his behavior. But he persisted.

At library time I stayed in the classroom with Lucas (he had not returned his library book and said he didn't want to go to the library anyway). I asked him why he thought I had kept him from the library today, and he knew exactly why. We began just to talk, and he was very open. I didn't want to lecture him. I wanted to try and get through to why he is so unhappy. At one point I just wanted to cry for him. He asked me why he had no friends, and I explained that whenever anyone tries to be his friend he hits, bites, or kicks them and people don't like that. I told him that he had to be nicer to others and they'd be nicer to him. He then asked, "How can I like other people when I don't even like myself?"

What a horrible thing for a 6-year-old to be going through. No amount of discipline is going to solve Lucas's problem. He seems crushed, feels he can't do anything right. He has no self-esteem at all. I could only encourage him and point out all that he has to offer all of us. At the end of our talk he seemed more convinced of his worth, but our one little bull session alone can't change him. As we walked down the hall to the library from the class, he reached over and took my hand to walk with him.

At that point I felt something very special. He had confided in me and that made me happy. And he showed me how much he needed encouragement. . . . I don't want Lucas to be a puppet—doing everything I ask him to do without any comment. I just want him to be a happy little boy for once in his life (I have never seen Lucas laugh).

3/9: Today I made a special point to talk to Lucas individually. I feel that he needs the extra attention desperately. He had a show-and-tell today. As much as I have mixed feelings about this activity, I was glad to see him get involved. His show-

and-tell was a poem he had copied for his mom. . . . He did a neat job, and I made sure that I praised his good work.

Lucas, as Julie now understood, had not sprouted angel's wings. He was a troubled boy, and she knew she would be pressed to contend with him in ways that would protect the class from disruption and him from behaviors that alienated him from his peers. Now at least she understood him better and was not setting impossible goals for him or herself. Julie was shaken when Lucas asked how he could like other people when he didn't like himself. Had she realized that he was probably parroting a parent or teacher when he spoke those words, she might not have reacted so strongly.

Like Julie, Jane, too, came to realize that she had been expecting too much too soon. In her journal she explained that after much thought and soul-searching she came to realize that, to date, she had done little "actual teaching" in her cooperating school. She continued:

2/25: All I have done is just discipline these kids. But every time I think I am getting somewhere and have a few rules set up, they fall apart when Miss F. tries them. I like her and I think she has some fantastic ideas about teaching, but she has not helped these kids form any self-control at all. I don't know how to do it either and sometimes I feel down about it, but now I'm getting the feeling that I need time. This year, next year, I don't know when, but I'll help the kids in my class.

Dorothy had a different problem. After 1 week of student teaching she had that desperate feeling that is so common to the student teacher: They do not take me seriously. It is the sensation that leads the young teacher to yearn for Friday afternoon and to dread Monday morning. For the stout-hearted, that feeling is also a challenge. Dorothy was stout-hearted. At a critical time she did not collapse, even under the turmoil she experienced:

1/14: The substitute was unable to come, so I had to take complete control of our class. I had discovered that the children did not take what I said to them seriously, because all I had been doing was threatening and not carrying things out. I kept telling April, Horace, and Thomas to stop running around the room and making jokes during my explanation of their arithmetic assignment. Was I going to be beaten by this? I decided I would not.

As soon as I got the rest of the class settled down and doing their math (accomplished this by telling them at 1:15 I would collect their papers), I took April, Horace, and Thomas out in the hall. I discussed with them how they were disturbing the class, plus I gave them an opportunity to explain their behavior. Well, all they could do was giggle and make smart remarks. Therefore, I proceeded to take them to the principal's office.

When we got there I became sick all over—the only thing I could picture was him calling their parents and the beatings they would get at home. All of a sudden I felt sorry for them and wanted to cry and tell the principal to forget it. But it was too late, and thank God he only made them stand in the corner outside his office. I'm really afraid that if he had mentioned calling their parents, I would have asked him not to. Someday I'll have to face such a situation—and how am I going to handle it? I really don't think I can answer until I'm in the actual situation, but I must get my logic together so I can support however I react.

1/15: Continued having problems with Horace, Thomas, and Martin. Therefore I kept them in the room while the rest of the class went to a film. I wanted the punishment to be constructive, so I had them help straighten up the room, then made them sit in their seats for approximately 5 minutes. Then we four went to the film.

Firmness, plus understanding, combined with perseverance and use of problem-solving techniques like COURAGE, is necessary in coping with disruptive students.

THE STUDENT WHO STEALS

Discovering that students are stealing is upsetting. One student teacher, Celia, told about an incident that we mention only to alert others to the need for care in safeguarding valuables and avoiding temptation for children and adolescents.

6/2: I got to school late and parked my car in the last faculty spot, adjacent to the student lot. I had more than I could carry in the car and left my tape recorder and papers on the front seat. I came out between first and second periods, but the tape recorder was gone.

Celia was student teaching in a suburban high school. Sandra, whose journal appears here, was assigned to an elementary school:

3/23: An unfortunate incident: While we were out on a nature walk, someone took money from my pocketbook in the coat area of our room. There is one fifth-grade boy in another class who has a record of doing this. I reported it to the school the next day because it wasn't discovered until I got home.

Thefts of this kind occur for a variety of reasons. Some are obvious ones like wanting (or needing) money for its own use. Others are indirect ones, like getting back at an authority figure for what has been perceived as an injustice, abuse, or grievance of some kind.

A student teacher should take preventive and self-protective measures. If you are victimized and the guilty party has been identified, it is wise to avoid indignation. Instead, react like the rational authority who disapproves of the behavior: Apply appropriate discipline and try to get the individual to face up to the reasons for the offense.

One of us had an experience many years ago that was different from Sandra's in that another pupil's property was taken. In general, the reasons for such thefts are somewhat different from those perpetrated against the teacher. Although the child or adolescent can be motivated by the overpowering desire to have the money or the property taken, it can also be instigated by envy of another student's success, beauty, popularity, relative wealth, athletic skills, and so on.

In the experience just referred to, one of us was the teacher of a seventh-grade class in which Ralph was seen going through the backpack of another boy, Lewis. The teacher was not surprised by this behavior because Ralph, who was husky for his age, acted the part of the bully with weaker boys after school and surreptitiously tried to provoke fellow students in class. The following is an approximate account of the interaction between the teacher and Ralph at the end of the class period after the other students had been dismissed for lunch.

Teacher: Ralph, is there something you want to tell me?

Ralph: What about? I don't know what you're talking about.

Teacher: About what you did in class this period.

Ralph: I don't know what you're talking about. I worked on the reports.

Teacher: [looking intently but not angrily] You don't know what I'm talking about?

Ralph: [shifting uncomfortably in his seat] Well . . . no . . . I don't.

Teacher: Let's just sit here until you remember what you did this period, apart from some work. Something you did that you should never do.

Ralph: [after a moment's pause] What's the big deal? I didn't take anything.

Teacher: You didn't take anything?

Ralph: No.

Teacher: Well, just to be sure, let's get Lewis in on this. We'll have him examine his bag right here in front of us.

Ralph: No! Don't call him. I'll give it back.

Teacher: Mmmmm . . .

Ralph: I just took a Scout badge. I'll give it back. [He gets up to leave.]

Teacher: Hold on, Ralph. What are you going to say to Lewis?

Ralph: [looking puzzled and angry] I don't know.

Teacher: If you go to Lewis this way you'll just cause even more trouble for yourself. I'll give you a few more minutes of my time to help you prepare.

Ralph: [angrily] What do you want me to say—I stole your Scout badge? Here it is?

Teacher: I offered to help and you got angry. Is that what you do when people try to help you?

Ralph: Nobody helps me. I don't need it.

Teacher: Don't need it?

Ralph: [after a long pause] I'll say I'm sorry. I'll say I won't do it again.

Teacher: Yes, Ralph, and that's a good thing to say.

Ralph: [at peace for the first time] Can I go now?

Teacher: When will you see Lewis?

Ralph: In the cafeteria.

Teacher: All right. You may go now. But I want to see you again after you've spoken with Lewis.

Although aspects of this vignette are dated (in particular, a Scout badge might not be the first thing seventh graders would think to steal nowadays), the teacher's strategy is not. The objective is clear: to handle the situation in the most constructive way possible. This means that Lewis's property will be returned and Ralph will learn from the encounter. A change in his behavior is the goal.

The teacher did not cause Ralph to become defensive, did not get aroused by Ralph's initial belligerence, and did not get angry when Ralph denied that he had engaged in any untoward behavior. The teacher, through an understanding approach that involved following Ralph's feelings closely, sought only to have Ralph remedy his behavior. The teacher knew that a heavy punitive approach would do much less for Ralph than one that elicited his thought and behavioral change.

EXPECTING THE UNEXPECTED

Expect the unexpected because it will happen. It is part of what makes a career in education continually challenging and stimulating. Some of the behaviors and events we consider to be unexpected include: fights; tobacco, drug, and alcohol use; weapon discovery; health emergencies such as epileptic seizures or diabetic ketoacidosis; a suicide attempt by one of your students; the death of one of your student's parents, the appearance of strangers in class; and eruptions at parent conferences between divorced or separated spouses. By expecting the unexpected you will be less surprised when events occur, and therefore better able to cope with realities.

We all know that we are supposed to "keep our cool" when faced with such events, but the question is how to do that. The best way is through preparation and rehearsal. Preparation means:

1. Knowing your students.
2. Knowing the resources in the school, including people you can count on in an emergency (e.g., a fellow teacher, nearby colleague, principal, vice-principal, school counselor, nurse, custodian, your most reliable students, etc.).
3. Mentally practicing the process of cooling down the atmosphere and feeling good that you were able to take control of the situation.
4. Imagining each of the "unexpecteds" just given happening, following through until you have dealt with each to your satisfaction.

Here is advice from experienced educators on handling common "unexpecteds" (Westling & Koorland, 1988):

• Fights: Firmly order the students to stop and separate. If they do not respond to your command, send for help and repeat the order. When they stop fighting, get all students back to work. At this point you want them involved, no matter in what. Later, in an atmosphere of calm, discuss the fight with each of the two students separately and apply class and/or school rules and disciplinary measures. Finally, talk with them about how such fights could be avoided in the future.
• Stealing: If you know who was the thief, find a time to discuss the action privately. If the theft is admitted and the item returned, the punishment should depend on whether this was the first offense. If the student does not confess, although you have no doubt that he or she is guilty, explain that you are disturbed both by the act and the denial. If the behavior is part of a persistent pattern, inform the guidance counselor or school psychologist. If you have no clues as to who committed the crime, do not punish the entire class, no matter how frustrated you may be.
• Foul language: Inquire whether there is a school or class rule about this. In your own class in the future, if there are no school rules, you may wish to make your own and announce and firmly enforce them.
• Health problems and physical accidents: Deal with the immediate situation, (e.g., a seizure, a fainting spell, a vomiting student, a bathroom accident) and then call for the school nurse or another person assigned to handle such problems. Do not move the student unless you have proper medical training; unless school rules allow it, do not administer drugs of any kind before speaking with the school nurse or a doctor. Prepare a written report of the incident, perhaps on a standard school form. Someone, perhaps you, will be expected to inform the parent. Be sure to plan for such occurrences in advance by having medical gloves on hand to protect you and others against contact with any bodily fluids.

With mental rehearsals and experience you will learn to take the unexpected in stride. That does not mean you will ever find it a favorite part of being a teacher. Zoey, who completed her student teaching in an elite, upper middle-class suburban school, heard what was considered flatly unacceptable language in the school community. The incident happened quickly, and Zoey, then halfway through her student teaching, did not know how to react. As she described in her journal:

> 11/12: I was standing with other teachers at recess but was clearly the only one who heard. I believe it was Mark (a really good kid) who, forgetting himself, yelled "shut the fuck up." I whipped my head around and saw him leaning in toward someone. In my mind, the other boy must have said something pretty hurtful. So both were at fault. I made eye contact with one of the onlooker boys (I don't teach him). He knew I heard. I just stared for a minute or two. I guess I was waiting to see if it would escalate. I should have gone over there, I suppose. But I don't know what I should have said. I certainly wouldn't have given a detention. In my mind, so many other things are more wrong. And after four years of college dorms, I've been deadened to obscenities. The words are used so frequently now they've lost their shock value, at least to my generation. But I realize that by not doing anything I may have been labeled a "cool" teacher, and I don't want the "good" kids to be scared off. That language might have frightened me in 8th grade. But *Mark* is such a good kid. I really want to talk to someone about this, but I feel like everyone at school will be too judgmental.

Despite the fact that the incident took place during recess, and therefore out of view of the majority of her students, Zoey found it highly troubling. It led her to consider not only her own values, but also those she as teacher might be obligated to encourage. Her experience illustrates both the importance of thinking about such unexpected incidents before they occur and the necessity of becoming familiar with classroom, school, and community expectations and policy to effectively cope with them when they do arise.

GROWTH IN COPING

Few of the student teachers' journals we collected or the interviews we conducted had 100% happy endings. What they reported was the mixture of successes and failures characteristic of real life. Many student teachers showed enormous growth during their few months of student teaching. Among their other accomplishments, the successful student teachers had become more effective in maintaining a disciplined class.

They learned that they, themselves, were ready to make the transition from student to teacher. In that process, they came to understand that teachers cannot help students by pretending to be their peers or by avoiding the use of the authority assigned to them. They discovered that being a classroom leader is not the same as being a martinet. At the same time, however, they realized that freedom in an orderly system that has its own rules is different from the anarchy of a laissez faire, do-as-you-choose classroom. Most important, they came to understand that although they had learned much in a matter of mere months, it was only a beginning, just as it was intended to be. Years of opportunity for growth as a teacher lay ahead.

A study of the journals shows that student teachers began at different levels with regard to their ability to manage a class and ended at different levels, too, just as you would expect. Among those who encountered and successfully overcame the toughest discipline problems, however, there was one common element: They all employed a systematic problem-solving process in working things through. In other words, although most of them did not have access to a prepackaged problem-solving plan like COURAGE, they did, on their own, develop and follow procedures much like COURAGE.

This meant that these successful student teachers used whatever information they could piece together about the problem they faced to develop one or more solution strategies. Because they had journals, they could look back and see what thoughts they had since Day 1. Without their journals, they could not have detected the changes that took place in their thinking, and they would have had difficulty remembering clearly what their earlier reactions were.

The most successful student teachers worked persistently at specifying the problems they were facing and struggling to understand them. To accomplish this, most talked their thoughts and ideas over with their fellow professionals (in and out of seminar) and with friends.

By the end of their assignment, successful student teachers had begun to come to terms with the real life of the teacher. Some students, they realized, came to school unhappy, angry, and belligerent. They had learned to contend with those emotions, and especially the behavior that they stimulated.

Malvina was well into her term as a student teacher in the sixth grade of a New York City school, still working only with individuals and small groups. She saw firsthand how classroom management problems are compounded when a student suffers from chronically uncontrollable angry outbursts. By the end of her assignment, she had learned how to effectively cope with this.

3/6: During the math lesson (which followed the morning reading period), Richard started banging and whistling. Mr. B. spoke to him privately by going up to his desk. The disturbances continued, but Mr. B. ignored him. The noise was beginning to have its effects on the rest of the class. I hesitated, but finally decided it wasn't worth it to the rest of the class to let the commotion go on. I asked him to stop; he now put away the mirror that Mr. B. told him to stop playing with. The disturbances continued. I asked him if he wanted to come to the back of the room so I could baby-sit for him. He was unwilling to come and I wasn't going to physically force him. The noise still continued. I took my chair and my work and sat next to him. I kept him calm enough so he did not upset the whole class (and I felt that was crucial).

Student teachers like Malvina who have gone to disciplined schools and then to college are upset at first when a boy like Richard (age 13 and above average in height and weight) bangs on his desk and whistles with no evident provocation, and furthermore continues after his teacher tells him to stop. Two months later, Malvina, who had been stunned by his behavior earlier in the term, handled it in stride. She also had an experience with Richard that gave her hope, very tentative, but hope nevertheless.

> 5/10: I had my first good experience with Richard today. The kids were allowed to make Mother's Day cards. Richard wanted some help in writing something. I had him respond to "What does your mother do for you?" He mentioned close to ten things. I listed them in a nice poetic arrangement. He just sort of looked at me in the end and said distinctly and with feeling, "Thank you, Miss R." Mr. B. saw and heard him do it and nodded to me. He apparently felt as I did. I had really "reached" Richard for a moment—and that's a hard thing to do.

Malvina had indeed reached Richard. Her success, momentary though it might have been, shows how much in the way of understanding, attention, and support some students in our schools need. This can be done only on an individual basis, and to do that, teachers typically require more assistance and smaller classes than they get. But as in Richard's case, small attentions such as Malvina gave can help, even if not enough to reverse the damage and present distress. In any event, Malvina's hopes were set back a few days later.

> 5/14: During a morning lesson time, Mr. B. indicated he had to step out for a moment. I continued with the lesson. All of a sudden a chair is turned over and Richard starts shouting. I had seen Richard go off like this once or twice before. He climbed to a chair, to a desk and kept challenging and baiting Harold to fight him. Harold, normally very patient with Richard, wouldn't put up with it any longer and started to fight. The rest of the class grew rather quiet and inactive. I moved to the back of the room and attempted to separate the boys by placing myself between them. Harold came (with my urging and pulling, if I remember correctly) to the front of the room. Richard kept baiting him and he began to fight. I called to the boys in the class and asked for some help. I had them hold Harold back. I also had worked hard to calm Richard, telling him it couldn't be settled by fighting in school and that I didn't want to be hurt. I took Richard out of the room.

By this point in the term Malvina had become almost expert at handling these crises, even to the extent of soliciting the help of the other students. Following the principle that there can be no learning in a class devastated by conflict, she took action to quell the fight and win a degree of tranquility. Malvina began to look for a pattern to understand Richard's behavior and she found one.

> 5/21: I noticed something rather interesting about Richard. At the end of the [field] trip today he began to "go off." I have the feeling that when things begin to go too well, Richard finds something to "go off" for. During our trip today Mr. B. and I were able to give him more attention—instead of making him happier, he acts up. And it's been true when things get good in the classroom too. This also fits with his answer to the psychologist's form when he said he usually expects bad or unhappy things to happen. How do you deal with a problem like this?

Some people are so accustomed to "things going wrong" that not only do they expect it, but they also make it happen. They help bring about problems so that the world behaves in the only way they know. They are not happy in that state, but they are at least accustomed to it. A teacher's task working with Richard (and those like him) is to try to help him learn and grow, to become accustomed to things going well. Malvina tried to do that, but she had no illusion about the obstacles both within Richard himself and in the circumstances in the school.

If we are to be effective classroom managers in coping with tough problems, we benefit by taking both a broad and a narrow view of the situations we face. We ask ourselves what, if anything, we might be doing to create or maintain discipline problems and, further, what we might be able to do to curb them. At the same time we are aware that some disruptive behavior has been stirred up elsewhere, perhaps by conditions at home or by those in school but not in our classroom. In this case, too, a logical problem-solving technique like COURAGE will help us develop techniques useful in managing the classroom and coping with tough problems.

CRITICAL ISSUES

- What is your reaction, emotionally and behaviorally, when a student disrupts the class?
- What approaches will you feel comfortable using to handle disruptive students? Intimidating students? Students with low self-esteem?
- What steps can you take to prevent outbreaks in class?
- Consider an "unexpected" event you have faced or heard about—perhaps learning a child was abused, or confronting a student who cheated, stole, or fought. How was the situation handled? What could be done differently next time?
- What help do you feel you need to learn to manage the "tough problems"?
- What results have you had in applying a problem-solving method like COURAGE to tough problems?

PART IV

Today and Tomorrow

11

The Student Teacher as a Person

TOPICS

- Coping With Controlled Exhaustion
- Reacting to Being Criticized
- Discovering That Teachers Are People
- Overcoming Self-Doubt
- Coping With Stress
- Coping With Legal and Ethical Issues
    - Getting to Know Relevant Educational Law and Legal Issues
    - Getting to Know Relevant Educational Ethics Codes
- Becoming Socialized as a Teacher
    - Coaching
    - Peer Involvement
    - Legitimacy
- When Coaches Don't Coach: Appreciating the College/University Supervisor's Support
- Growing in the "School of Hard Knocks"

In actuality, student teachers as people are hardly separable from student teachers as preprofessionals. Only for the sake of emphasis do we have a chapter of this kind.

In this chapter the focus is on the people behind the student teachers and the human emotions they experience. We present nine kinds of experiences common to student teachers. All of them have the potential for promoting personal growth.

COPING WITH CONTROLLED EXHAUSTION

Many student teachers find their experience exhausting. Knowing that their future career depends on success during this period, they invest their whole self into it. Contending with the behavior of unruly, disruptive, and unmotivated students takes a further and heavy toll of energy and peace of mind. Beyond that, the tension from being under observation by itself is fatiguing. This last factor is sometimes compounded by overt and covert differences about important matters, most significant of which is whether the student teacher will be permitted to teach in a way that fits his or her personal style.

Besides all this, sometimes the student teacher has further academic requirements to meet during this time. Then there is one's personal life. "How can I leave the worries and pressures of my class behind," the student teacher wonders "so that I can enjoy tonight's get-together with my friends?" Here is Joyce, halfway through her student teaching:

> 2/11: Boy, it's Friday. TGIF. Change of pace for a weekend. Teaching can really get you down. I haven't developed the ability to leave school at school. Maybe it's because I'm always so busy planning for tomorrow.

> In my opinion, teaching this quarter has made me aware of the stamina I'm going to need if I get a regular position. Like, I'm almost totally exhausted after 5 or 6 weeks. What will I be like after 5 or 6 months! Beats me.

At points the time pressures can become so great that even medical appointments are put off as low priorities. Ruby wrote:

> 2/18: I had a lot of trouble controlling the class, perhaps because it was Friday or perhaps it was just because I hadn't been here on Thursday. . . . I went back to do my bulletin board and it took me from 3:00 to 7:15, which meant that I had to cancel my doctor's appointment. I'll have to get my iron shot Saturday.

When it seems there is no time to complete the planning, grading, and self-reflection necessary for a productive day at school, student teachers often make the mistake of cutting out what college students often deem expendable: sleep. Unlike their college classmates, however, student teachers need to be wide awake at 8 a.m., with no possibility for an afternoon nap. As Janice began to realize, proper rest is essential for teaching at one's best:

> 1/10: Five hours of sleep is enough to kill you. I'm in finals mode and it's just day #2 of full-day teaching. In many respects today went better than the first. Things went fairly smoothly, although we had a fire drill first period, so no movie (after I so carefully timed everything out at 1 a.m. last night). I must get to sleep earlier tonight!

Some fatigue is due to inexperience in performing a task that is in itself tiring. Gary, a high school English student teacher, explained:

> 3/11: This week, at last, I got the chance to read the students' papers. I wrote comments and put grades on them (lightly in pencil). Great, but I feel I've been through

the meat-grinder. Four classes turned their papers in on the same day (it's the end
of the marking period). How much of this can you stand? Or do you get used to it?

As demanding as student teaching is, most individuals muster the energy
and the hours necessary to emerge from it stronger as teachers and people than
they were at the beginning. Awareness of the limited time frame is one positive
factor. Even more important is the conviction that this road leads to a lifetime
profession.

If exhaustion is sapping your strength, take steps to adjust. Set aside sufficient
time each day for sleep, relaxation, pleasure, reading, exercise, a favorite television show, or playing the piano. Frequently, the emotional demands of student
teaching, not just the long hours, bring about that exhausted feeling. Putting your
life into balance, with time set aside for pleasurable activities, will help you
manage your emotions and combat that feeling of exhaustion, both now and in
the future. You owe it to yourself—and to your students—to wake up in the
morning rested and relaxed enough to teach with energy, enthusiasm, and grace.
Some of the suggestions in the section on coping with stress later in this chapter
will help you contend with exhaustion.

REACTING TO BEING CRITICIZED

Criticism is an essential ingredient in the development of professionals. Artists,
actors, and athletes depend on it to enhance their growth in their respective
fields. We as teachers need it, too.

Teachers regularly use imaginative ways to translate their classrooms into effective learning environments; that is, classrooms that are physically and psychologically conducive to learning. When their innovations are effective, they
excite and generate great interest. However, one cannot expect that every new
idea will work as planned. Some do not. Criticism and self-criticism, as long as
these are constructive, help the teacher learn from ideas that did not work as expected, and therefore develop professionally.

As for student teachers, criticism may be forthcoming for a number of reasons and most of all because a method used was simply not effective. Sometimes
a method is not used effectively because it has been learned from a professor's
lecture and then applied to an inappropriate situation. In other instances, the
method may fail because it is too different from what students are accustomed
to. Sometimes, as a result of the "strangeness" of a method, criticism may come
from quite an unexpected source, as Laura discovered:

1/29: Today was a good day with one exception. One of the girls told me that a boy
said I was a stupid teacher. That really hurt. I couldn't figure out why he would
have said it. I hadn't reprimanded him or anything like that. The only thing I could

think of was that I had done some things differently from Mrs. W., so that maybe that's why he thought I was stupid. It was a blow to my ego, but I suppose it won't be the only time it will happen.

Hearing criticism from one's students is infrequent. Most criticism will come from cooperating teachers, as the very purpose of student teaching is to have practical experience accompanied by vigorous and constructive critiques. For some student teachers, however, the criticisms are difficult to cope with, even when the student recognizes them to be valid. With time, self-confidence, and a growing comfort in the classroom, criticism becomes increasingly easy to accept and to use.

Occasionally, however, a difference in temperament or teaching style leads to ongoing, difficult-to-deal-with criticism such as Lynn was subjected to:

3/5: Today was another bad day. Mrs. S. thought I took too long doing the math paper with the children. She felt the children would grow to dislike math if the papers were drawn out too long. I must be in a sensitive mood because I really feel low. I mean, her criticisms really got to me. I'm beginning to doubt whether I'll ever make a teacher and in fact if I want to be one. If I had to teach this way in a regular teaching position I don't think I could last.

Mrs. S. criticized Lynn for the same faults day after day. Why? Mrs. S.'s way of teaching worked. By that we mean that what she did (i.e., employing a crisp, thoroughly controlled form of drill), she did effectively. She believed that it was in the students' interest for Lynn to use this same mode of instruction. However, Lynn resisted, preferring an approach she had used during an earlier school field experience.

Lynn's journal alerted the college supervisor to this problem, and a conference with Mrs. S. and Lynn softened the cooperating teacher's stance and Lynn's strong reaction to criticism. Lynn then tried Mrs. S.'s method and found that she could work with it, a discovery that gave her more confidence in the classroom and also increased her repertoire of teaching skills.

The skills you develop during student teaching are often very different from those you acquired in your education courses. In those courses you were responsible for more abstract learning, writing papers that demonstrated your understanding of concepts and a broad base of knowledge. But when you teach you need other skills: personal presence, the ability to hold youngsters' attention, flexibility in planning, and "eyes in the back of your head."

Your cooperating teacher's role is to help you learn these skills. Still, these are new skills and you may have difficulty rapidly incorporating them into your repertoire of behaviors and blending them with your college learning. You may feel angered, frustrated, and uncomfortable when your cooperating teacher criticizes you. If his or her criticism gets you down, use COURAGE and consider ways of dealing with the problem, such as having a discussion with your supervisor.

Maureena's comments show that she finally recognized the benefit of her co-operating teacher's criticism:

> All term long Jan criticized my teaching. Day after day. I didn't keep the kids interest (hey, they are high schoolers and almost adults), I didn't stick to my schedule every period (hey, I finished all the units on time), etc. But listening to her and working hard paid off. When I got my written evaluation and letter of reference, I was *mucho* pleased. They were very positive.

DISCOVERING THAT TEACHERS ARE PEOPLE

Perhaps you can recall an experience years ago when, by chance, you encountered a teacher of yours in a supermarket or at a mall. You may have been surprised to see her engaged in so prosaic an activity as shopping. One of the rarely discussed benefits of the student-teaching experience is the opportunity it provides to shatter myths. Teachers are people; they are very human.

The humanness of teachers leads them at times to be less than saintly in their personal behavior. You will find when you spend a free period in the faculty lounge that teachers do not often discuss Schopenhauer's philosophy or Greek tragedies or even the newest educational practices. They often discuss their classes and students but just as often they discuss their children, their families, football games, vacations, dates, and yes, school gossip.

Some student teachers come to their first teaching experience with "stars in their eyes," expecting their teacher peers to be like the idealized version of one or two exceptional teachers in their own past. What disenchantment to witness teachers expose their feet of clay, as Amy reported.

> 3/1: The time I spent in the teacher's lounge today disillusioned me. All I heard was malicious gossip. I wonder what they said about me when I walked out!

> One day during one of my free periods, I was on the phone for about 5 minutes with my roommate. I had been in the midst of some personal problems, and was in a foul mood; however, I managed to keep my voice slightly above a whisper when she asked me how school was going. . . . I was later informed that one of the teachers who had a reputation for eavesdropping at every chance had heard my conversation and repeated it. This is one example of how the teachers in this school constantly work against one another. It is true that what I said was not complimentary; however, the important thing, as far as I am concerned, was that my attitude did not conflict with my teaching, which was my sole reason for being in the school.

Perhaps the behavior of the informer in Amy's case could be attributed to an excessive and mindless loyalty to the school; or, to be charitable, even to a more admirable motive: concern about Amy's dissatisfaction and a desire to have her obtain more assistance. Regardless of the eavesdropper's motive, the lesson is the same. Use the same good sense in sharing thoughts about your school experience in the teacher's room as you would in the staff room in any other organization. As Amy painfully learned, it is hardly the place to talk in uncomplimentary terms about your employer.

Ira also reported an example of the demystification of the teaching profession. He attended a faculty meeting and soon discovered that the process of school governance, far from being romantic, is often a bore and a drudge, even as it is essential.

> 3/22: What a day of enlightenment; I attended a "Teachers' Meeting" today after school. It is absolutely amazing how people can and do blow such little things completely out of proportion. I never before heard such argumentation and heated discussions over such petty items. To hear some of the conversation you would never guess that these were all educated people talking.

Over time, Ira will come to appreciate the importance of staff meetings that give teachers the opportunity to contribute to policymaking in their school building. As more school systems move toward decentralization, such meetings will assume increased importance. Even if the principal or chair of the meeting is not effective as a group leader and much time is wasted, the bottom line is this: You can only put in your view and work for change in faculty meetings if you are present and participate.

Teachers can, of course, be excellent as instructors without actively participating in teachers' meetings or, for that matter, socializing in the teachers' room. You make your own choices. Whether you choose to isolate yourself or not, you should do it with your eyes open, recognizing, on the one hand, that teachers are indeed human and behave like human beings. On the other hand, you can learn a great deal from out-of-classroom interactions with teachers. You will also come to see that the welfare of your professional group depends on its organizational strength.

OVERCOMING SELF-DOUBT

One of the toughest obstacles to overcome in teaching, as in almost every human endeavor, is self-doubt. It usually does not announce itself or make itself known in obvious ways. It comes on wearing different cloaks. For Elaine, who had been having a relatively good time of it as a student teacher, it first took the form of insecurity about the future.

> 3/25: Besides not feeling well, I really didn't want to go to school today. I am worried about my plans for next year, about finishing courses this year, and I am preoccupied with other things. Since I am teaching, I feel kind of left out of college life. I feel like I've already graduated and am in a world of my own. I guess I'm getting kind of scared about the insecurities of the future and it is affecting my interest in teaching.

Elaine had been excessively demanding of herself. Does that kind of drive make one an exceptional teacher? The answer, unequivocally, is no. People who constantly demand more of themselves rarely find any lasting satisfaction in their accomplishments. They whip themselves so unmercifully that, even apart from any concern we might have about their personal contentment, they are so stressed that they are subject to cracking under the strain of any new tension.

Elaine was so stressed that her confidence and self-esteem showed signs of erosion in the presence of a substitute teacher. Note that these losses were not caused by any identifiable behavior on the part of the substitute, but rather by Elaine's conclusion that under a set of new circumstances, the hospitalization of her cooperating teacher and the arrival (March 31) of a substitute, she had to prove herself all over again.

> 3/30: Today did not go well at all—I didn't get "good vibes" from the kids nor did I feel much was accomplished. I am so frustrated by the fact the kids are dependent on adult direction; also, the room, the way it looks is not making me too happy. I wonder if I am being "lazy" and not doing enough. Today I found out Mrs. R. had gone into the hospital and I had the full responsibility for the kids—it was all on me. I am glad today is over.

> 3/31: Today was no better. I feel as if the substitute was looking at me very curiously and saying to herself: She doesn't know what she is doing—I would do it this way. I "won" Mrs. R.'s respect, and now it's as if I have to prove myself all over again. I think I'm afraid to assert myself today with her. I don't know my limit or how far I should go. I'm beginning to wish everything was over.

> 4/1: I have the same doubts today as I did Tuesday and Wednesday. I had the confidence that what I was doing was right, but now I'm beginning to wonder. Having to win approval of the substitute is really putting pressure on me. I seem so uncreative and unimaginative compared to her. I don't know. I feel as if I'm doing a terrible job with the class. I don't think I'm enjoying my experience as much as before. I sense I can do it, but I feel her critical eyes all over me all the time. I'm glad the day is over!

On 3/30 Elaine learned that her cooperating teacher had gone to the hospital. She was alone with the children, and there was no substitute teacher. She felt "lazy" as if, when there was no one present whose approval she had to win, she did not have to expend energy. She was also concerned with the "looks" of things. Ironically she, who seemed so dependent on how other adults react to her, was frustrated that the kids were dependent on "adult direction."

By 3/31, her self-doubts reached the point at which she was projecting them on the substitute; that is, she acted as if she knew, without being told, that the substitute had a poor opinion of her. (Chances are the substitute had never been in a class with a student teacher, and she herself had to adapt to a new situation.) Elaine told us that she had to win the respect of the cooperating teacher and felt she had to start all over and do it again with the substitute.

On 4/1, her confidence ebbed as she compared herself with the substitute. Instead of benefiting from this opportunity to observe still another person's work as a teacher, Elaine used her observations to put herself down—nothing short of that. Instead of seeing teachers as colleagues from whom she could learn, she saw them as threats. She felt "critical eyes all over me all the time." With her supervisor she even raised the possibility of quitting.

Fortunately for Elaine and for everyone concerned, she had a capable and sensitive supervisor. In the margin of her 3/31 journal entry the supervisor wrote, "Elaine, we need to talk!" At the end of her 4/2 journal entry she noted:

> Elaine, bring this week's journals and let's get together. I've observed you and I know several things about you: (1) You have fine qualities. (2) You are doing many good things. (3) You are sensitive. (4) You are willing to try. The question is why don't you know this? In my own opinion, you have the potential of becoming an exceptionally good teacher, not just average, and I guess I'm wondering how we are seeing this at such opposite extremes.

Having a minicrisis of self-doubt, is part of life. It should not be the cause for withdrawing from teaching unless, at the end of the student teaching and after very careful analysis, a person decides the field is not for him or her. Instead the individual should do what Elaine did with help from her supervisor. First, she examined her journals. Through that process, she discovered that she was faced not with the problem of becoming a teacher, but with the problem of becoming an adult. She saw that she was dependent on the approval of her cooperating teacher, which we hasten to add is different from wanting healthy approval for her work (in the form of positive criticisms and a good grade).

Through conversations with her supervisor and others, Elaine saw that she constantly struggled with an urgent sense of anxiety that if she—her classroom or her teaching—did not look right to people, they would consider her a complete failure. Having seen this, Elaine learned to catch herself when she was having irrational thoughts that made her tense. When she felt others were criticizing her teaching and doubting her ability, she reminded herself of what was fact: She had been assured already that her work was much more than passable. After this crisis, Elaine completed her student teaching with relative ease.

Self-doubt is like any of the other problems student teachers encounter, and can be effectively dealt with in the same manner. If self-doubt begins to concern you, address it squarely. Use COURAGE or another logical problem-solving plan to delineate the issues, outline alternatives, and develop a solution.

One of the best ways to counter self-doubt is by being open to good feelings. If you allow yourself to experience positive thoughts, they will permeate your life. Brenda is a good model. As evident in her journal entries, she celebrated the good feelings she had during the course of her teaching day even though she knew she had much room for improvement. Brenda benefited from her ability to pause and praise herself for what she had already accomplished, noting that it not only furthered her professional development, but also carried over into her personal life.

> 1/28: I feel more confident than yesterday: the children responded more to me when I took over the morning routine, more than yesterday. For the first time I worked individually with a child . . . also I observed Kelly today. I'd like to help him deal with his bad temper. I'm starting to think about the meaning of being a teacher, and how I must think of myself as a teacher. It's really a nice feeling being loved, having the children hang on to you and hug you, but I must begin to think of what they are learning. Aren't they learning dependence by hanging on to me? What am I trying to teach them?

> I feel that I must gain more confidence in myself (and I feel confident I will) in order to be more effective not only as a teacher, but as a person.

> 2/13: I found that some confidence I am gaining here is spreading into a lot of my relationships outside of the classroom. I had been feeling stagnant, like I wasn't changing anymore, but now I feel more change and more confidence in dealing with both my Sunday school class and with certain close friends of mine, particularly ones I found it hard to talk to. I feel more able to talk now. I feel less afraid.

Student teaching is often a professional stepping stone and a transition point as you move forward into adulthood. No longer solely a student, you are on the front line, sharing responsibility for directing the education of others. This responsibility requires new skills and ways of thinking about yourself so that you come to fully enjoy your professional work. The transition is gradual, but most student teachers find that by the end of their teaching experience, the title "Mr." or "Ms." no longer sounds foreign. Although the name is but a symbol, it represents something more. Effective student teachers acquire a confident adult identity, at least in the confines of the school building, well before many of their college classmates.

COPING WITH STRESS

Daily life is often saturated with stress. Life events like a death in a family, a divorce, an illness, and unemployment create stress, but so do positive events like a marriage, a promotion, and a vacation. Furthermore, life's daily hassles such as commuting, cleaning, and shopping can be stressful. Psychologists have come to understand that individuals cannot live a stress-free life. We can, however, learn to cope with stress in effective and constructive ways rather than living with tension and headaches or, worse yet, resorting to alcohol, drugs, or other addictions as an escape.

Before we review good coping techniques, let us look at some findings about stress in student teaching. Forty-four secondary-school student teachers (some graduate, some undergraduate) completed a questionnaire in their last week of student teaching designed to gather information that might enable faculty to reduce the stress of student teachers (J. B. Davis, 1990). The respondents were asked questions about when they felt the most stress during student teaching, how intense it was, what factors contributed to the stress, which of the factors they considered the major cause of their stress, and what preventive measures might be taken.

Forty-three of the 44 said they experienced stress during student teaching. They used words like the following to describe how they felt: pressured, anxious, overwhelmed, tense, and overburdened. Given a choice as to what point during their student teaching they felt most stressed (beginning, middle, end, throughout), beginning was chosen most, but throughout was chosen almost as often.

The respondents listed these reasons, among others, for their stress at the beginning: new experience, new role, leaving college, entering the work world, unfamiliar setting, unfamiliar people (teachers, students), ambiguity about the role, and ambiguity about evaluation. The reasons the student teachers felt stress throughout their student-teaching assignment included time pressure (not enough time to plan lessons, construct tests, grade papers, etc.), classroom situation (problems in maintaining control, dealing with unmotivated students, etc.), and the cooperating teacher (the expectations and demands of that teacher, sometimes combined with a lack of direction or a personality clash).

J. B. Davis's (1990) study reported some silver linings. First, although the student teachers felt stressed completing their day-to-day school activities, most said that their feelings of stress would come and then be gone for a time. Another silver lining was in connection with the intensity of the stress: On a scale that ranged from slight to intolerable, on the average the student teachers chose moderate. Occasional, moderate stress can be managed, especially if you learn how to reduce its intensity and prevent the occurrence of some of it.

Lazarus and Folkman (1984), two psychologists well known for researching and writing about stress, proposed three useful ways to cope with stressful times:

1. Prevent stress to the extent possible. Do so by being prepared for each class, by being prepared for unexpected events, by learning all you can about classroom management, by having a thorough understanding of what the cooperating teacher expects of you, by arriving at school on time, by not carrying another job during the student teaching term, and so forth.
2. Modify stressors to the extent possible. Do so by arranging a conference with your cooperating teacher if uncertainty about his or her demands is stressful, by modifying your classroom behavior so that you can keep a better eye on the students, by applying your discipline plan as soon as student chatter irritates you, by being flexible in your daily lesson plans, and so forth.
3. Modify your reactions to stress to whatever extent possible by keeping things in perspective. Remind yourself that although student teaching is important, it is not the end all and be all of your life. Remember that there is life after student teaching. Here is how you can do that. Let us say that a few students are particularly

troublesome one day or that the cooperating teacher seems to ignore you on a particular afternoon. It is good to be able to appreciate that their own life's circumstances probably account for their behavior; do not allow it to depress you. Another way to modify your reactions to stress is by maintaining a balanced life. Do that by taking special care to incorporate relaxation and pleasure into your days during the student-teaching period.

Remember also that you alone are not going to solve the problems of the children or adolescents you are instructing. You may make a small impact, but you are working with them for only a short period of time. Year-long teachers, and to an even greater extent parents, counselors, mentors, tutors, and religious leaders, are likely to have more opportunities to help students, troubled or not, than you can in a short student-teaching stint.

COPING WITH LEGAL AND ETHICAL ISSUES

Legal and ethical issues belong in a chapter on the student teacher as a person because they touch on our personal thoughts and individual values. Although many student teachers find the thought of understanding complex laws and ethical codes rather daunting, knowledge of them is essential.

Getting to Know Relevant Educational Law and Legal Issues

Some U.S. laws are so relevant to the teaching profession that teachers need to be acquainted with them. We already discussed IDEA and ADA in chapter 7. We also briefly introduced laws related to suspected child abuse and neglect in chapter 10. Child abuse and neglect fall under the jurisdiction of state and local governments, so laws differ somewhat by state. All states, however, require that reasonable suspicion of abuse resulting in physical injury be reported in a timely fashion, which in most cases is 24 to 72 hours after an educator becomes aware of the situation. Almost all states have similar laws for abuse or neglect resulting in emotional or mental injury. Laws demand this even if reporting the suspicion violates confidential or privileged communication between teachers or counselors and students (Fischer et al., 1999).

You may not be involved in these matters. We introduce them to acquaint you with the fact that education law is extensive. Moreover, education law is by no means limited to issues about children with disabilities and children who are abused.

For example, some legal issues are relevant to classroom management and discipline in general. Consider teachers who must contend with both verbal and physical forms of disruption in their classrooms. How may they respond to the following?

- Verbal disruption: For example, a student screams and curses and refuses to leave the room.
- Public or private property damage: For example, a student smashes an electric globe of the world.
- Personal threat: For example, a student's behavior involves injury or the threat of injury to another student or a teacher.

From a legal point of view, verbal control, the major form of restraint, is generally acceptable, as is forceful behavior in defense of self or others. Forceful behavior under other than defensive conditions and touch control (or the laying of hands), however, are likely to be unacceptable in your jurisdiction.

The overriding question with regard to force revolves around the definition of reasonable force. Force may take the form of (a) verbal control, such as the teacher's use of oral and body language; (b) touch control, such as the use of a firm grip, leverage, or pain; and (c) defense, which is a teacher's forceful behavior to protect herself or someone else from injury.

Sexual misconduct, a legal issue that has become increasingly acknowledged and visible in the workplace, is also of central importance to today's educators. Long-standing school practices, such as hugging a high school senior who has just gotten into college or assisting a kindergartner struggling to buckle his or her pants, have been modified or changed because of the possibility, however small, that such acts could be misconstrued. Many school districts instruct teachers to always leave the door of their classroom open whenever conferring with just one student, regardless of age or gender. Similarly, they warn against physical contact of any kind between teachers and students.

In his article "Two Rules for Professional Conduct," music educator Stufft (1997) explained how he carefully considers alternatives to making physical contact with student musicians when he wishes to correct hand positioning on an instrument: "'Can I do it by example first?' 'Can I use pictures?' 'Can I use another student as a role model?'" (p. 42) he asks. If he does make physical contact with a student, he ensures that he does it gently and "while standing at a respectable distance" (p. 42). Other music teachers, he noted, often ask permission before touching a student: "May I correct the position of your left hand on the violin?" (Stufft, 1997, p. 42). Following such precautions protects both students and teachers. If you do not have information about what is permitted or advisable in your school, plan a meeting to discuss this legal issue with your supervisor.

Getting to Know Relevant Educational Ethics Codes

Ethical issues arise over a wide spectrum of behavior on the part of both teachers and students. We present a few ethical issues to illustrate the questions they raise and some coping (as well as preventive) measures you can take concerning these issues. We also introduce you to an educator's code of ethics.

As a student teacher you may not have to make difficult decisions that involve complex ethical issues. You may, however, witness your cooperating teacher involved in that kind of decision making, perhaps in connection with cheating on exams or homework or in deciding how to discipline a student. You may, like Karen, even have strong differences over school policy.

> 1/6: I have a difficult question, I think an ethical one, and it's about a situation that really annoys me. Sally had her head down on her desk during today's history lesson. After I assigned the class seat work and everyone had begun working I approached her and asked what was wrong. She hesitated a bit and finally said something like, "It's that time of the month."
>
> She really looked terribly uncomfortable, so I suggested she go to the nurse and get an aspirin. She returned in 10 minutes to tell me that the nurse couldn't do anything for her, that school nurses were not permitted to dispense unauthorized medication. I had aspirin in my purse and was about to give her one when my cooperating teacher stopped me (she had been out of the room earlier when I had sent Sally to the nurse), saying it was against the rules. I really felt it was an awkward situation. Why should Sally have to suffer? Why shouldn't I have given her the aspirin?

We can empathize with Karen's frustration. At the same time we can appreciate the importance of regulations. Many rules that have been established by the school and school board are for the protection both of students and teachers. (The occasional student could be allergic to aspirin or develop a serious medical problem from ingesting it.) Because the dispensing of medication of any kind brings to bear all sorts of legal questions, it is best to advise students like Sally to bring their own medication to school on those days they feel they might need some.

Karen's annoyance is understandable. She knew that the aspirin in all probability would have relieved Sally's discomfort and she found it hard to accept a regulation that disallowed it. She is not alone in having that feeling. There is another side, though: If you were to provide assistance in the form of medication for menstrual pain, at what point would you stop? Earache? Toothache? Digestive problem? Broken toe?

To learn the particulars of the relevant laws in your state, discuss the issue of medication with your school nurse. The deeper issue is the ethical one, namely, the right thing to do in a situation like that with Sally, and like that raised by Larry in the following journal log:

> 3/26: By chance I overheard several students in the hall talking about book reports which were due today. One said, "I was too busy so I handed in an old book report of my brothers'." These are the questions that ran through my mind: What should I do? Tell my cooperating teacher, talk to the student directly, or ignore the whole thing?

This kind of problem has been present for decades and is only growing as technological advances make it easier and easier for students to transfer material from the Internet and other sources into their own papers—with or without acknowledging the source—with the click of a mouse (Bodi, 1998; Walker, 1998). No matter how tempting it may be to "ignore the whole thing," such a choice would be unwise. It would certainly not be helpful to the student. To act professionally and ethically, you must cope with the problem in a constructive, nonpunitive way. Your aim should be to teach, not to make the student suffer.

As a student teacher, you will want to share the information with your cooperating teacher. He or she will have to decide how to deal with the problem. For your sake in the future—all teachers are confronted with some form of cheating, usually with many more varieties than they like—and because your cooperating teacher might ask for your thoughts, you should consider how you would handle such a situation. For example, you might first ask the student why he or she cheated and what the consequences of doing so are. Then, you might ask the student how he or she proposes to resolve the problem created. Finally, tell the student what your intentions are. Your actions would probably depend partially on the student's responses to your queries and could range from no penalty (if the student was genuinely sorry and promptly submitted his or her own book report) to failure. Note, however, that some schools have a zero-tolerance policy toward cheating and suspend students for it regardless of motivation. In that case, you have no choice but to report the incident to the administration.

In addition, consider how in the future you might reduce the incidents of cheating in your classes. For example, before the first take-home writing assignment, you could devote a class period to discussion and role plays about what constitutes honest scholarship (e.g., how reference books, Internet Web sites, critiques, and other sources must be documented, how much parental or peer assistance is acceptable, whether or not computer spell checkers and grammar checks are allowed, etc.). As part of this discussion, emphasize why cheating is a poor choice. Students might be reassured if they understand that there is an opportunity to turn in rough drafts of assignments before they are due or submit a rewrite if they are disappointed with their initial grade. Before the first in-class test, you might want to take the preventive strategy of rearranging the classroom into a "test-taking" position that reduces the possibility of eyes wandering from one paper to the next. Finally, you might want to review the literature on what leads students to cheat in the first place.

Bushway and Nash (1977) reviewed past studies on when and why cheating occurs; they revealed the following:

1. Cheaters and noncheaters differ in some personal and behavioral characteristics, including cheaters (a) being lower in school achievement, (b) being closer to others in their class, and (c) being more tense and anxious.
2. Situational factors are important, including (a) the moral climate of the school, (b) the likelihood that students could be successful at attempts to cheat, and (c) the teaching style of the teacher (e.g., assignments and tests that are too difficult, or use of the curve in grading).

3. There are many different reasons for cheating, ranging from avoiding strict punishment at home to pressure to obtain high grades for college admission to scoring at a level that allows participation in interscholastic sports.

When planning discussions about honest scholarship with students, it is important to note that students and teachers often understand cheating differently. McLaughlin and Ross (1989) administered questionnaires about cheating to 130 middle-class high school students in Memphis, Tennessee, and 10 administrators and teachers. The research attempted to answer the following questions: What types of behavior do students classify as cheating? How serious an offense do students view each particular type of cheating? How often do they practice those types? How do students' responses to these questions about cheating compare with the responses of administrators and teachers?

The vast majority (90% or more) of the students classified both copying during an exam and looking at notes during an exam as cheating. Faculty, administrators, and students showed considerable agreement about what constituted cheating, although faculty and administrators classified more behaviors as cheating and regarded more of them to be serious. For example, all school personnel, but only 69% of the students, classified "allowing someone to copy homework" as cheating. Also, faculty considered allowing another student to copy on a test to be more serious a violation than students did.

Although students knew what behaviors were unacceptable, they cheated frequently. Some admitted to copying homework, and even taking turns in doing that.

During your student teaching you will be guided by school rules and your cooperating teacher when confronted with ethical issues such as cheating. You should use this time period as an opportunity to think about your own values. When you have your own class you may decide to take action to discourage cheating and similar unethical acts early in the school year.

In connection with thinking about ethical issues and discussing them with colleagues, you may find the National Education Association's (NEA) "Code of Ethics of the Education Profession," shown in Table 11.1, helpful. Approved in 1975, the Code appears in the annual NEA Handbook.

BECOMING SOCIALIZED AS A TEACHER

After years as a student, how, during the student-teaching experience, do you make that step to the other side of the desk? An interesting study by Friebus (1977) examined the process by which student teachers transition from student to professional.

Friebus interviewed 19 student teachers six times each. To ensure representativeness, he selected student teachers with assignments that varied on several relevant dimensions (grade level, school neighborhood, supervisory arrangements, etc.). Three of his crucial findings are discussed next.

TABLE 11.1

Code of Ethics of the Education Profession

Preamble

The educator, believing in the worth and dignity of each human being, recognizes the supreme importance of the pursuit of truth, devotion to excellence, and the nurture of democratic principles. Essential to these goals is the protection of freedom to learn and to teach and the guarantee of equal educational opportunity for all. The educator accepts the responsibility to adhere to the highest ethical standards.

The educator recognizes the magnitude of the responsibility inherent in the teaching process. The desire for the respect and confidence of one's colleagues, of students, of parents, and of the members of the community provides the incentive to attain and maintain the highest possible degree of ethical conduct. The Code of Ethics of the Education Profession indicates the aspiration of all educators and provides standards by which to judge conduct.

The remedies specified by the NEA and/or its affiliates for the violation of any provision of this Code shall be exclusive and no such provision shall be enforceable in any form other than one specifically designated by the NEA or its affiliates.

Principle I

Commitment to the Student

The educator strives to help each student realize his or her potential as a worthy and effective member of society. The educator therefore works to stimulate the spirit of inquiry, the acquisition of knowledge and understanding, and the thoughtful formulation of worthy goals.

In fulfillment of the obligation to the student, the educator—

1. Shall not unreasonably restrain the student from independent action in the pursuit of learning.
2. Shall not unreasonably deny the student access to varying points of view.
3. Shall not deliberately suppress or distort subject matter relevant to the student's progress.
4. Shall make reasonable effort to protect the student from conditions harmful to learning or to health and safety.
5. Shall not intentionally expose the student to embarrassment or disparagement.
6. Shall not on the basis of race, color, creed, sex, national origin, marital status, political or religious beliefs, family, social, or cultural background, or sexual orientation, unfairly—
   a. Exclude any student from participation in any program.
   b. Deny benefits to any student.
   c. Grant any advantage to any student.
7. Shall not use professional relationships with students for private advantage.
8. Shall not disclose information about students obtained in the course of professional service, unless disclosure serves a compelling professional purpose or is required by law.

Principle II

Commitment to the Profession

The education profession is vested by the public with a trust and responsibility requiring the highest ideals of professional service.

In the belief that the quality of the services of the education profession directly influences the nation and its citizens, the educator shall exert every effort to raise professional standards, to promote a climate that encourages the exercise of professional judgement, to achieve conditions which attract persons worthy of the trust to careers in education, and to assist in preventing the practice of the profession by unqualified persons.

In fulfillment of the obligation to the profession, the educator—

1. Shall not in an application for a professional position deliberately make a false statement or fail to disclose a material fact related to competency and qualifications.
2. Shall not misrepresent his/her professional qualifications.
3. Shall not assist any entry into the profession of a person known to be unqualified in respect to character, education, or other relevant attribute.
4. Shall not knowingly make a false statement concerning the qualifications of a candidate for a professional position.
5. Shall not assist a noneducator in the unauthorized practice of teaching.
6. Shall not disclose information about colleagues obtained in the course of professional service unless disclosure serves a compelling professional purpose or is required by law.
7. Shall not knowingly make false or malicious statements about a colleague.
8. Shall not accept any gratuity, gift, or favor that might impair or appear to influence professional decisions or action.

—Adopted by the 1975 Representative Assembly

Coaching

Friebus (1977) found a surprisingly large number of individuals who, during the course of a student's internship, took on a role similar to that of an athletic coach. The coaches acted as someone who "guides and advises the trainee, provides . . . encounters with new activities, and challenges to old identities" (p. 264). The coaches included, in order of importance, the cooperating teacher, college supervisor, other teachers in the school, self (the student teacher), professors, students, principals, friends, relatives, and student-teacher peers. These people coached by providing ideas about classroom management, information about teaching, encouragement, performance evaluation, and certain expectations.

That the cooperating teacher should top the list, followed by the supervisor and other teachers at the site, is not unexpected. The high score for "self" is surprising, however, and it suggests that student teachers are using their own observational skills and sensitivity to learn "how things work" and to generate advice for themselves. How does this work? Friebus (1977) provided this interchange between an interviewer (I) and a student teacher respondent (R):

I: Did the mid-term review give you a sense of progress?

R: Didn't need it. My progress came from within myself, was evaluating myself.

I: Who is your main indicator of progress?

R: Me, you can tell me I'm excellent but if I don't have the feeling within myself it doesn't mean anything.

I: If you had problems or a question about what you were doing, who was your main source of information?

R: First and foremost it was me.

Peer Involvement

Friebus (1977) found that contacts student teachers have with their fellow student teachers serve two important functions to becoming socialized in the profession. First, peer comparison allows student teachers to compare notes and see how their situation stands in relation to others. Through this process they assess whether they are teaching a fair share of lessons, whether they are overworked or underworked, and so forth. A second function served by peer involvement is support and comfort; that is, having much in common, peers are ideal people with whom to share the varied feelings and inevitable dilemmas student teachers encounter. Out of the sharing can come some profitable exchanges and useful ideas.

Legitimacy

A third area Friebus (1977) examined is legitimacy. The student teacher's grow-ing feeling of holding a professional identity is molded in part by how others be-have toward her or him in the new role. Such behaviors might include obedience by students in response to the student teacher's directions, an invitation from a fellow teacher to join her for lunch, a comment by a parent acknowledging the difference the student teacher had made for his child, and so on.

Friebus found that students and the cooperating teacher produced the most in-stances that legitimized the student teacher's role as teacher. That the students top the list is a fascinating example of human interaction. Student teachers, who devote so much of their energy to helping their learners develop academically are, in turn, helped by the learners to develop professionally and feel like an adult leader in the classroom.

Very likely, you, too, will be socialized through your interactions with your "coaches," peers, and students. Among your coaches, one of the leading ones will be you.

WHEN COACHES DON'T COACH: APPRECIATING THE COLLEGE/UNIVERSITY SUPERVISOR'S SUPPORT

Repeatedly, the experiences of our student teachers point to the crucial role of the college supervisor and cooperating teacher. Children can be expected to be-have like children and teenagers like teenagers, and when 20 or 30 of them are together, there are bound to be problems, even just those that naturally stem from people living and working in close proximity. For student teachers, the major purpose of the apprenticeship experience is to learn to take these problems in stride so they may be dealt with effectively.

If you have your cooperating teacher and college/university supervisor on your side and have their advice and especially their support, your chances of having a valuable, even if difficult, teaching experience is increased many times over. But in those instances when the cooperating teacher is hostile toward the student teacher and competitive with her or him—especially when these attitudes are covert and masked by occasional acts of false solicitousness—then the stu-dent teacher can have her or his confidence and self-esteem shaken to the core. Kate had such a cooperating teacher.

1/27: I went home Friday feeling quite discouraged. After three days of student teaching I still felt like a stranger with my cooperating teacher and even with the kids. After listening to everyone's glowing accounts of their experience in Thurs-day's curriculum class and reflecting on my own experience, I was really de-pressed. I thought about it all weekend and tried to explain my feelings to my friends. But I couldn't seem to verbalize exactly what the problem was. I had been so realistic over vacation, but I guess I was picturing things like they were at the end of my field experience, a wonderful relationship with the teacher. Probably I was expecting too much too soon. Also I was used to kids who craved extra attention. Now faced with kids coming from a totally different background who are much cooler in their reaction to strangers, and a cooperating teacher who seems aloof, I have to modify my expectations. All these things were running through my head.

After 2 months of frustration—of no support from her cooperating teacher, despite ever increasing effort on her part—her confidence was undermined to such a point that she wrote the following:

3/29: I am beginning to experience this feeling of anxiety creeping over me. As I make the valiant effort to finish my proposal for my course in School and Community, my mind keeps wandering. I feel very confused. I keep thinking I should throw my proposal down and concentrate on tomorrow morning, but then I realize that the kind of situations I need to prepare myself for just can't be planned. My lessons are ready to go, the materials are set, but . . . .

I don't think I would be so scared except that I feel the issue of taking total control, rather than seeming like a logical, natural step, is beginning to feel like an insurmountable hurdle. Maybe the problem is that I am still unclear.

Maybe I am looking for a simple solution when there is none. I'm afraid to show doubt in myself because then everyone else will doubt me. But at the same time the doubt is beginning to overpower me. Where is all my self-confidence? I know, it's sitting on three and a half years' worth of papers, test grades . . . and somehow I haven't managed to translate it into the real world.

How can a person try so hard and not even come close to achieving a desired goal? Maybe it's the wrong goal? Maybe the answer is that I care too much and I'm getting sick of "maybe's."

The story has a happy ending. Kate's supervisor helped her recognize what Kate herself had surmised, that her cooperating teacher had been a destructive force, a person rare among cooperating teachers. The cooperating teacher seemed intent on giving Kate nothing but negative feedback or, at best, no comments whatsoever. Kate completed her 10-week period and went on to another student-teaching experience in a middle school during which she became finally convinced that she had the makings of a superb teacher. The second school offered her a position, which she accepted.

Ideally, the student teacher and cooperating teacher form a working team, directing their efforts toward common goals. When this does not happen, when the student teacher does not get the support he or she needs, the best resource available is the supervisor. Although supervisors typically will be ready to listen at any time and particularly as soon as the lack of support begins to become a problem, it is likely that they can be most helpful after the student teacher has begun to apply the first steps of a problem-solving approach like COURAGE.

Occasionally others in the school building—precisely those people who are supposed to help a student teacher become socialized—do not work in a student teacher's best interest. Whether hostile and competitive or merely insensitive, they can also undermine a student teacher's confidence as he or she works to assume an adult role. Janice describes two such situations in her journal.

12/8: Mrs. M. asked if she could switch lunch duties with me. Because it was pouring outside and the choir risers were set up in the gym, "recess" was in the lunchroom. I certainly didn't mind covering for her. During the usual announcements about dismissal [when the teacher speaking informs students of the various teachers who will dismiss them that day], Mrs. C. *completely* ignored me although I had told her I was covering for Mrs. M. It seemed pretty clear it wasn't just oversight. Those teachers who are "on duty" stand up, those who are "off duty" continue eating their lunch sitting down. When Mrs. M. explained that Mr. W. would be dismissing along with her, I was standing right next to him, yet she did not mention my name. It was hurtful, but more than that, embarrassing when done in front of the entire grade. So she's telling them I'm not a "real" teacher?

This was exacerbated when I went over to the high school during a free period to pick up materials. I didn't introduce myself when I went into the office since the same three people there were those who had mortified me when I went to the high school in November. The woman at the desk again assumed I was a high school student, though I asked a question no student would. When I explained, she was even ruder . . . "with that hair cut . . . " and "you look so young . . . " I was near tears; I am very conscious of my dress because I know I look (and am) young. After what happened this afternoon, I could take no more. The other woman at the desk said, "You must get sick of hearing that." I didn't answer—maintained a cold, professional stance and tone. Then walked right out of the building into the rain and sobbed in my car.

Again, applying COURAGE or a similar problem-solving approach is essential. It is vital that student teachers take action when unfairly criticized, attacked, or ignored. The best defense is to continue to act with the utmost professionalism and to seek help when needed. Most people in schools support student teachers and these true coaches, along with your college/university supervisor, are ready and willing to help smooth the way as you become socialized to the profession. Be sure to let them know if you are encountering repeated problems.

GROWING IN THE "SCHOOL OF HARD KNOCKS"

Dorothy had a gift for teaching. This was apparent to her supervisor early in the term, although her cooperating teacher never recognized it. Despite the obstacles she encountered, Dorothy achieved a great measure of success with her class through dogged persistence, imaginative plans, and the honest expression of her feelings.

> 1/20: This morning the class was misbehaving and I lost control of myself. Tears started rolling out, and I said to the class, "I don't understand you kids. I go home every night and work on new and interesting things for you to do and I receive no response or respect from you. All you can do is disturb the class. Do you realize I do these things only because I care about you and what will happen to you in the future if you don't learn?" No discipline problems the rest of the day. But I do realize I need to control my emotions, and it is something I will have to work at.

Again and again Dorothy found renewed strength and inspiration from the students themselves. The following journal entry conveys the kind of devotion to students that becomes apparent to them and elicits their warm and positive response.

> 3/3: It's the usual Friday. The children are tired and restless. Very excited about the weekend, questioning me about leaving. Timmy kept saying in reading group that they were going to spring a surprise on me, and Larry would say, "Be quiet, Timmy." The school counselor came in and talked to me today, and I told her that it had been a hard quarter plus a period of shattered dreams and idealism; that I found out that many things the university teaches you cannot be used; also, that I feel the structure of schools increases discipline problems and that every time I punished a child I thought: We are punishing him for many things he cannot help, things forced upon him by the school and home environment. It ran through my mind, and every night I go to sleep thinking of this. But as my father and I discussed, I have to teach the child the appropriate behavior set up for him by this society or he will have many difficulties adjusting later. . . . Isn't it sad that this is what is happening every day in many schools?

Institutions that educate teachers help them develop conceptions of what schools should be like. Sometimes student teachers and beginning teachers who have fine aspirations have not had the experience in the "school of hard knocks" to appreciate the power of the principle of inertia. The status quo is not easily changed, and those who learn that fact of life and understand the reasons for it are more likely to work for modest, realistic goals. Dorothy learned that fact of life and, although saddened, was strengthened by it. Even under these less-than-ideal circumstances, her devotion to her students paid off by making a difference in many of their lives.

Dorothy was fortunate in being able to mobilize herself so that she did not suffer from continuing doubts, no matter how discouraging a day or week she encountered. She felt early on that in her situation, the cooperating teacher was more enemy than ally, and that the only kind of criticism that she could depend on getting was the kind that put her down. However, she would not allow that relationship to be defeating.

Dorothy was reinforced by the support she received from both the supervisor and her colleagues in the student-teaching seminar. For one thing, her classmates agreed that her cooperating teacher was being grossly unfair and unhelpful. For another, when she heard how her fellow student teachers received extra support from their cooperating teachers, she was reassured that most teachers actually are helpful to newcomers and that her unfortunate experience should not dispel her expectation that she would in the future find herself working with kindly people.

Near the end of her teaching, Dorothy used her journal to define for herself the role that her cooperating teacher had played and to put her experience in perspective. This prepared her to appreciate her last 2 days and to take full and clear note of the children and of their feelings toward her. Like every other teacher—of kindergarten, 6th grade, 11th grade, or university—who gives students the feeling that he or she genuinely cares and works for them unstintingly, Dorothy got the evidence that her students cared and that she had been important to them.

> 3/9: I must admit I had fun with the class today, because for the first time I stopped worrying about pleasing Ms. K. We had our usual reading in the morning, but in the afternoon we did choral reading and had the boat race with the children screaming. I read stories to them, then we had gym together. It was great. The class even talked about how much they enjoyed it!

> 3/10: What a day! The children brought me earrings, pins, a rabbit, and a lamp plus a letter that meant a lot to me . . . .

> Sometimes I feel Ms. K. was truly trying to stifle my progress! She definitely had me feeling like a failure on and off through the entire quarter, but thanks to a great deal of thought I gave it Wednesday and Thursday, and encouragement from my supervisor, I have come to realize I am capable of being a very human teacher. Reconsideration of myself plus positive responses from the children and my supervisor helped.

> Ms. K. laughed when she saw several of the children crying over me leaving. I feel sad that these children had to suffer this hurt, but I feel good about it too because I realize I have radiated some warmth toward these children which I feel is very necessary in a healthy human development. Geraldine said to me, "I want to tell you before you leave that you are the best teacher I have ever had." Another little girl said she was going to kidnap me. Then Lisa said I was better than the teacher she had before she came to this school. I realize now that instead of listening to Ms. K. so much I should have listened to the children's responses to me all quarter, because I did know they enjoyed me, but instead I worried about Ms. K. and my evaluation.

I'll miss the children, but I feel like a thousand pounds have been taken off my shoulders.

Such are the dramas in the life of the student teacher. They are moving and they are yours to appreciate. Those who choose teaching, knowing it is an occupation of decision making and intense human interactions, are likely to have relatively good endings to their own dramas.

CRITICAL ISSUES

- How am I coping with the exhaustion and stress that student teaching typically brings?
- How am I handling—and benefiting from—criticism?
- In what ways is constructive self-criticism part of my thinking? How am I countering self-doubt?
- What am I doing to prepare for the legal and ethical issues that arise in classrooms?
- In what respects am I already feeling like a teacher?

12

From Student Teacher to Teacher

About a century ago, Freud said that the mark of adulthood was the achievement of satisfaction through work, sex, and family. Although some of Freud's ideas have fallen from the preeminent position they held in years past, most people would agree with his statement about adulthood. With regard to work, no one would deny that for many people, having a career is one of the highest priorities in life. That, after all, is the ultimate goal toward which you have been striving.

True, there may be mornings during the student-teaching period when you would like to toss the alarm clock out the window and go back to bed. Most days, though, you will find student teaching a challenge, as well as the route to a secure career. Moreover, you will enjoy the satisfaction—so important in life—of being identified with an organization (a school), of being part of a group of coworkers (faculty and staff), of utilizing a body of knowledge about students (stages of cognitive development), and of having a discipline (language or science) and developed skills (to teach students to read, to converse in French, to solve physics problems) to share.

Looking forward to next year, your wish is probably like others in your position: to feel successful in the classroom. As a recent study shows, this feeling is important in separating those who stay on and make teaching their career and those who leave after 1 or more years.

The investigator, an experienced teacher (Yee, 1990), queried current and former teachers to find out what led most to remain in the field and some to leave it. She found that remaining in teaching and deriving satisfaction from it is associated with:

- Workplace conditions such as positive support from administrators and peers, positive community and parent attitudes toward the school, and adequate budgetary support for the school.
- Extrinsic benefits such as favorable pay and job security, promotion opportunities, and schedule and vacations.
- Intrinsic benefits such as seeing oneself successful as a teacher, viewing students as the chief source of intrinsic reward, and feeling a sense of professional growth.

All three categories are important. The first one (workplace conditions) helps make the third (intrinsic benefits) attainable, and the second one (extrinsic benefits) can surely make life more pleasant. Still, there is no formula that can predict who will remain in teaching and who will not.

Some teachers, Yee found, stay for the extrinsic benefits (e.g., summer vacation) even when they are not getting satisfaction from the intrinsic ones, the work itself. That condition is not unique to education; you may have already encountered lawyers, consultants, accountants, and others who are unhappy with their work but stay for the extrinsic benefits. But the fact that we share this condition with other professions does not make it any more satisfactory, either for the unhappy teacher or the unfortunate students.

Yee (1990) also examined the effects frustration with lack of classroom success had on teachers. She concluded that some who fail but do not physically leave the profession "withdraw emotionally and psychologically, effectively retiring on the job" (p. 120).

We believe that the careers of many teachers who became dissatisfied or frustrated did not have to turn out in that unhappy way. Perhaps they might have had more favorable career outcomes if their circumstances had been different during the early, crucial stages of their teaching. This chapter is designed to help you move forward as successfully as possible into the next step in your career—to assist you in effectively making the transition from student teacher to teacher.

ESCAPE FROM FREEDOM

A quality job search, an expert in the area wrote (Kimeldorf, 1993), involves much time and the willingness to expose yourself to the risk of being rejected. Every step of the search is time consuming, from networking and contacting potential employers to scheduling and preparing for interviews. Furthermore, even the most talented applicants will receive some letters of rejection. In the face of such letters, the effective job search requires you to persist. Most of those who do so will find a position.

It is useful to consider the psychological as well as practical factors involved in the job search process. When Fromm (1976) chose the title *Escape From Freedom* for one of his books, he captured the essence of a problem that plagues many of us. We want the satisfactions of adulthood yet at the same time we have much anxiety about them. (The anxiety is sometimes at such a low level of consciousness that we realize it only vaguely.) What we are experiencing is a throwback to an earlier time in our life when we wanted at one and the same time to imitate the behavior of an older brother or sister or a neighbor's child but did not want to give up being mom or dad's little boy or girl. We wanted to stay overnight at a friend's house (or later go out on a first date), but how much "safer" it was to stay at home!

Elements of the insecure or frightened child lead us to "do and not do" at the same time, to go after a job opening and yet to drag our feet, to take the initiative in arranging for an interview and yet manage to leave doubts in the interviewer's mind about our single-minded interest in being a teacher in that school. If we are not careful, these elements can lead to self-sabotage, making us a day late in submitting an application or 10 minutes late in arriving for an interview. They induce us to "forget" to contact the faculty member we met in the teachers' room in our student-teaching school who said she knew of an upcoming position in a nearby school district.

Having such anxieties and ambivalent feelings do not make you abnormal, nor do they ordinarily require professional counseling. By being vigilant during your job search, you can guard against any self-destructive behavior they may cause.

Ask yourself, have I established a plan or am I going about the search process without direction? Am I following my plan faithfully or so haphazardly as to raise suspicions about conflicting motives (e.g., to want to find a job and to not want to find a job)? Is the plan operating effectively? Am I getting responses to applications? Requests for my college placement credentials? Appointments for interviews? If the answer is negative to any of these questions, remember that

COURAGE can be useful not just in the classroom, but also in situations such as this. Consider using problem-solving techniques to avert pursuing a plan that will not produce opportunities.

PREPARING FOR THE JOB HUNT

Studies about how people land a job consistently show that friends and acquaintances are among the top sources of leads. It pays to "talk up" your job hunt, to let it be widely known, to encourage others to give you tips about openings and to follow them vigorously. A personal contact usually means that you are more than just another candidate to those who schedule the appointment. It means that in circumstances when you are among a group of equally qualified finalists, you have an edge. Of course, you will also be at an advantage if you student teach in a district that hires most new teachers from its pool of student interns (Kolze, 1988).

As you are engaging in your job search, you should take advantage of your college or university's placement bureau, if one is available. This office may send records you place on file out to potential employers for you (no matter to how many positions you apply) at little or no cost. As a result, you will not have the burden of asking professors or others to write and send letters of recommendation repeatedly. Further, you will be building a file at the placement office good for a lifetime's use. Should you apply for another position 1, 3, or 10 years from now, all you will need to do is update the file. Remember that determined job hunters are prepared at any minute to mail a résumé, letters of recommendation, and a letter of interest, all concise, to the point, striking, and well written.

Your Résumé

To present yourself to prospective employers, you will need a personal résumé. Learning to compose a strong and appropriate résumé at this point will help not only in getting your first job, but later ones as well. Write a résumé so that the potential employer scanning it knows almost instantly the highlights of your background. Because your résumé plays such a crucial role in your job search, we suggest you consult a recent book on résumé writing or the section on that topic in a book like Moffatt's (2000) *How to Get a Teaching Job* or Warner and Bryan's (1997) *Inside Secrets of Finding a Teaching Job*. In addition, you might want to check whether your university's career counseling center offers a workshop on résumé writing.

Writing a strong résumé is a time-consuming task, much like writing a term paper that would earn an A in the toughest English class. You will have a stronger final product if you write a draft and put it aside for a day or two before reviewing and revising it again. After preparing the next draft, ask others for comments and criticisms.

In Table 12.1 we present the kinds of information that should be included and a recommended format with explanatory footnotes. Modify both of these (content and form) to your personal taste and especially to highlight your particular strengths.

If your experience cannot be subsumed under the given headings, add others. For example, if any of your writings have been published, by all means include them under a "Publications" heading. Similarly, if you have been a volunteer (e.g., in a "Y," 4-H club, or Scout camp) or have engaged in public service (e.g., a voter registration drive), include such items under an appropriate heading. The résumé is, after all, a vehicle to present yourself well and give recipients a clear notion of what you are capable of doing.

Although everything relevant should be included in your résumé, the document should be brief and to the point. As Chris Smith did in Table 12.2, use concise phrases to make your résumé easy to read. Finally, to state the obvious, make sure your résumé is visually appealing, printed on durable, professional paper, and organized in a way that does not look busy or crowded.

Your Portfolio

As part of your teacher education courses, you may have developed a portfolio, or collection of self-selected materials illustrating your growth in teaching and educational philosophy. If not, you may want to develop such a portfolio to accompany and support your résumé and application.

In a survey of 65 school administrators responsible for aspects of the hiring practice, 48% said they would spend only 3 to 10 minutes reviewing an applicant's portfolio (Newman, Smolen, & Newman, 1993, cited in Montgomery, 1997). For that reason, it is advisable to keep portfolios short, perhaps 6 to 8 pages of text with additional supporting material neatly organized into appendixes (Seldin, 1993). With so little space, it is essential to make optimal use of each line of text.

Newman et al. (1993) asked administrators to identify what they looked for in beginning teachers and how such competencies could be documented in a teaching portfolio. The recommendations were as follows:

1. A commitment to lifelong learning. This should be made clear in a written statement of one's educational philosophy.
2. Effective communication skills. This can be illustrated through inclusion of correspondence with parents and students as well as by the effectiveness of one's written educational philosophy.
3. Sound motivational strategies. This can be illustrated through inclusion of a classroom organization and management plan.
4. Effective classroom management. Again, the classroom organization and management plan can make this clear.

TABLE 12.1
Recommended Components of Your Résumé

Name and contact information, including:

- Full name
- Mailing address
- Phone and fax numbers
- E-mail address

Position desired, including:

- A short description of what sort of teaching job you seek

Education, including:

- High school information:
  - Name and location of high school
  - Year diploma awarded
  - Grade point average (GPA)
  - College/university information:
  - Name and location of college/university
  - Degree and year awarded
  - GPA
  - Academic majors and minors
  - Optional: Classes taken, particularly those relevant to your desired teaching position

Honors and awards, including:

- Grants and scholarships received
- Honors and awards received in college/university
- Major honors and awards received in high school
- Honors and awards received elsewhere

Extracurricular activities, including:

- Athletic, artistic, community/public service, or other activities you are or were involved in—focusing on college/university work but mentioning major high school activities as well
- Leadership positions held in any activities or clubs

Certification:

- Any teacher certification you have or are preparing for, even if it is in a different state from the job for which you are applying

Experience, including:

- Student teaching/internship information:
  - School name, location, and grades/subjects taught
  - Dates of experience
- Any other teaching, camp counseling, or other relevant experience (e.g., working with children by tutoring, lifeguarding, coaching, etc., or teaching/counseling adults in any capacity)
- Optional: Other work experience that is not relevant to the job you are seeking

Membership in professional organizations

Optionally, a brief description of personal information such as hobbies, travel, etc.

References, including:

- The names and addresses of three to five individuals—such as your cooperating teacher and college/university supervisor—who can knowledgeably discuss your teaching skills, as well as your academic and personal traits
- If names and addresses are not provided, you should write "References available upon request" at the bottom of your résumé.

TABLE 12.2

Sample Résumé

Chris Smith

P.O. Box 54321	chris-smith@stateu.edu	1234 Main Street
Collegetown, NY 12345	Fax: (321) 777-7777	Hometown, CA 98765
(321) 555-5555		(789) 999-9999

POSITION DESIRED History or Social Studies teacher, Grades 7–12
Basketball coach

CERTIFICATION Plan to take National Teacher Examination, June 2002

EDUCATION **Lincoln College,** Collegetown, New York
B.A., May 2002 (expected) GPA: 3.27 (through 12/01)
Major: Secondary Education Minor: History

King High School, Hometown, California
Diploma, June 1998 GPA: 3.65

SELECTED HONORS AND AWARDS
- Carnegie Scholarship, Lincoln College, 2001 ($1,000 award)
- Top GPA for the semester, Alpha Beta Gamma (Fall 2000)
- Most valuable player, King High School basketball (1997, 1998)

EXPERIENCE *Student Teacher, Northside High School, Collegetown, NY*
Student-taught three sections of 9th grade World History and one
section of 11th grade American History
January 2002–March 2002

Camp Counselor, Beautiful Scout Camp, Lake City, ID
Counselor for boys and girls overnight camp, ages 8–13

Responsibilities included management of children during all parts
of the camp experience, including lifeguarding at the pool, help-
ing with arts and crafts, supervising cooking and outdoors activ-
ities, as well as managing dining and bedtime routines
June–August 1998
June–August 1999
June–August 2000 (head counselor)
Camp Director: Mr. John Revere

Joe's Corner Grocery, Hometown, CA
Cashier at local grocery store

1996–1998 (full-time in summers of 1996–1997, part-time
otherwise)

EXTRACURRICULAR ACTIVITIES
Alpha Beta Gamma, Lincoln College, Collegetown, NY
- Community Service Director, 2001–2002. Organized four ma-
jor community service projects.
- Social Manager, 2000–2001. Administered budget of $10,000
to plan social events.

Intramural Basketball, Lincoln College, Collegetown, NY
- 1999–2002; Captain, 2002

(continued)

Varsity Basketball, King High School, Hometown, CA
- 1995–1998; Co-captain, 1997, Captain, 1998

Choir, King High School, Hometown, CA
- 1994–1998

TRAVEL EXPERIENCE

Summer in Europe
- June–July 2001; Traveled in Western Europe, visiting numerous historical and cultural sights of interest

REFERENCES

Kelly Baskin, Ed.D.
Associate Professor of Education
Lincoln College
Collegetown, NY 12345

Yolanda Garcia, M.A.
Chair of History Department
Northside High School
Collegetown, NY 12345

John Revere
Camp Director
Beautiful Scout Camp
Lake City, ID 77777

George Yakahama, Ph.D.
Professor of Education
Lincoln College
Collegetown, NY 12345

---

5. Understanding of characteristics of learners. This can be illustrated through a teacher's inclusion of personal lesson plans.
6. Ability to plan and sequence instruction. This can be illustrated through inclusion of personally developed unit plans.

Using this information, Montgomery (1997) recommended that the following items, each supplemented by an appendix, be included in a student teacher portfolio:

1. A brief, reflective essay that provides a self-assessment of the beginning teacher's strengths, weaknesses, and professional goals.
   - Related appendix: Analyses of lesson plans and journal entries reflecting problem-solving skills.
2. A brief, reflective essay that outlines the beginning teacher's philosophy of classroom management.
   - Related appendix: List of classroom rules, explanation of rationale for those rules, sample letter to parents explaining management system, classroom rules, and reasoning behind outlined rules.
3. A brief, reflective essay that describes instructional methods and approaches to be used in the classroom.

- Related appendix: Sample lesson plans and assessments.
4. Description of any special projects or activities planned and carried out during student teaching (optional).
  - Related appendix: Captioned photographs or other supporting information.

The materials in your portfolio should be organized in a logical sequence, with the résumé and table of contents placed first. Make the portfolio neat, easy to read, and pleasing to the eye.

Although time consuming, the effort invested in preparing a portfolio is worthwhile. A portfolio contains a much more complete picture of you as a teacher than you could possibly convey orally during a brief interview. Moreover, the process of preparing a portfolio enables you to reflect on just those issues that potential employers deem most essential. This means that you are all the more prepared when arriving for your interview.

GETTING CERTIFIED

Once you have successfully completed your state's academic requirements for certification as a teacher, you should submit a formal application to your state's department of education. Your college supervisor or other personnel can advise you about the process. Typically, one official is designated as the institution's certification officer and serves as a liaison with the appropriate person in the state department of education.

Candidates in about three quarters of the states must pass one or more of the tests of the National Teacher Examination (NTE) before being certified. Additionally, many states require that candidates pass one or more state-administered tests designed to supplement or take the place of an NTE test. Be sure to contact your state department of education to obtain a list of required examinations.

The Educational Testing Service (ETS), which designed the NTE more than 50 years ago, introduced a new version in 1995. The tests are administered in three stages. The first, known as PRAXIS I, is taken early in a student's career to enable candidates to have plenty of time to get additional instruction, if they should fail the first time. The test at that stage is on basic skills (reading, writing, and mathematics).

The Stage 2 tests, PRAXIS II, which evaluate content-area knowledge, include the three tests of the NTE Core Battery: General Knowledge, Communication Skills, and the Principles of Learning and Teaching. PRAXIS II also includes subject assessment and general and content-specific teaching knowledge tests. These multiple-choice and computer interactive tests are taken shortly before or after graduation. The Stage 3 tests, PRAXIS III, include evaluations of classroom teaching, portfolio reviews, listening and oral response tasks, video stimuli, and essays.

If the thought of these tests is stressful, remember that after 16 or more years of school and college, you are "test-wise." You know what information to obtain about an exam you are scheduled to take, and you know what and how to study. Prepare. Also remember that in planning your course of study your institution undoubtedly took into account the kinds of assessments required for certification.

Assistance in preparing for the PRAXIS tests is available from several sources. ETS publishes a variety of helpful materials, including *Tests at a Glance*, which offers you test descriptions, sample questions, and test-taking strategies. This booklet may be downloaded from the ETS Web site (www. ets.org). A printed version may also be obtained, without cost, by phoning 1-609-771-7395.

To help prepare for PRAXIS II, you may find it helpful to consult one of many commercially prepared test-preparation books. Available at many libraries and bookstores, these books provide full-length practice tests for the NTE Core Battery and sample questions for the most frequently taken specialty-area tests. Besides the correct answers, the authors give helpful explanations and advice on test-taking strategies.

BEGINNING THE JOB SEARCH

Keep in mind that personnel in two school districts know you better than any others. They knew you even before you started your job hunt. The first is the one you attended. True, they have not observed you teach. On the other hand, they have knowledge about your character and personality and about the kind of student you were. Together, these add up to a lot of important information about a potential teacher. It is very much to your advantage if your former teachers pass the word on to hiring principals that they know that you are a dependable and conscientious person, or that students will appreciate you as a teacher.

The other district is the one in which you do your student teaching. They have seen you as a teacher. They do not have to depend on letters of recommendation or your grade in student teaching to make a judgment about your teaching ability; they have much more reliable evidence: what their own eyes and ears have given them. The school district may not want to lose you. Let them know as early as possible if you plan to apply for openings they will have.

Most likely, you will want to cast your net beyond those two school districts in your job search. You should identify the school districts in the geographic area(s) in which you are willing to live and follow leads you generate through your networking. When ready, you can contact these districts to obtain application materials and learn about the hiring process.

Request job applications in advance so you can prepare and carefully edit your materials: a cover letter, the application, and your résumé. Remember that you want to present yourself in such a way that will make your application stand out favorably and, concomitantly, you want to avoid flaws that will make it easy for the selection committee to reject your application. These flaws include misspelled words, applications that do not conform to instructions, résumés that are not professional in appearance, and so forth.

One day you will receive a phone call or letter informing you that you are a candidate for a position and inviting you to come for an interview. It is a thrilling moment: The hiring official was already impressed enough to make you a candidate.

THE INTERVIEW

Preparation for the Interview

The personal interview is your opportunity to exceed whatever assessment has already been made of you—that is, to show that you are at least as good as your résumé and placement credentials indicate and as good as your college supervisor and cooperating teacher have rated you. In short, the interview provides you with an opportunity to show that you are an excellent choice for the vacant position.

We have frequently been asked about preparation in anticipation of the interview. Our answer is deceptively simple: Prepare yourself to be yourself. A relaxed and spontaneous person is typically self-confident, prepossessing, and interesting. A person's chances are enhanced if these qualities are apparent to the interviewer.

Of course, you will also want to prepare for an interviewer's questions. Interviewers will want to learn several things about you: Why do you want to be a teacher? Why did you choose the level (or the field) that you are in? What makes you think you can be a good teacher? What is your teaching philosophy? What are your strengths and weaknesses? What do you expect will be your greatest problem the first year on the job? What classroom management style will you adopt? What kind of school would you like to teach in, with what kinds of children? Are there questions about the position or about the school that you would like to ask?

Questions like these are both fair and appropriate, and you should expect them. Spend time developing and organizing your thoughts about how you might answer these and similar questions. After doing this, you might want to record or tape your answers, or at the very least, speak them out loud. Ask yourself, did my responses sound professional? Did I reflect my needs and goals while also keeping in mind the needs and goals of the potential employer?

Another way to prepare for a job interview is by role playing. With your student-teacher colleagues, or with friends or relatives, you can simulate the real-life experience. Ask your role-playing partner to be, in turn, a male interviewer, a female one, tough, gentle, talkative, passive, directive in questioning style (e.g., How many credits in sociology did you take?) versus open-ended (e.g., Tell me about yourself).

Practice answering a range of questions asked over a 30-minute period. Begin with open, get-to-know-you questions like, "Tell me about your training at college/university." Then answer questions about your student-teaching experience and problems you might face in the classroom ("How would you handle [such and such] a discipline problem?"). Then have your partner look at your résumé and generate tougher questions like, "What did you do in the summer and fall of 1999? Nothing is listed on your résumé" or, "What are your goals over the long run as a teacher?"

After some experience as the applicant or candidate, trade off with your partner and play the role of employer or interviewer, an experience that gives you the opportunity of seeing the selection process with that functionary's perspective.

You will also find it helpful to discuss the interview and job hunt with your college supervisor. Do that, also, with those who have been through it most recently: last year's graduates, who are now in teaching positions.

In addition to the interview, some schools—particularly independent (private) ones—will ask job applicants to teach one or more class periods, or parts thereof, during the course of their school visit. If given this opportunity, rejoice! As a student teacher you have learned to effectively instruct, inspire, and manage a classroom of children or adolescents. Now you will be able to showcase your skill and enthusiasm in the sight of potential employers. When the teacher, department chair, or division director contacts you with the subject matter or lesson to be covered the day of your visit, carefully prepare your lesson plans. Make sure you employ a variety of techniques (lecturing, leading discussion, raising questions, fielding questions, etc.) during the short time period made available to you.

The Interview Itself

At last your interview day has come. Be on time! Dress for a formal interview; looking professional certainly helps in making a positive impression. Be prepared to share important information about yourself and to seek information about the job that is not readily available elsewhere.

As a general rule, if you are relatively comfortable during the interview, your relaxed state will help the interviewer. Consciously or otherwise this will tend to elevate the rating you are given.

There are various ways to relax yourself prior to the interview. One of them, a simple exercise that you can use unobtrusively while sitting in the waiting room, calls first for you to breathe in deeply through your nose, exhale slowly through your mouth. Then, after a few inhalations, and while continuing the breathing, think about relaxing the top of your head, inside your head, your eyes, your face, neck, and so on, downward until you reach your toes. As you do so, remind yourself of the years of training you have had.

During the interview, be yourself. Answer the questions posed straightforwardly. Share your strengths. Show your enthusiasm, energy, and determination.

Do not hesitate, when appropriate, to ask questions. Learn about the school's history, about the community it serves, and about plans for next year. While you convey who you are and what you seek, try at the same time to present yourself in ways that will make the interviewer or hiring committee "look good" if they choose you.

Another important factor to consider during job interviews is the kind of nonverbal messages you send. In one study (Amalfitano & Kalt, 1977), photographs of a male and a female (supposedly job seekers) were shown to 44 interviewers at an employment agency who were then asked to rate them. In some pictures the job seekers were looking straight ahead; in others they were looking down. Although the only difference between the photographs was where the individual was looking, those applicants making "eye contact" (by looking straight ahead) were more likely to be hired, and were rated as being significantly more alert, assertive, dependable, confident, and responsible. They were also seen as having more incentive.

Other researchers (Young & Beier, 1977) found that head movement and smiling are important nonverbal communication factors during job interviews, although not as powerful as eye contact. What is especially important about their experiment is that these researchers randomly chose half their participants to display eye contact, smiling, and head movement, and half to minimize it. Those told to display it, whether it was their personal style or not, were rated as more deserving of the job than their counterparts in the other group.

When you return home from an interview, make notes in your journal about it and assess how it went. Use COURAGE to plan future interviews, especially if you left this one with any sense of regret or disappointment.

If you have two successive experiences that left you feeling that things did not "click," it is vital that you take action. A first one might offhandedly be attributed to an outside factor—the personality or values of the interviewer (e.g., does not want a male teacher in a primary grade)—but a succession of interviews that leave you with negative feelings raises questions about your part in the exchange.

We are not suggesting that repeated failure at obtaining a position is due to your inadequacy. People specializing in job searches suggest that the typical applicant experiences multiple rejections before being hired (Kimeldorf, 1993; Sonnenblick, Basciano, & Crabbe, 1997). Of course, job market conditions and your areas of specialty can be major factors. Our view is only that a critical appraisal of your interviews will help you better prepare for future interviews, now or at later stages in your career. They will also help you maintain a positive attitude.

We draw the following conclusions about interviews from educational administrators and specialists in the field of employment counseling:

1. Consider in advance what is likely to occur during your job interview.
2. Work at developing self-confidence about upcoming interviews. Use any methods that help you relax and give you a positive outlook.

3. Think about the questions that are likely to be asked. Prepare responses that you can give comfortably, taking into account both your own beliefs and the realities of the position.
4. Decide what you wish to convey about yourself as a person and a prospective teacher.
5. Plan appropriate ways to describe your experiences in college and at work. Highlight your activities with children or adolescents, and communicate your special academic, artistic, and athletic interests.
6. Attend to your nonverbal communication. Look at the interviewer, engage in eye contact, and find occasions to smile.
7. Check whether you are communicating effectively by observing the nonverbal behavior of the interviewer. Is he or she attentive or distracted, responsive or bored? Modify your behavior as needed.
8. With the questions you ask, work at better knowing the interviewer and the school system he or she represents.
9. At the conclusion of each interview, use COURAGE to review the flow of it from beginning to end, taking note of the affect as well as the content.
10. Soon after each interview make a follow-up contact with the interviewer. In this letter (or e-mail or telephone call if conditions require faster contact), remind the interviewer of your appointment and thank him or her for the time given you. Also use the opportunity to briefly refresh the interviewer, if appropriate, about your qualifications and strengths.

THE REJECTION LETTER

Unhappily, you may receive one or more letters notifying you that you were not selected for a position. If that happens, remind yourself that it is the norm to get turned down. Do not put yourself down. Instead, use this as an occasion to mobilize yourself for further activity in the job hunt.

If you receive repeated rejections, one possibility is that the competition is very great. Others are that your letter and résumé do not do you justice, your letters of reference are not helpful, or that you convey a defeated attitude in your interview. An appointment at your college career counseling or placement office is warranted at such times.

If your field of teaching is especially oversupplied, another plan might involve trying for a different teaching level, such as 7th grade instead of 12th grade, or preschool instead of kindergarten; or a different setting, such as a training program in industry or an adult program for senior citizens. You may also want to consider job possibilities in other, possibly less desirable, geographic areas.

Determined job hunters will systematically review newspapers, professional magazines, and other print sources containing job listings. They will visit job fairs. They will also spend time online as many school districts now regularly post job openings on their Web sites. Job hunters open to teaching positions in an independent (private) school should consider registering with a teacher placement service. Information about these recruitment agencies, which offer their services free of charge to graduating college seniors, may be accessed through the National Association of Independent Schools Web site (www.nais.org).

Above all, remember to keep a positive attitude. Job searching is not easy, but like in other areas of student teaching, those who approach it systematically ultimately prevail.

Nancy wrote about a not uncommon series of events. You may find that the quest for a job is complexly interwoven into the rest of your activities. For example, you may find yourself competing with a friend or classmate for a position or wondering if your philosophy of education will jive with those in the school where a position is open.

1/10: Today I called the principal at the other junior high. There's a possibility that I may have a "real" job next quarter. I'm going to the junior high on Monday to observe, talk to the two English teachers, and be interviewed. I'm uptight about it. I really want this job, but I've never gone for an interview before.

1/11: Problem: One of the girls I teach with also wants the job. That's fine. But the principal told me about it first. That's not the right thing to do. Lynn was hurt, and I feel bad about it. If I get the job she'll be bitter. Worse yet, we're good friends. We've both said that we wouldn't let it mess up our friendship, but one of us will probably be hurt. Of course, maybe neither of us will get the job. That would hurt, too. She hasn't filled out her application yet. I'm going to tell her that I have an interview on Monday. I think it's important to be honest with her. She'll be full of questions that I won't want to answer. I sure wish there were two jobs open . . . !

1/15: Today I had my interview. They are very traditional at this school. I'm afraid that they're afraid. They don't want a liberal. They asked me about grammar and how valuable I thought *Romeo and Juliet* was for ninth-grade students. What can I say? As far as grammar goes, I said that I thought it was a tool to be used in communication. I felt better after I talked to the two English teachers. They are conservative, but not so subject-oriented that they lose their humanity. I think they are doing some good, human things.

1/26: I didn't get the teaching position. Neither did Lynn. He hired a woman with 3 years experience. I feel sort of bitter and I have no right to. No one owes me anything.

2/15: What can I say? Looking back at my journals I see a definite change in attitude and I know the cause. I wanted that job and I didn't get it. I felt bitter. Then I got depressed. What was I going to do after graduation? What about the future? Know what I decided? Nothing. But it doesn't bother me anymore. I'm going to enjoy the spring.

Nancy worked through her disappointment and readied herself to enjoy her final term at college. Soon after writing the next journal entry she returned to the business of planning the next steps in her career, and she found a good position.

THE ACCEPTANCE LETTER

One day the mail carrier will deliver the letter you have been waiting for. You have been selected, and after your acceptance and some necessary formalities, you will be officially appointed. Assuming that you are a spring graduate, you will be fortunate to get that letter in the spring. However, it may come in June or late in the summer because some teachers resign or take leave at that late date for such reasons as another job, a spouse's transfer to another area, pregnancy, illness, or a late retirement decision.

Whenever you get your letter, enjoy! After your celebration you can turn to the challenging task of preparing to teach your own class or classes.

PREPARING FOR THE JOB

When you walk into your own classroom in the fall, the experience will be very different from that of walking into your student-teaching assignment. On the one hand, you will better understand the feeling of being the teacher; you will know how to prepare, present, and evaluate a lesson; you will be accustomed to witnessing conflict of one kind or another and having to deal with it; and you will be comfortable being evaluated, and evaluating yourself. On the other hand, something you never before experienced will happen: You will enter a class that is going to be your class. There will be no cooperating teacher who has the ultimate responsibility, and no university supervisor to consult. Their absence may arouse two different feelings in you: satisfaction commingled with mild anxiety.

The new experience confronting you has the inevitable and unavoidable components of all growth-potential challenges: opportunities and risks. It places new responsibility on you as it encourages you to put your knowledge and creative ideas to work. You will hardly have to start from scratch because you will be given a curriculum guide to follow. If anything, you may complain that there are too many constraints. Yet, no guide replaces you—your style of leadership, your style of conducting the class, and your personality as you relate to students.

Susi wrote this letter to her college supervisor not many days after she took over a class of her own:

9/10: I've been a real live teacher for one week, and I've been bursting to write you since day one. I can't begin to tell you how appreciative I am to you for reminding me all semester that when I'm in my classroom things can be different. All summer that tempting challenge to try new things has been in the back of my mind, and now I'm having a fantastic time exploring the myriads of educative processes.

> I am learning slowly the delicate blend of freedom and control that is essential to a happy productive classroom. I am disappointed that the school insists on a formalized workbook program in reading and math. It amazes me that people are still convinced children learn best circling and X-ing workbook frames. I had hoped I could have worked some total programs myself. As it is, with the constraints, I am forced to supplement as best I can with more active learning experiences.

Susi delighted in having her own class and in experimenting with some of her ideas. She also very early on began practicing one of the preeminent principles of teaching: As she gracefully put it, "I am learning slowly the delicate blend of freedom and control that is essential to a happy productive classroom."

The combination of freedom and control is important not only in the teacher's work with students, but also in the teacher's professional role. For example, Susi experienced both the freedom that comes from leading her own class and also the constraints of a school-imposed workbook program. Rather than being devastated by it or wasting energy railing against it, she found ways and time to supplement the school program with the more active learning experiences she valued.

Soon after you sign your teaching contract you will be given the school district's curriculum guide or course of study for your class or courses. If you are fortunate and still have a number of weeks before the term begins, study the curriculum guide and, within the limits set by it, develop your lesson plans for at least the first few weeks in the term. Is that being overprepared? We think not. If new teachers do what they can in advance, they will have more time in the fall to deal with what cannot be entirely prepared for—like the inevitable "unexpecteds." Moreover, they will have time to enjoy the nonwork parts of their lives.

As you prepare your lessons, remember the attention span of your students. You will do yourself a great service if you also bear in mind the obvious fact that their enjoyment will make a world of difference in their attitudes and attention. In all probability, you can attest to the validity of this statement on the basis of your own recollections of school and college courses.

You can take several steps in preparing for your new position. First, following advice in chapter 2, become acquainted with the school building and the community it serves. Also, learn about the best form of transportation from your home to school, the parking arrangements, your schedule, the school calendar, the teacher organizations, the school secretary, the librarian, the nurse, and the custodian.

You will find it helpful to get the names of other teachers at your grade level or in your department and especially other new teachers, who you will want to get to know early in the term. If you have difficulty remembering names and faces, ask the school secretary for a copy of the class roster and faculty list as well as class pictures or yearbooks. Learning your students' names before the first day of classes allows you to personally call on students from day one, accelerating the development of a quality relationship. Making sure you learn both teachers' first and last names ensures you can address colleagues appropriately and comfortably both in the halls and in the privacy of the faculty room or teachers' lounge.

If you know you will be teaching in your own classroom, plan initial seating arrangements and desk and table positions in an intentional way. Will you be able to walk between the rows or clusters? Can a person sitting in every seat see the board(s) clearly? Does the positioning of students foster or hinder class discussion?

During the weeks before you begin teaching you will want to design bulletin boards and wall displays. Consider how you will make the room warm and friendly, how you will showcase student work, and how you will use posters and charts to enhance your teaching. Also think about ways you can give students— whatever their age—ownership of the space by allowing them to help in the design during the first week or weeks of school. You want to make the classroom a happy, comfortable, student-friendly place from day one.

THE FIRST DAY AS TEACHER

You know quite a bit about that initial day before you even walk into your classroom for the first time. You know, for instance, that both you and the students will be excited and a bit uncertain about what the year will hold. You know that right from the start you want to present yourself as the adult leader who will insist on maintaining a sane working environment. You know, too, that the students, fresh from a summer's vacation, will be bubbling over with news to share with friends. How, then, will you show them that you will be a fair adult leader who works in their interest?

The first day of class is an important one. From the moment students set eyes on you, you start conveying your expectations of them by word, deed, and attitude. If you are positive in your reaction to a student's question, other students will take note, and you encourage questions in the classroom. If you react positively to student initiatives, you encourage them, too. If you are negative to private conversations during a classwide discussion, you discourage that behavior. You will more likely discourage it constructively if you explain, like a rational authority, that such sideline discussions disturb the class, and that you want everyone to contribute to the group discussion.

If you think much of the chatter in the classroom the first day is a carryover of the long summer vacation, you might choose to organize small-group or whole-class discussions (or other activities) focusing on the vacation for two purposes: to get it out of students' systems and to mine the very rich material of the vacation months. Whatever your method, you will want to convey to the class from the outset that you require cooperation on the part of all students.

CATEGORIZING STUDENTS BY NEEDS

Another activity helpful to you on the first day is to begin to make mental notes about the students in your class(es). To help you direct your attention to individuals, begin to classify them into several functional categories:

1. The spontaneously active students who enjoy school and participate eagerly. They are as important as any others, but need no special attention at this time, except the opportunity to be active in the learning opportunities that you arrange.
2. The interested but marginally active students. They are not a high priority at this time; however, just as soon as possible, you should encourage them to participate before the first group of "activists" takes over in a discussion.
3. The passive, withdrawn students who seem "out of it." Because such children and adolescents feel more like observers than participants, they will need your attention early. That could take the form of a warm hello, a friendly glance in their direction, a question to encourage involvement, or assistance in a project or assignment.
4. The turned-off students who at first seem to be passive, but are not so at all. They are quiet because they have no wish to be in school and no interest in class activities. They are quietly angry in an environment that they experience as alien and hostile. You can begin the process of trying to identify them so that, as the weeks progress, you can try various ways of helping them.
5. The disruptive students who come to school on the first day of class with learned patterns of behavior that could soon alienate classmates and school personnel. Although their attitude is not personally directed at you, you must deal with it from the opening bell. Along with a warm offer to these students to join the class goes the unequivocal message that disruptive behavior will be dealt with instantly at its first appearance.
6. The informal class leader, a student who has great influence over peers. The student may be in that position because of past achievement, physical presence, personal charisma, or other reasons. This influence, which can be used for good or bad purposes, should be valued by the teacher and brought into service to the class. For example, such a person can be a force in the classroom by being a model of good class citizenship. To make positive use of the student and at the same time make the class experience productive for him or her, you will need to see the student as something other than a threat to your leadership. If you begin to react defensively, remind yourself that you are the responsible authority and that your job is to use all resources to make the class a valuable experience for all your students.
7. Students with physical or mental disabilities. The only special attention they might require is that which their disability calls for. Examples are placement in front of the room because of a visual or aural disability, additional time for writing because of a motor or learning disability, and protection and support because their difference may lead other students to tease or isolate them. If you do not receive it, you should request the IEP and advice on all your special-needs students from the principal, counselor, psychologist, school nurse, or other person assigned the responsibility of overseeing their welfare.

HUMOR

When 1,000 students between the ages of 13 and 17 were asked what makes a good teacher, the most frequently mentioned characteristic was having a sense of humor (79.2%); this scored above making class interesting (73.7%) and having knowledge of their subjects (70.1%). When asked what characteristics constitute the worst teacher, the fact that they are dull or have a boring class (79.6 %), in students' opinions, outweighed the fact that they do not explain things clearly (63.2%) or show favoritism toward students (52.7%; "Students Say," 1997).

Humor is a great human resource and an invaluable addition to any classroom lesson. It can serve many purposes, including anxiety reduction. Perhaps you have noticed that tension rises when a speaker and an audience first encounter each other and that it speedily dissipates if the speaker begins with a relevant cartoon, joke, or humorous story. Both speaker and audience feel a great sense of relief as uncertainty gives way to smiles and laughter.

Humor will reduce the students' anxiety and your own and will make class more interesting and appealing. Moreover, it pairs well with the firm class control that is a keystone to effective teaching. If you feel comfortable using humor, build it into your lesson plans. If you do not feel 100% comfortable with it, remember that humor does not have to take the form of jokes or planned skits; it can naturally emerge from the glow of students' personalities and excitement of school life. In a retrospective report at the end of the term, Patty described how the humor of her classroom brightened the student-teaching experience:

5/30: It was almost impossible to exist in my classrooms without a sense of humor. This is probably true in every classroom. Laughter is a great remedy too. Even days when I entered the classroom in not the best of moods, something would happen to lift me.

Be alert to cartoons, humorous news items, and appropriate anecdotes that you can use to leaven the serious business of learning. One of the authors tells this joke to his college class during the first minutes of the first day of each term:

Here we are. The vacation is over. Reminds me of a story a neighbor told me about what happened in her house a few years back.

It was the first day of school and she heard her son's alarm clock ring, but after a few minutes he still wasn't down for breakfast.

So what could she do? She went upstairs, knocked on the door and said, "Johnny, Johnny, get up. It's after seven! You'll be late for school."

"Okay," he grunted. But as soon as his mother left the room he rolled over to snooze some more.

A few minutes later the mother walked back upstairs, pounded a little harder on the door, walked in and said with more authority, "Johnny, you must get up right now. Breakfast is on the table."

"I'll be right down," Johnny said assuredly. But as soon as his mother left the room he pulled the covers over his head.

Five minutes later—still no Johnny and breakfast was getting cold. The mother trooped back upstairs, walked in the room and this time pulled the covers back and said, "Johnny, get up right this second. You are going to be late for school if you don't hurry."

"I don't want to go to school," Johnny moaned.

The mother replied: "But you have to go to school, Johnny. You are the principal."

Besides well-worn jokes like this one, other forms of humor can help you establish a serious, yet comfortable, working atmosphere from the first day on. For example, many concepts you teach can be illuminated by examples that are themselves comical and that make learning a more lively and involving process for students. Further, humorous role playing can be used (e.g., Columbus coming ashore in America and finding a Wendy's, or Shakespeare completing a manuscript and not being able to find a photocopy machine or the zip code of his publisher).

The classroom situation itself gives rise to humor, although the kind that degrades or humiliates anyone should be strictly discouraged with the reasons for that clearly spelled out: "We don't do things in our class to hurt anyone. We can learn and enjoy ourselves without that."

THE EVENINGS OF THE FIRST WEEKS

At the end of each day during your first weeks it will be helpful to review and evaluate your experience, perhaps by making entries in your journal. In what ways did you meet the objectives you had set? In what ways not? What will you do about objectives you did not meet? Should they be a part of tomorrow's objectives? How can you use COURAGE to solve the problems you face?

Also, ask questions at another level. Review the day's events and ask these questions: What made me feel good? Can I build more of that in my plans for tomorrow, later this week, next week? What about the events of the day that made me feel bad? Was it in my relationship with the students? Which ones? What do I feel about them? Why do I feel that way? What can I do tomorrow so that when that day ends, I will not have the same bad feelings?

Engaging in this type of thought session and making journal entries will probably seem like a colossal chore when you come home tired and want to relax and go to bed. There is, after all, a whole year to solve problems. However, experience has shown that if you struggle with your problems during the first days and weeks, the ones that follow will be far simpler.

Questions presented here and others important in your personal situation should be on your agenda every day after school until you feel at ease, self-confident, and in control. Then you can consider them weekly. By that time you will in all probability have made assessment an integral part of your professional way of life, an engrained habit that separates the real professionals from the generally mediocre teachers.

THE REAL WORLD

In the world you enter when you start your first teaching job, you will not find perfection and you will be disappointed if you expect it. It is wise to set high standards, but not to expect the unachievable in an imperfect world. Yes, the real world has beauty, abundance, health, and compassion, but it also has unhappiness, ugliness, poverty, physical and mental illness, and brutality. Students in your classes will not have entirely escaped at least some of the awful experiences in the second set of conditions. They may not be free of those experiences when they come to class and, therefore, they may not be able to achieve what they might have under other circumstances.

If you take a position in a school where student performance falls below—perhaps considerably below—national or state achievement norms, you must learn to live with that situation if you are to develop your effectiveness. Schools are currently under enormous pressure to raise students' level of achievement. You will be, too. However, by setting realistic achievement goals, you will enable your students to get maximum benefit from your teaching and, in this way, help them raise their performance levels. Under these circumstances you should find satisfaction in witnessing a fifth-grade child attain the fourth-grade level in a given subject when that child entered your class performing at the 2.5 grade level.

Teachers are often in a position not greatly different from physicians. They also serve people who, for a variety of reasons, are not up to national "norms" (in their case physically). They succeed in sustaining life in patients like that, but often at a less than optimal level of health.

The medical profession has its roots in a great humanistic tradition, and so does teaching. Among other activities, the medical profession strives for ways to alleviate health deficiencies from past abuse and neglect. The educational profession strives to overcome students' past disadvantages, even if it cannot eliminate them entirely. Our nation will be immeasurably stronger when it institutes major programs to prevent health deficiencies and economic and educational disadvantages. We hope that time will come soon.

Whatever challenges you face, remember that ours is a profession of worth. We serve humankind whether we teach 2 or 20 or 200 students a year. We can do that best when our eyes are wide open to the realities of the world and the school in which we work.

CRITICAL ISSUES

- In detail, what steps should I take to prepare myself for finding a job? Consider emotional preparation as well as tasks you must complete.
- What must I do to ready myself for my first teaching position?
- How can humor be useful in my classroom?
- How can I use COURAGE and other problem-solving techniques I learned from this book and in my courses as my career unfolds?
- How will the lessons of my student-teaching experience be useful in my career?

References

Amalfitano, J., & Kalt, N. (1977). Effects of eye contact on the evaluation of job applicants. *Journal of Employment Counseling, 14,* 46–48.

American Association of University Women. (1992). *How schools shortchange girls.* Annapolis Junction, MD: Author.

American Association of University Women. (1995). *Growing smart: What's working for girls in schools.* Annapolis Junction, MD: Author.

American Association of University Women. (1999). *Gender gaps: Where schools still fail our children.* New York: Marlowe & Company.

Asch, A. (1989). Has the law made a difference? In D. K. Lipsky & A. Gartner (Eds.), *Beyond separate education: Quality education for all* (pp. 181–205). Baltimore: Brookes.

Bloom, B. S. (Ed.). (1956). *Taxonomy of educational objectives: Cognitive domain.* New York: McKay.

Bodi, S. (1998). Ethics and information technology: Some principles to guide students. *The Journal of Academic Librarianship, 24,* 459–463.

Bradley, R., & Teeter, T. (1977). Perceptions of control over social outcomes and student behavior. *Psychology in the Schools, 14,* 230–235.

Burns, R. C. (1993). Parent involvement: Promises, problems, and solutions. In R. C. Burns (Ed.), *Parents and schools: From visitors to partners* (pp. 9–20). Washington, DC: National Education Association.

Bushway, A., & Nash, W. (1977). School cheating behavior. *Review of Educational Research, 42,* 623–632.

Chavkin, N. F., & Williams, D. L., Jr. (1988). Critical issues in teacher training for parent involvement. *Educational Horizons, 66,* 87–89.

Chess, S., & Thomas, A. (1987). *Know your child.* New York: Basic Books.

Clandinin, D. J., & Connelly, F. M. (1992). Teacher as curriculum maker. In P. W. Jackson (Ed.), *Handbook of research on curriculum* (pp. 363–401). New York: Macmillan.

Clapp, B. (1989). The discipline challenge. *Instructor, 99,* 32–34.

Cohen, M. W., Mirels, H. L., & Schwebel, A. I. (1972). Dimensions of elementary school student teacher concerns. *The Journal of Experimental Education, 41,* 6–11.

279

Copeland, W. D. (1978). Processes mediating the relationship between cooperating teacher behavior and student–teacher classroom performance. *Journal of Educational Psychology, 70,* 95–100.

Copeland, W. D. (1987). Classroom management and student teachers' cognitive abilities: A relationship. *American Educational Research Journal, 24,* 219–236.

Daher, J. (1994). School–parent partnerships: A guide. In C. I. Fagnano & B. Z. Werber (Eds.), *School, family and community interaction: A view from the firing lines* (pp.111–132). Boulder, CO: Westview.

Davis, G. A., & Rimm, S. B. (1998). *Education of the gifted and talented* (4th ed.). Boston: Allyn & Bacon.

Davis, J. B. (1990). Stress among secondary school student teachers: Factors which contribute to it and ways of reducing it. *The High School Journal, 73,* 240–244.

Diamond, L. (1999, Dec. 5). Leaping. *The Florida Times-Union,* Jacksonville, FL. [on-line]. Available: http://www.jacksonville.com/tu-online/stories/archives/.

Doyle, W. (1986). Classroom organization and management. In M. C. Wittrock (Ed.), *Handbook of research on teaching,* (3rd ed., pp. 392–431). New York: Macmillan.

Ensminger, M. E., & Slusarcick, A. L. (1992). Paths to high school graduation or dropout: A longitudinal study of a first-grade cohort. *Sociology of Education, 65,* 95–113.

Fant, H. E., Hill, C., Lee, A. E., & Landes, R. (1985). Evaluating student teachers: The national scene. *Teacher Educator, 21*(2), 2–8.

Finn, J. D., Pannozzo, G. M., & Voelkl, K. E. (1995). Disruptive and inattentive-withdrawn behavior and achievement among fourth graders. *The Elementary School Journal, 95,* 421–434.

Fischer, L., Schimmel, D., & Kelly, C. (1999). *Teachers and the law* (5th ed.). New York: Longman.

Friebus, R. J. (1977). Agents of socialization involved in student teaching. *Journal of Educational Research, 70,* 263–268.

Fromm, E. (1976). *Escape from freedom.* New York: Holt, Rinehart & Winston.

Gardner, H. (1983). *Frames of mind: The theory of multiple intelligences.* New York: Basic Books.

Gardner, H. (1993). *Multiple intelligences: The theory into practice.* New York: Basic Books.

Goldenberg, I. I. (1969). Reading groups and some aspects of teacher behavior. In F. Kaplan & S. B. Sarason (Eds.), *The psycho-educational clinic papers and research studies* (Vol. 4, pp. 109–118). Boston: Massachusetts Department of Mental Health.

Gonzalez, L. E., & Carter, K. (1996). Correspondence in cooperating teachers' and student teachers' interpretation of classroom events. *Teaching and Teacher Education, 12,* 39–47.

Grant, L., & Rothenberg, J. (1986). The social enhancement of ability differences: Teacher–student interactions in first- and second-grade reading groups. *Elementary School Journal, 87,* 29–49.

Harty, H., & Mahan, J. M. (1977). Student teachers' expressed orientations toward education while preparing to teach minority and mainstream ethnic groups. *Journal of Experimental Education, 46,* 34–41.

Hatfield, T. A. (1998). The future of art education: Student learning in the visual arts. *NASSP Bulletin, 82 (597),* 8–17.

Hearne, J. C., & Moos, R. H. (1978). Subject matter and classroom climate: A test of Holland's environmental propositions. *American Educational Research Journal, 15,* 111–124.

Hoy, W. K., & Woolfolk, A. E. (1990). Socialization of student teachers. *American Educational Research Journal, 27,* 279–300.

Johnson, D., & Johnson, R. (1989). *Cooperation and competition: Theory & research.* Edina, MN: Interaction Book.

Johnson, D., & Johnson, R. (1991). *Teaching students to be peacemakers.* Edina, MN: Interaction Book.

Jones, M. G., & Vesilind, E. (1995). Preservice teachers' cognitive frameworks for class management. *Teaching and Teacher Education, 11,* 313–330.

Jussim, L. (1990). Social reality and social problems: The role of expectancies. *Journal of Social Issues, 46,* 9–34.

Kainan, A. (1994). *The staffroom: Observing the professional culture of teachers.* Brookfield, VT: Ashgate.

Kaplan, D. S., Peck, B. M., & Kaplan, H. B. (1997). Decomposing the academic failure–dropout relationship: A longitudinal analysis. *Journal of Educational Research, 90,* 331–343.

Kauffman, J. M. (1999). Commentary: Today's special education and its messages for tomorrow. *The Journal of Special Education, 32,* 244–254.

Kimeldorf, M. (1993). *Educator's job search: The ultimate guide to finding positions in education.* Washington, DC: National Education Association.

Kindlon, D., & Thompson, M. (1999). *Raising Cain: Protecting the emotional life of boys.* New York: Ballantine.

Knapp, M. S., & Woolverton, S. (1995). Social class and schooling. In J. A. Banks (Ed.) & C. A. M. Banks (Assoc. Ed.), *Handbook of research on multicultural education* (pp. 548–569). New York: MacMillan.

Koeppen, K. E. (1998). The experiences of a secondary social studies student teacher: Seeking security by planning for self. *Teaching and Teacher Education, 14,* 401–411.

Kolze, R. C. (1988). Finding first-rate teachers. *The American School Board Journal, 175*(7), 29, 41.

Krathwohl, D. R., Bloom, B. S., & Masia, B. (1964). *Taxonomy of educational objectives: Affective domain.* New York: McKay.

Lazar, A., & Slostad, F. (1999). How to overcome obstacles to parent–teacher partnerships. *The Clearing House, 72,* 206–210.

Lazarus, R., & Folkman, S. (1984). *Stress, appraisal and coping.* New York: Springer.

Li, Q. (1999). Teachers' beliefs and gender differences in mathematics: A review. *Educational Research Volume, 41,* 63–76.

Liben, L. S. (1995). Psychology meets geography: Exploring the gender gap on the National Geographic Bee. *Psychological Science Agenda, 8,* 8–9.

Lloyd, M. A. (1994, November). Maintaining vitality in the classroom. *APS Observer, 7,* 11–13.

MacMillan, D. L., Gresham, F. M., & Forness, S. R. (1996). Full inclusion: An empirical perspective. *Behavioral Disorders, 21,* 145–159.

Madsen, C. H., Jr., Becker, W. C., Thomas, D. R., Kosen, L., & Plager, E. (1972). An analysis of the reinforcing function of "sit-down" commands. In M. H. Harris (Ed.), *Classroom uses of behavior modification* (pp. 169–182). Columbus, OH: Merrill.

Maker, C. J. (1982). *Curriculum development for the gifted.* Aspen, MD: Aspen.

Manning, M. L. (1998). Gender differences in young adolescents' mathematics and science achievement. *Childhood Education, 74,* 168–171.

McLaughlin, R. D., & Ross, S. M. (1989). Student cheating in high school: A case of moral reasoning vs. "fuzzy logic." *High School Journal, 72*(3), 97–104.

Miller, J. H. (1997). Gender issues embedded in the experience of student teaching: Being treated like a sex object. *Journal of Teacher Education, 48,* 19–28.

Moffatt, C. W. (2000). *How to get a teaching job.* Boston: Allyn & Bacon.

Montgomery, K. (1997). Student teaching portfolios: A portrait of the beginning teacher. *The Teacher Educator, 32,* 216–225.

Murwin, S., & Matt, S. R. (1990, April 7). Fears prior to student teaching. *The Technology Teacher, 49,* 25–26.

Newman, C. J., & Licata, J. W. (1986–1987). Teacher leadership and the classroom climate as predictors of student brinkmanship. *The High School Journal, 70*(2), 102–110.

Newman, C., Smolen, L., & Newman, I. (1993, February). *Administrative responses to portfolios prepared by teacher candidates.* Paper presented at the annual meeting of the Eastern Educational Research Association, Clearwater, FL.

O'Connor, A. M. (1999, Aug. 24). Learning to Look Past Race. *Los Angeles Times* [on line]. Available: http://www.latimes.com/archives/.

Otto, R. G. (1998). Keeping compliant with 504, ADA and IDEA. *School Business Affairs, 64,* 9–16.

Packard, K. L., Schwebel, A. I., & Ganey, J. S. (1979). Concerns of last semester baccalaureate nursing students. *Nursing Research, 28,* 302–304.

Paechter, C. F. (1998). *Educating the other: Gender, power and schooling.* London: Falmer.

Persell, C. H. (1977). *Education and inequality: The roots and results of stratification in America's schools.* New York: The Free Press.

Persell, C. H. (1993). Social class and educational equality. In J. A. Banks & C. A. M. Banks (Eds.), *Multicultural education: Issues and perspectives* (2nd ed., pp. 71–89). Boston: Allyn & Bacon.

Piaget, J., & Inhelder, B. (1969). *The psychology of the child.* New York: Basic Books.

Reynolds, A. (1992). What is competent beginning teaching? A review of the literature. *Review of Educational Research, 62*(1), 1–35.

Rosenthal, R. (1973, September). The Pygmalion effect lives. *Psychology Today, 7,* 56–63.

Rosenthal, R. (1985). From unconscious experimenter bias to teacher expectancy effects. In J. Dusek (Ed.), *Teacher expectancies* (pp. 37–65). Hillsdale, NJ: Lawrence Erlbaum Associates.

Rosenthal, R., & Jacobson, L. (1966). Teachers' expectancies: Determinants of pupils' IQ gains. *Psychological Reports, 19,* 115–118.

Salvia, J., & Ysseldyke, J.E. (2001). *Assessment* (8th ed.). New York: Houghton-Mifflin.

Sarason, S. B. (1982). *The culture of the school and the problem of change* (2nd ed.). Boston: Allyn & Bacon.

Sarason, S. B. (1990). *The predictable failure of educational reform.* San Fransciso: Jossey-Bass.

Schloss, P. J. (1992). Mainstreaming revisited. *The Elementary School Journal, 92*(3), 233–244.

Schwebel, A. I., & Cherlin, D. L. (1972). Physical and social distancing in teacher–pupil relationships. *Journal of Educational Psychology, 63,* 543–550.

Schwebel, M., Maher, C. M., & Fagley, N. S. (1990). *Promoting cognitive growth over the life span.* Hillsdale, NJ: Lawrence Erlbaum Associates.

Seeman, H. (1988). *Preventing classroom discipline problems: A guide for educators.* Lancaster, PA: Technomic.

Seiler, W. J., Schuelke, L. D., & Lieb-Brilhart, B. (1984). *Communication for the contemporary classroom.* New York: Holt, Rinehart & Winston.

Seldin, P. (1993). *Successful use of teaching portfolios.* Boston: Anker.

Seligman, M. E. P. (1991). *Learned optimism.* New York: Knopf.

Shavelson, R. J., & Stern, P. (1981). Research on teachers' pedagogical thoughts, judgments, decisions, and behavior. *Review of Educational Research, 51,* 455–498.

Slavin, R. (1994). *Cooperative learning: Theory, research & practice.* Boston: Allyn & Bacon.

Slavin, R., & Shaw, A. (1992). *Success for all: A relentless approach to prevention and early intervention in elementary school.* Arlington, VA: Educational Research Section.

Smith, J., & Souviney, R. (1997). The internship in teacher education. *Teacher Education Quarterly, 24,* 5–19.

Sonnenblick, C., & Basciano, M., & Crabbe, K. (1997). *Job hunting made easy.* New York: Learning Express.

Stevens, R. J., & Slavin, R. E. (1995). Effects of a cooperative learning approach in reading and writing on academically handicapped and nonhandicapped students' achievement and attitudes. *The Elementary School Journal, 95,* 241–259.

Students say: What makes a good teacher? (1997). *Schools in the Middle, 6*(5), 15–17.

Stufft, W. D. (1997). Two rules for professional conduct: Two basic rules can help education professionals stay out of trouble in the area of sexual harassment. *Music Educators Journal, 84,* 40–42.

Tanner, D., & Tanner, L. (1995). *Curriculum development: Theory into practice* (3rd ed.). Englewood Cliffs, NJ: Prentice Hall.

Tauber, R. T. (1999). *Classroom management: Sound theory and effective practice* (3rd ed.). Westport, CT: Bergin & Garvey.

Tichenor, M. S. (1998). Preservice teachers' attitudes toward parent involvement: Implications for teacher education. *Teacher Educator, 33,* 248–259.

Tompkins, J. R., & Tompkins-McGill, P. L. (1993). *Surviving in schools in the 1990's: Strategic management of school environments.* Lanham, MD: University Press of America.

Uegh, S. G. (1999, June 22). The changing faces of Maine at state's most diverse school: Tolerance rules but color defines cliques. *Portland Press Herald,* Portland, ME. [on-line], p. 1B. Available: http://www.portland.com/archive/index.shtml.

Unrau, N. J., & McCallum, R. D. (1996). Evaluating with K.A.R.E.: The assessment of student teacher performance. *Teacher Education Quarterly, 23,* 53–76.

Vygotsky, L. S. (1986). *Thought and language* (A. Kozulin, Trans.). Cambridge, MA: MIT Press. (Original work published 1934)

Walker, J. R. (1998). Copyrights and conversations: Intellectual property in the classroom. *Computers and Composition, 15,* 243–251.

Walther-Thomas, C., Korinek, L., McLaughlin, V. L., & Williams, B. T. (2000). *Collaboration for inclusive education: Developing successful programs.* Boston: Allyn & Bacon.

Warner, J., & Bryan, C. (1997). *Inside secrets of finding a teaching job.* Indianapolis, IN: Park Avenue.

Weinstein, R. S., Madison, S. M., & Kuklinski, M. R. (1995). Raising expectations in schooling: Obstacles and opportunities for change. *American Educational Research Journal, 32,* 121–159.

Westling, D. L., & Koorland, M. A. (1988). *The special educator's handbook.* Boston: Allyn & Bacon.

Williams, J. L. (1995, February). *Differences between cooperating teachers and student teachers in their assessment of student teacher performance: Potential threats to a successful relationship.* Paper presented at the 75th annual meeting of the Association of Teacher Educators, Detroit, MI.

Winebrenner, S. (1992). *Teaching gifted kids in the regular classroom: Strategies and techniques every teacher can use to meet the academic needs of the gifted and talented.* Minneapolis, MN: Free Spirit Publishing.

Yee, S. M-I. (1990). *Careers in the classroom: When teaching is more than a job.* New York: Teachers College Press.

Yell, M. L., & Drasgow, E. (1999). A legal analysis of inclusion. *Preventing School Failure, 43,* 118–123.

Young, D., & Beier, E. (1977). The role of applicant non-verbal communication in the employment interview. *Journal of Employment Counseling, 14,* 154–165.

Author Index

Subject Index